HOW TO
COOK YOUR
DAUGHTER

HOW TO COOK YOUR DAUGHTER

A MEMOIR

Jessica Hendra

WITH BLAKE MORRISON

HARPER ● PERENNIAL

NEW YORK ● LONDON ● TORONTO ● SYDNEY ● NEW DELHI ● AUCKLAND

HARPER ● PERENNIAL

A hardcover edition of this book was published in 2005 by HarperCollins Publishers.

HOW TO COOK YOUR DAUGHTER. Copyright © 2005, 2019 by Jessica Hendra and Blake Morrison. All rights reserved. Printed in the United States of America. No part of this book may be used or reproduced in any manner whatsoever without written permission except in the case of brief quotations embodied in critical articles and reviews. For information, address HarperCollins Publishers, 195 Broadway, New York, NY 10007.

HarperCollins books may be purchased for educational, business, or sales promotional use. For information, please email the Special Markets Department at SPsales@harpercollins.com.

FIRST HARPER PERENNIAL EDITION PUBLISHED 2019.

Designed by Kris Tobiassen

Library of Congress Cataloging-in-Publication Data has been applied for.

ISBN 978-0-06-288833-4 (pbk.)

19 20 21 22 23   LSC   10 9 8 7 6 5 4 3 2 1

FOR MY DAUGHTERS,

JULIA AND CHARLOTTE,

WHO CHANGED EVERYTHING.

CONTENTS

PART I

MAY 2004

I PULLED THE BOOK FROM THE SHELF AT BORDERS and read the names first. The title: *Father Joe: The Man Who Saved My Soul*. Then the author: Tony Hendra, my father.

That's when I noticed the hands.

There is no face on the jacket of my dad's memoir. Just a cassocked body of a monk, shot from the shoulders down, hands folded across what looks like a Bible. They are strong, sinewy hands, and they may belong to a priest or perhaps just a model posing for the cover. Still, I couldn't help but see something different.

They reminded me of hands that had once held a child. That had pushed back her white-blond hair and carried her off to bed. That had felt beneath her nightie. That had explored a little girl.

They reminded me of my father's hands.

Of course they couldn't *be his*, I thought. *He wouldn't have volunteered to dress up for the cover just to save the modeling fee, would he?*

Donning religious garb had been something of an obsession with my father. It had been his way of sticking it to the Catholic Church, an institution that he simultaneously revered and resented, and I could remember at least three or four pictures of him playing a priest or a cardinal, or even the Pope.

But this book wasn't billed as a parody. In fact, it had just been described by the nation's most influential newspaper as one of the greatest spiritual memoirs ever written.

A day earlier, I had come home to a phone call after a long and sweaty run, the sort I take every morning, no matter the weather or occasion. I ran on my wedding day and the morning after, never mind that it was below freezing and snowing. Running was my obsession, and my husband, Kurt, a character actor whose face you'd know quicker than his name, had grown used to my many foibles. He even helped me laugh at them. He understood that I couldn't cook more than maybe four dishes, and that, if we ever had dinner parties, I'd just buy something from the store and guiltily accept whatever compliments came my way. He knew that I never bought a hair dryer because, for some reason, I could never quite figure out how to use it effectively. He accepted that, at thirty-nine, I still struggled knowing my right hand from my left, and that my dyslexia made it difficult for me to read even my own handwriting. He even figured out my secret: I tried to compensate by making my writing illegible (if I couldn't read it, no one would!). And Kurt loved me anyway.

On the phone was Rudy Maxa, a former newspaper reporter and columnist better known to National Public Radio listeners as "The Savvy Traveler." He had been the best man at our wedding and is a dear family friend. "Listen, have you seen the *New York Times Book Review* this morning?" he asked.

"No Rudy." I smiled. "I live in Los Angeles now, remember?"

Rudy didn't laugh. "Well I think you should take a look at it. There's a lead review of your dad's new book. And it's a rave. I mean a *rave*. You may find it surprising."

I wiped my forehead. "Surprising in what way, Rudy?" I felt as though he was trying to tell me something without really wanting to say it.

"I know you said your dad was writing a book about a priest," he said, "but this book . . . well, it sounds like a confessional."

"A what?"

"A confessional. The review says, quote, 'It belongs in the first tier of spiritual memoirs ever written.'"

The first tier of spiritual memoirs? "What else does it say?" My voice had grown weak. I was reluctant to ask but too curious not to. When my father had first mentioned the book to me in passing two years earlier, he had called it "a biography of sorts." I should've known to attach more meaning to the last two words—"of sorts"—rather than the first two. "Of sorts" was the sort of caveat my father loved to offer.

"Just go online and read the review yourself," Rudy said. "You might have something to say about the book. If you do let me know. I can get you to the right people."

The offer seemed odd, but I suspected Rudy knew more than he wanted to share. It was no secret to him that my dad and I had a difficult relationship. I wasn't sure exactly what my husband had told him, but he had told him something, if not the whole story. Rudy had been in the newspaper and magazine business for years, and at one time—coincidentally—he was the Washington writer for *Spy* when my father was its editor-in-chief. If he said I should read the review, then I would.

Kurt downloaded and printed it for me. "You read it," he said. "I'll go amuse the girls." Our daughters, Julia and Charlotte, were six and three years old.

And so I closed the door and sat down in our playroom/office to read a review that began this way: "Saints are perhaps always best evoked by sinners. And it would be hard to think of someone more at ease in the world of modern sin than Tony Hendra."

Modern sin? At ease? Did the reviewer really have any idea the nature of my father's sins?

The book indeed was a biography—of sorts—about a Benedictine monk named Father Joseph Warrilow. For most of his life, my dad had known Father Joe, first meeting him when he was fourteen on a trip to an abbey off the coast of England on the Isle of Wight. Since then, the two had remained friends, and the book told the story of how Father Joe helped my dad, now sixty-two, come to terms with all he had done wrong.

I had met Father Joe twice before he had died a few years ago, and I knew him to be as my father—and the review—described him: an incredibly special man. What I didn't recognize were the descriptions of my father, of his life, or of the sins that he had confessed. The reviewer wrote of my father's sexual adventures and how none of them was truly "sinful." How Father Joe's great gift was to relieve him of misplaced sexual guilt. And I asked, incredulous, as I read it, *How could my father write about this? About sex and sin and misplaced guilt?*

Then came the phrase that I could not forget. Tony Hendra, it read, "spares us no details of his own iniquities as a parent. . . ." I reread it a few times. *Spares us no details of his own iniquities. What does that mean?* For a moment, I thought: *He's finally come out with it.* But I saw from the rest of the review that, of course, he had not. All I wanted to do was to call this reviewer and shout, "How do you know he spared no details! Oh, he spared you *a lot* of details because if people knew the details, no one would have published this 'biography of sorts!'"

I paced in circles holding the review in my hand, ignoring the cries of "Mommy, we're hungry" coming from outside the door. I had locked it so I could cry without scaring the poor girls who were now rattling the door handle. Finally, I pulled myself together enough to go outside. I had been a professional actress for about twenty years, and though never as accomplished as my husband, I'd met with some success when I first came to Hollywood. But after I had Julia, I focused more on mothering than acting, and my most unforgettable role—as Dejar in *Star Trek: Deep Space Nine*—is remembered less for my acting and more because of the audience: Trekkies who log every character. That's not to diminish my convincing portrayal of a "Cardassian female . . . [who] posed as a scientific colleague of Ulani and Gilora and attempted to sabotage a joint Cardassian-Bajoran scientific effort to place a subspace relay in the Gamma Quadrant." At least, that's how StarTrek.com describes it. Now, a much tougher role awaited me. I had to put on a happy face for my daughters. But as I mixed and poured pancakes and talked with them, distracted, I couldn't escape the review, the book, and what, if anything, I should do about it.

Of course, I had to read *Father Joe*. The book sounded so different than the one Dad had told me about in France two years earlier. But maybe there was something that alluded to bigger "iniquities." Or maybe . . . maybe there was some note that made it clear that the author left some events out of his "confession" for the sake of those he hurt. *Yes, that would be enough*, I decided. Some eloquent version of "I omitted details of my first family's troubles to protect my children's privacy." So my husband, my daughters, and I headed to the local Barnes & Noble.

As we walked into the bookstore, I asked Kurt, "What section do you think it's in?"

"Try fiction," he deadpanned.

In fact, the book had been in the biography section . . . before it sold out. "We had a few in," a clerk offered, "but they all went today. Should have more in next week. Can we hold a copy for you, ma'am?"

"No, thank you," I told him. "I'll try somewhere else."

Maybe it was better this way, Kurt reasoned. "At least you can sleep tonight without it burning a hole in your bedside table, Jess."

But I was up for hours anyway. I simply couldn't shake that phrase: "Tony Hendra spares us no details of his own iniquities as a parent." I imagined my father in his Upper West Side apartment reading the review, the phone ringing all day with calls from friends, his agent, his publisher. "Congrats on the fabulous review, Tony! You deserve every word of it. It's just such a wonderful book!"

Did he experience even one moment when his conscience pricked at him? Was he lying awake too, thinking about what he hadn't mentioned? Did part of him squirm because he knew that not all of the praise was deserved? Or had he justified what he had done, had he buried it so deep that he was sleeping soundly, basking in the glory of the writer's dream, a rave in the *New York Times?*

First thing the next morning, Memorial Day, I dragged Julia and Charlotte out to get the book. We tried Borders this time, and I went straight to the biography section. That's where I first saw the hands.

I carried the book to the checkout counter, my two little girls trailing me. The clerk was in his early fifties—a friendly face, maybe the manager—and I handed him the book face down. He turned it over. "I just read a great review of this book in the *New York Times* yesterday."

"Really?" I answered flatly.

"Yeah, I was a big fan of the *National Lampoon* back in the 1970s. Been following this guy Tony Hendra for a while."

"Oh."

Without thinking, I handed the clerk my credit card. "That's weird," he said. "Your name is Hendra too. Any relation?"

"No, no relation," I said quickly. For the first time in ten years, I regretted not taking my husband's name.

"Just a coincidence, huh?"

"Yeah, just a coincidence."

"Well, enjoy," he said, bagging the book and handing it to me.

As I walked from the store, I heard the little voice, the one that told me I had lied. But it was coming from beside me. "Mommy, doesn't 'relation' mean someone in your family?" It was Julia, my six-year-old fact-checker.

"Yes, it does mean that." What else could I say?

"Why did you tell that man you were no relation to Grandpa Tony? Didn't Grandpa write that book?"

"Uh, yeah."

"So you lied to that man?"

"I guess I did."

"Why?"

"I don't know honey. I just didn't want to talk about Grandpa Tony right now."

"Oh."

I was safe. Then: "Mommy, was it a white lie?"

Help!

"Yes, I suppose it was a white lie," but Julia looked troubled, and I felt awful. I was almost forty, but I had become that little girl again—vulnerable, anxious, and lost. My feelings about my father had been in remission. I was happily married with two wonderful daughters. I'd beaten an eating disorder or at least tamed it. I'd pulled my life together. And now, like a complicated cancer, those feelings were back.

For that, for how I felt at that moment at Borders and in the weeks that followed, my father would call me a victim, a member of what he cleverly termed the "Sally-Jessy-Raphael culture." A person determined to live in the past. Of course, it was easy for him to say that, and at times, I wasn't sure he was entirely wrong. When he'd call the house in the years before *Father Joe* was published, just the sound of his voice on my answering machine started an emotional chain reaction that made me feel crazy. "Hey Jessie. It's me, Dad," he'd say. "Give me a call, will you?" A simple message. But for me, nothing that involved my father was simple. Like the "biography of sorts" that became my father's "confessional," every phrase that he uttered seemed meant to be parsed. Every inflection told a story. I couldn't help myself, and each time I heard his voice, I was reminded of how very complicated our relationship had become.

One day it might have been the way he said "Dad," drawing out the sounds and ending strong on the last "d." Or the fact that he continued to call me Jessie, the name I had as a little girl. In my teens, I had dropped the "ie" ending, just as my sister had gone from Kathy to Katherine and my mother from Judy to Judith. When my father left us, we had, without a single word between us, shed the names we knew when my family lived together, as if signaling some metamorphosis. That's what it *had* been, a metamorphosis. We had all grown up—my mother, my sister, and me. But not my father. Responsibility was never his strong suit, and only my grandmother, his brother, and his two sisters ever called him by his Christian name, Anthony. To the world, and no matter how old he became, no matter that he became a best-selling author, he preferred to remain, simply, Tony.

Or maybe I'd feel inexplicably thrown by the message he left: *Give me a call, will you?* It wasn't so much a question. My dad seldom asked anything. It was just an assumed command, as though through charm or force of personality, he could simply will the response he expected, the response he felt he deserved. Years ago, when their accents hadn't yet dulled from decades of living in the United States, my parents' voices fell somewhere between the Rolling Stones and the royal family. Now, his voice had mellowed, like my mother's, and retained just a slight British accent. The closed "a" sound. The silent "l." The enunciation that comes from using the front part of the mouth and the lips to form the words.

And if it wasn't his voice, it might be the hands on the cover of his book—hands that probably weren't my father's but seemed to taunt me nonetheless.

It all seems so ridiculous, doesn't it? So horribly tedious when I think about it. But maybe things will make more sense when you hear the rest of my story, when you learn how I got to this place. I knew in my heart that it was never really about what he said or how he said it, or even whether he modeled for his book. But every time I heard his voice, each time I saw him, I would simply try to preoccupy myself by focusing on the trees to avoid the forest, to try to escape the question that nagged at me: *Should I have this man in my life at all after what he did? Wouldn't it be better, wouldn't it be less agonizing, to never talk to him again?*

When I brought home *Father Joe* that Memorial Day, I felt as though my dad had left me another message, this one long, involved, and unavoidable. I needed to know whether something beneath those folded hands might somehow help me finally understand him, whether something in those pages might help me reconcile the events that, sadly, had come to define my life.

1.

RED MILL ROAD

FOR MANY CHILDREN, DEATH IS ONE OF THEIR FIRST vivid memories. Usually, it's a grandparent or great aunt, someone distant, someone old. You see your parents cry, perhaps for the first time. And it startles you. But they console and soothe you, they reassure you because they know that you can't possibly understand death, not when you are just four years old.

For me, the man who died was in his twenties—about the same age as my mother and father. And though I was four and too young to understand exactly what had happened, I was old enough to be scared.

They found him in his Hollywood apartment, and those who knew him—my parents included—gathered the next day in the living room of a friend's house. I was sure—absolutely convinced—that his body lay somewhere in that house. I still remember how I clung to my mother, my wide eyes searching the pale, shocked faces. They seemed at least as scared as I was, huddling on the couches as if they were telling secrets—whispering and hushed, as though whatever killed their friend lurked just around the corner. They said he'd "OD'd," but of course, that meant nothing to me. Then "choked on his own vomit." Then: "Poor Chris. Heroin killed him." What I saw, what I was *sure* would happen in just a few seconds, was the man walking toward me, covered in vomit, snarling with his nose and mouth and body dripping with this black goo "heroin." Behind him there'd be a trail.

Heroin. I wanted nothing more than to get away from that house, to go play with my sister, Kathy, in the sun, to go home to Laurel Canyon. But I had to stay here with adults who seem as bewildered as me. And I was terrified: *Would Heroin get me too?*

It's not the most ideal of childhood memories. But you have to consider the time (1969) the place (California) and of course, the parents. Mine had come thousands of miles from England to experiment with the Southern California scene of the late 1960s. They were born during the Second World War, part of the generation that would be responsible for the Swinging Sixties. My mother grew up in Wimbledon, a suburb of London. Her father, Alfred Christmas, owned a chemist's shop. She, her sister, and her brother lived with my grandmother and grandfather in a mock Tudor house built on a lot leveled by a V-bomb in the waning years of the war. My grandfather spent his time growing roses and humming. Kind but emotionally reserved, he had a habit of walking with his arms behind his back, his right arm bent with the hand clutching his left arm, as if holding himself back. My grandmother proved warmer than her husband. On our visits, she played with us and baked jam tarts and Victoria sponge cakes for afternoon tea.

One of her great sorrows was her name: Doris. My grandmother said my great-grandparents had planned to name her Kathleen. But at her christening, when the godfather was asked to name the child, he announced—much to the horror of the assembled relations—"I name the child Doris." And Doris she would stay. When I heard the story some years ago from my mother, I asked, with a degree of skepticism, what any American of my generation would: "Why didn't her parents say anything?" At the same time, I was saying to myself: *because they were English.* As I can attest, the value of keeping silent for the sake of maintaining family peace seems to run in our veins.

Doris and Alfred named their second child—my mother—Judith. But for much of her life, Judith was Judy. I imagine it must have been hard being called "Judy Christmas." As I told my mother during one of my more obnoxious moments as a teenager, it seemed a name more suitable for a stripper than for an intellectually gifted and talented girl like my mom, who became the bright light of her family by earning a place at Girton College, University of Cambridge.

Anthony Hendra, my dad, was born the son of a stained-glass maker and raised in rural Hertfordshire, the region in which Jane Austen set *Pride and Prejudice.* Even as a child, he seems to have been eccentric. My grandma Georgina told me how little Anthony used to ram his tricycle at top toddler speed into a brick wall over and over and over again. "All day long, just riding right into the wall," Grandma Georgina said with a smoker's laugh. My uncle recounted how my father, then a teenager and obsessed with becoming a monk, instructed his brother and sisters to send letters to the Pope recommending one Anthony Christopher Hendra for sainthood. The Pope failed to respond.

My father, like my mother, was tremendously gifted intellectually. To his family's surprise (but no one else's), he easily won a scholarship to Cambridge. Initially, he resisted accepting the place, having already decided on his vocation as a novice in a Benedictine monastery. But at the insistence of the more senior monks, he went off to the university.

It was at Cambridge in about 1962 that my parents met. By this time, my father had put his monastic aspirations in the deep freeze and instead embraced the world of earthly delights. By the end of her senior year, my mother was very pregnant. At twenty-two and dreaming of success as a comedian, my father was understandably reluctant to marry. My mother, more in love with my dad than he was with her, could neither face an abortion nor give the baby up for adoption. So, unsure of what was going to happen, she continued on with her pregnancy. In her Cambridge graduation pictures, though unmarried and visibly with child, my mother wears her gown and rounded stomach with pride. She smiles into the camera defiantly, holding her diploma over the spot where her illegitimate baby—my sister, Katherine— grows. She is beautiful, her long hair untidily looped in a Bronte-like bun, a concession to the formality of the occasion. My grandparents stand awkwardly on either side of her: my grandfather in his gray Sunday best, my grandmother in a Queen Mother hat. To me they look confused, caught between the pride they feel in their daughter having graduated from the best university in England and their mortification over her obvious "condition."

In the end, sometime after my sister's birth, my parents did marry, and they spent their honeymoon night in Paris. My mother said it was wonderful. My father said it rained and called it the worst night of his life. And so their marriage began.

In 1964, a year before I was born, my parents immigrated to America—first to the East Coast, a place where my father had visited to test the comedy waters. He and his stand-up comedy partner, Nick Ullett, had met with some success there, and the opportunities in the States seemed greater than in London. I was born in New York, where my parents had a fifth-floor walk-up apartment on the Upper East Side of Manhattan.

Not ones for baby-naming books, my parents turned to the pages of the *Collected Works of Shakespeare*, just as they had when my sister was born. She was named Katherine after the long-suffering but tough-as-nails Katherine of Aragon in *Henry VIII*. I became Jessica from *The Merchant of Venice*.

Our names foretold our futures. Kathy spent a childhood as "Thunder Thighs," a name my father coined for her. She persevered by throwing herself into her studies. Today, she's a doctor.

My name seems even more prescient. At the end of *The Merchant of Venice*, Jessica faces a decision a daughter dreads: to follow her heart, thus betraying her father, or to stay true to him and betray herself. And so I was given not a name that I hated, like my grandmother's, or a diminutive one as unfitting as my mom's, but one that foreshadowed a future that no one in my family could have imagined.

By the time I was born, my father had begun his career as a satirist and comedian. At Cambridge he performed with John Cleese and Graham Chapman. Soon after coming to America, the comedy team of Hendra and Ullett appeared on *The Ed Sullivan Show* (Dad and Nick believed Sullivan understood less than half of what they were saying but loved their accents). Dad was brilliant, charming, witty, and gregarious, especially to those who didn't know him well. But he struggled. Despite his talent, he couldn't crack the TV world. What he wrote was too racy, too clever, or just not right. And so, Hollywood wouldn't be for us—or, more aptly, for him.

I have only two other vivid memories of California—whirling around and around on the Mad Hatters Tea Party Ride until I threw up all the treats I had consumed for my sixth birthday and waking up in a shaking bed to the sound of breaking glass and the eerie rumble of an earthquake. For me, death by overdose, Disneyland, and earthquakes summed up L.A. in the late 1960s.

I do, however, remember the day we left Los Angeles in the early summer of 1971.

My mother prodded me gently. "Jessie, you need to wake up." It was still dark in the room where Kathy and I slept, and I could hear only faint twittering from the birds in the fruit trees in the garden. For a second, I wondered if there was another aftershock from the earthquake—if my mom was waking me to stand under a doorway until the hanging light fixture in the living room finally stopped swaying. But the world appeared still, and Kathy was already sitting up in bed, her brown hair messy.

"We have to leave today," my mother reminded me.

Yes. Leaving. Today we'd be starting a drive that would take us all the way across the country, back to the house in New Jersey where I had lived when I was two. I sat up. Despite the mixture of memories, I didn't want to leave this place. There was my school on Wonderland Avenue, my friends, the playground down at the bottom of the canyon. But maybe the house where we were going wouldn't shake like this one. Maybe Heroin wouldn't be there. And they did have winter, with real snow and everything. *What did it feel like? Did it smell? What was it like to be really cold? What was it like to be bundled up in a big coat, a scarf, and boots as I had seen in the stories at school?*

My mother told us we could keep our nighties on. There was no point getting dressed if we didn't want to. Still groggy, Kathy and I walked through our bedroom doorway, along the hallway, and followed my mother's slim, tall figure out the front door of a house that we would never see again.

My father was loading bags into the Volkswagen bus. He moved quickly and, despite being in one of his "heavy stages," looked strong as he hefted the bags. The bus was white, with brown-and-red paisley curtains on the back. Its look was shabby but friendly, as though it were saying "It might be tough, man, but I'll do my best to get you there." In the back lay a mattress, the closest thing we had to car seats. There, we would sleep at night and perch during the long days of driving.

"Why are we going now, Daddy?" I asked. "It's still dark."

"We have to leave before the landlord wakes up," he said matter-of-factly. "He's a vampire and just went to bed."

I was still groggy but that woke me up. "Oh," I said, not sure if my dad were joking. It was always hard to tell with him. Like the other night when the police had pulled us over for speeding. The cop shone a flashlight in the back seat of the car and told my father to take the "little girls home." When the officer walked away, my father turned to us: "They always take the children to jail first, you know, girls."

When everything was packed, we climbed into the VW, and Daddy started the cheery engine. Kathy and I lay down in the back. I clutched the tattered mass of wool that had morphed from a baby blanket into my most precious possession. I called it, simply, "Mine." Then I watched out the back window as Laurel Canyon disappeared.

"We're off!" my father shouted into the early morning light. And so we were, a family making its way across the country in the true American pioneer tradition. Except we were going from west to east. And my father, the comedian and satirist, wasn't looking to settle the country like the pioneers of the 1860s. He planned to unsettle it.

We drove all day and ended up spending that night somewhere in the Utah desert. But the job of getting to New Jersey was proving hard for the valiant VW. The next morning, I woke up to the sound of a choked engine.

"For fuck's sake!"

The bus wouldn't start. My father smacked the steering wheel in frustration.

"Jesus Christ!"

He jumped from the van into the desert heat and began to have a near epileptic fit, his huge blue eyes growing larger and larger the more his anger mounted. Each word, perfectly enunciated in a fine English accent, exploded from his mouth.

"God . . . damn . . . mother . . . fucking . . . piece . . . of . . . *shit*!"

He hopped around the VW, kicking it and screaming, his longish blond hair bouncing up and down on his shoulders. His unbuttoned shirt flew out behind him. His white belly reflected the sun. Sweat popped from his face, and his usually flushed checks grew scarlet.

"Fucking . . . heap . . . of . . . fucking . . . *crap*!"

My mother sat in the front seat, completely silent, her face tense, her full lips set. We would come to know that posture well. Kathy and I kept quiet too, waiting for my father's eruption to subside. There was nothing else to do. After a while, he gave up kicking the VW and squatted glumly in the sand.

We waited in the desert for what seemed like an eternity. In the sweltering heat, the VW grew so hot, it sizzled to the touch. Then, suddenly, two shapes—bathed in intense sunlight—moved toward us from a car that just seemed to appear.

"Need some help?" one asked.

When we were chugging hopefully along again, Daddy told Kathy and me that the men who had gotten our car started were guardian angels of the desert, waiting under the scorching sun to help people like us. "The Mechanic Angels," he called them.

The VW averaged two breakdowns a state. On highways, on small country roads. Not that my sister and I minded. We were having a great time watching the country go by, eating diner pancakes in the early morning, listening to trucks hurl through the night when we pulled off the road to sleep.

Finally, tenacious to the end, the VW willed itself across the New Jersey state line and into the tiny town of Glen Gardner. It sputtered past the gas station and local bar, past the general store, down a small winding road that led over an old bridge and into the gravel patch at one side of a shadowy barn. My dad cut the headlights. We were home.

He carried my exhausted sister and me out of the van and into a darkness deeper than any I had experienced. The house was a huge black box in the night. I heard trees rustling, the call of an owl, and a low noise that sounded like running water. I held Mine close as my father carried me toward the house. In the morning, I woke up and fell in love with Fifty-five Red Mill Road.

My mother and father had bought the house soon after they arrived in America. They became instantly enamored of the rural townships of Hunterton County, where they had rented a small summer place in 1966. Perhaps it reminded them of England: lush, green, and with a relatively long history. Or maybe it was just because it was cheap.

My mother had been desperate to get Kathy and me out of New York for the summer. She looked in the *New York Times* for the least expensive summer rental available. That meant we wouldn't be heading to the Hamptons or the Cape but rather to unfashionable New Jersey. While exploring one day, my parents came upon the house on Red Mill Road. They scrounged together just enough money and bought it, renting it out during our years in L.A. Now we had returned, mainly because we were broke. Los Angeles had proved to be a place with a lot of talk and very few paychecks. My dad had retreated to the East Coast to try his luck writing for anything *but* television. And there the house stood, as if knowing we'd be back.

It had been there for more than two hundred years, surrounded by trees and fields, along a narrow country road that had once been even less—a cart path. By American standards, the house was ancient. And though it was neither large nor ornate, it was the sort of place that deserved respect. After all, it had been built by a blacksmith who dragged each of its hundreds of stones from the stream that ran a few yards from the front porch and from the fields that lay around it. The walls he constructed were so thick that from the outside, the house seemed much larger than it actually was. A covered porch ran along the front, and a small garden was nestled between it and a white picket fence.

Originally there were four rooms, two downstairs and two upstairs. Later, a kitchen—built not of stone but of wood—had been tacked to the side. And a bathroom was added upstairs. The living room had a low-beamed ceiling; small, paned eighteenth-century windows; and a large fireplace. Next door was a parlor of sorts that we called "the study." On either side of the old parts of the house were two sets of thin, winding staircases. Even then I knew they were incredibly dangerous. But that didn't stop Kathy and me from racing up and down them almost immediately. We'd start at the top step, then thump, thump, thump—down step by step, on our bottoms and collapse in a giggling heap onto the hard wooden floor of the living room.

Kathy and I were to have one of the upstairs rooms as our bedroom. It had two windows: one that overlooked the back lawn and another that gave us a view over the road and into the maple and oak trees that hid the stream. We could see the back of the small house—a blacksmith's forge—that stood across from us. For the moment it was empty. Its owner, my father's former partner Nick Ullett, was still in Los Angeles. Our room was decorated with pale blue wallpaper that had soft, red roses—the most beautiful pattern I had ever seen. A door separated my parents' room from ours. The simple layout of the house hadn't included hallways, but there was a small landing where one of the staircases ended. Then there was another door that, if opened, revealed the dark stairs that led to the mysteries of the attic, a place I feared to explore.

At the side of the house stood the wooden barn, sagging and blackened by age. At sunset, the bats that slept in the rafters all day left to prowl for food. My father made his office there, in a spartan upstairs corner. Whenever he worked there, I would run down the stone path that led from the house to the barn, open the creaky wooden door to his office and tip-toe up the stairs. Then I'd just sit and stare as he wrote. I loved to watch his hands.

He had bulky knuckles but long fingers that were far more nimble than they looked. I adored the way they flew over his typewriter, the keys tapping out a soundtrack to the words that appeared on the thin, yellowish paper. Then the music would stop, and there would be only the typewriter's patient buzz as it waited for my father's fingers to play again. In those moments, he would look out of the window above his desk, across the road, over the stream, and up into the field that lay on the other side of the river bank. He would puff long on the thin brown cigar that dangled from his mouth, dropping ash onto the floor. He seemed a world away, staring off into the field, deadly serious as he searched for a decent joke. His fingers would leave the typewriter and begin tapping on the wooden desk. First the thumb. Then the index finger. Then the pointer. Then the ring finger. And finally the pinky. Rat tat tat tat TAT. Rat tat tat tat TAT.

I remained quiet on the floor nearby, trying to roll my fingers the same way. But my fingers were too small, too light, and my barely audible taps lacked authority, style.

When he was finished writing for the day, Daddy turned off his typewriter, stood from his desk, and held out his hand. The veins shone greenish-blue against the pale whiteness of his skin. They seemed like huge, protruding pipes just under his flesh. When I looked closely, I thought I could see his blood pumping through them. I would take his hand and run my little fingers over the back of it, exploring the bumpy map. Then we would go down the office stairs together and out into the night.

The two of us walked in the fields or the woods around the house, exploring fallen trees, stopping to spy quietly on deer or rabbits. He'd tell me stories about the spirits that lived in the woods. I'd hold his hand tightly, reassured by those bumps on the back. They proved he was alive. They proved he was my dad. And as long as he was with me, nothing horrible could happen—to me or to him.

I loved our new house, but I still wonder what it thought of us. We weren't of the same world, what with our beat up VW and California clothes. What did it think of my parents, of their 1970s intellectual attitudes? I wonder if it took one look at my family and wished for the old days of long dresses and dark suits, the formality, the clear line between child and adult. In my family, it was hard to tell who exactly were the grownups. But, of course, the house took us in, silent, solid, ancient—sheltering a young family that, unlike it, was anything but stable.

Kathy and I spent what was left of the summer of 1971 exploring the fields, picking black-eyed Susans and Queen Anne's lace, running over the little bridge, jumping into the deeper parts of a stream; that was our greatest joy. We played mermaids and lounged on the rocks. We tried to fish with our hands and trekked up the river, jumping from stone to stone and discovering interesting mosses and funny bugs.

And at night, when we were exhausted and Daddy hadn't gone to New York to work, he would create the most incredible bedtime stories.

"All right girls, what will it be tonight?" he would ask.

"*The Adventures of Sergeant Teddy!*" I'd yell.

"*Elizabeth Big Foot!*" Kathy would scream.

"No, *Five Foot Six, Five Foot Six!*" Kathy and I would finally agree.

We both liked *The Adventures of Sergeant Teddy*, the sadistic sheriff of the toy room who tied up the Barbies and jailed the other teddy bears. We loved the stories about *Elizabeth Big Foot*—a young girl with an enormous foot that always got stuck in the bus. But *Five Foot Six* was our favorite. *Five Foot Six* was an eight-year-old boy who got his name from his unusual height. His parents treated him terribly. At dinner, they tied each strand of his spaghetti together and made him slurp it all at once. They tricked him into jumping into the swimming pool that they'd frozen solid. Or they blindfold him and told him they were taking him somewhere special for his birthday; instead, they made him sit for three hours in the car parked in the garage.

"Are we there yet, Dad? Are we there yet?" he'd ask, over and over again.

"Not yet, Five Foot Six," his father (*my* father) would answer.

They were dark, dark stories—modern-day Grimm's fairy tales. But Kathy and I loved them. We'd roll around our beds giggling and laughing at every word until my father's voice gave out.

For much of that first summer, Kathy and I felt as though we belonged in that house. Life seemed quieter there than it had in Los Angeles. And no, the house didn't shake. But then came fall—and school. That was where I first noticed how different we were, where I realized that the Hendras stood out like graffiti scribbled over a billboard ad for Wonder Bread.

Lebanon Township School (or Lebanon Township Jail, as it came to be called by those sentenced to attend class there) was a long, white, one-story building with a grassy playground. Inside it had been painted Board of Education green, and in each room—or, at least it seemed like each room—a portrait of President Richard Nixon looked down upon us. I think Spiro Agnew was there too—at least in spirit.

From the first day my mother dropped Kathy and me off, I couldn't escape how odd we were. The other mothers wore neat Carol Brady haircuts, pink lipstick, and polyester pant suits. My mother had long, straight hair and a makeup-free face and wore a T-shirt and jeans. Worse was that her British accent stood out, and she didn't drive a station wagon. I sensed I was in for trouble.

"Have a good time." Mom kissed me good-bye. I didn't want to let her go.

I trudged into my new classroom, never so aware of my shaggy white-blond hair, crossed right eye, and pigeon-toed feet. At the door was my teacher, Miss Mole. That wasn't her name, of course, but it should've been, given the enormous black mole she had on her chin. It had a long hair growing from it, even blacker than the mole itself. And no matter how hard I tried, I couldn't take my eyes off it. Its hideousness fascinated me. *Did Miss Mole know it was there?* I wondered. *Didn't she have a mirror? Come on, pull it out!* I watched it sway gently as she ordered us to stand for the Pledge of Allegiance.

At noon, the bell rang, and we grabbed our lunch boxes and filed into the cafeteria. Except I didn't have a lunch box, the most stylish fashion accessory for the elementary school student of 1971. I had nothing that bore the logo of *Bonanza*. No aluminum relief of Hoss or Little Joe, ever-so-slightly raised and painted on the front of the box. Not even *The Jetsons*! Just a crumpled brown paper bag from under our sink. Even before the days of community recycling, my parents were bag conservationists. I sat down at one of the tables. Some kids next to me were talking about one of the teachers.

"You know, Mr. Reposo, at wood shop, he ties you up in the closet if you're bad."

"I heard he once got a saw and cut a kid's finger off."

"No, he didn't cut it off. He grabbed a drill and just drilled a hole right through it."

I hoped that first graders didn't have to take wood shop.

I pulled my cheese sandwich from the bag. My mom's homemade bread came out in strange shapes with big holes in it. The thick-cut wedges of English cheddar cheese my dad brought back from New York fell through them and onto the table as I tried to take my first bite. I glanced at the kids around me; their bread was pure white, every slice exactly the same. And no holes! Their cheese was sliced thin, perfectly square, bright orange, and soft. Their carrots were sliced, peeled, and packed in the plastic wrap my parents refused to buy. They even had paper napkins—forbidden in our house. "Every napkin is a tree, Jessie," my father had told me. But at that moment, I didn't care about trees or preservatives. I just wanted a lunch that looked like everyone else's. I wanted my mother to wear a polyester-pants suit. I wanted even a sliver of plastic wrap.

Pouting, I gathered what was left of my lunch and threw it in one of the huge green trash cans that rimmed the cafeteria. I trailed out to the playground, which was crammed with shouting kids, and sought refuge behind the swing set.

"Hey, little girl! Stay in the playground! Do *not* go out of the marked playground area. Got it?" *Who was this girl with the bright yellow band across her chest and waist?*

"Okay."

I turned and fled into the crowd, making myself small on one of the benches. A kid my own age sat next to me.

"Did that safety yell at you?" she asked.

"A what?"

"A safety. They're just big kids that get to boss us around on the yard."

"Oh," I said.

The bell rang, and we headed back to Miss Mole.

That night at dinner, Kathy and I told my parents about school. Daddy became livid when he learned that we were saying the Pledge of Allegiance.

"You girls are not even *American* for fuck's sake. (Actually, I was, but Kathy had been born in England). I don't want my children pledging allegiance to *any* flag, especially not the American one," he told us. "I don't want you girls involved in any of that nationalistic crap. What a fucking country!"

He would write a note to the principal of Lebanon Township School, he promised, insisting that Kathy and I not say the pledge. All I could think of was Miss Mole telling the class to stand up, hands over hearts, her mole hair waving as she spoke. "Everybody *except* Jessica Hendra." I imagined her sharp voice as she said my name, her scowl, and the looks on the other kids' faces as they stared at the commie hunched over her desk. "We knew by her lunch she was weird," they'd whisper.

But Daddy was even more outraged about the safety who kept me away from the swing set. "Hitler Youth," he called her, not that Kathy and I had any idea what a Hitler Youth was.

"Was this girl giving you a Sieg Heil?" he asked me.

Thankfully, by the next morning, my father had forgotten about the note and protesting against the safety. He was busy getting ready to go to New York. There was more and more work for him at the *National Lampoon.*

My mother would shuttle him to the commuter bus that left from Clinton (about fifteen minutes from our house) and went into the Port Authority Bus Terminal. Many evenings, Kathy and I would go into Clinton with Mom to pick up Daddy. Sometimes, he would have spent the night—or even a few nights—in New York, and we always looked forward to seeing him again. Often, he would bring little goodies back from the city. I remember once he brought back some caviar and black truffles he had shoplifted from Bloomingdale's. Stealing from the "big stores" was "a moral imperative," he told me, flashing his loot proudly. "But never steal anything from a mom-and-pop store, okay, Jessie?" Of course I said yes, but I didn't understand at all. I didn't know what "imperative" meant, but I knew that stealing was wrong. Was my father a no-good thief or a modern-day Robin Hood?

Then one night Daddy emerged from the bus with his head wrapped in an enormous white bandage streaked with red where the blood seeped through. He looked like a bleeding Mummy, and Kathy and I were horrified. Later that night he told us the story of what had happened, and I was *convinced* he was Robin Hood.

2.

THE BROWNIES

HE WAS WALKING WITH A FRIEND DOWN IN SOHO LATE the night before when a car came speeding down the street and almost hit them. He yelled at the driver to slow down, and the driver did more than that. He stopped, backed up, and jumped out of the car, pulling a gun on my dad. Daddy thought that was it, that the man was going to shoot him right then and there in the face. But then the man heard a police siren coming toward them, and, instead of firing, he hit my dad over the head with the pistol and sped off.

I was thrilled and frightened by my father's bravado. I had seen him yell at a good many cars, and I believed his story. I would have believed *anything* he told me. I learned the truth only recently. My dad had, in fact, been pistol-whipped, but in a barroom brawl. It turns out he was defending a woman he was having an affair with at the time, something that would have been hard to explain to your six-year-old daughter, let alone to your wife. Regardless, my mother rarely questioned him about his often erratic behavior or about the increasing frequency with which he stayed in the city. Before cell phones and answering machines, it was harder to track people down. You could just disappear—and my father often did.

After Daddy's bloody return from New York, I became even more anxious about him going there. I worried he would yell at a car again and that, this time, he *would* get shot, hurt, or run over. That we would go to Clinton to pick him up from the bus, and he would come down the steps covered from head to toe with bandages oozing blood. Or worse, that he would not be on the bus at all—that he would be lying dead along side some New York street curb.

The days he stayed home in New Jersey to write were always better. On those days, I could keep track of him. I could relax and not worry so much while I played with our neighbor, Becky Bradford. We'd play dress ups, go in the stream, or just run around outside. Neither Kathy nor I were much for dolls, especially not Barbies, at least not around our house. Playing with Barbies meant enduring jabs by my father, who found the dolls absurd. As he put it, "Only in America would they make a doll for kids with tits like that."

If we wanted to play dolls, we would walk up the long gravel driveway to Becky's. Her mother, Connie, made us peanut-butter-and-grape-jelly sandwiches on spongy white bread while she inhaled Parliaments. Like most everyone but my mother, she wore the standard Brady haircut and pants suit of the normal mom. Best of all, she thought Barbies were cute. I could play for hours up at their house, reveling in Wonder Bread, Fresca, Barbies, and maybe even an episode of *Mighty Mouse*. The Bradford house was my portal to suburban America. I felt slightly guilty when I returned from a day at Becky's—as if I had been off doing something illicit. I wondered: *Could my parents smell the Hamburger Helper on my breath?*

I never stopped feeling awkward and out of place at Lebanon Township School. But there seemed one way to belong.

I had seen them sitting outside the A&P supermarket in Clinton. They always wore their hair in little bows or pig tails, and they dressed in crisp, green dresses; little caps; white knee socks; and brown shoes. The cookies came in neat packages laid out on the tables in front of them. And next to the boxes were pictures of the girls sitting around a campfire, putting up canvas tents, or holding the hands of grateful-looking old ladies. I wanted to be one of those girls. I wanted to look official and perky and go camping and sing songs. I wanted to sit outside of the A&P on Saturday mornings with my friends, giggling and selling cookies.

But I found out from the girls in my class that you couldn't just become a Girl Scout. You had to *earn* that green uniform. You had to make it through the Brownies.

I decided not to tell Daddy about joining the local Brownie troop. If he thought the safeties at school were Nazis . . . well, I had a feeling that he wouldn't approve of the uniformed Brownies. It was always easier to tell my mother about such matters. She said if I wanted to go to the next troop meeting, that was fine.

I would go to the first meeting without the official brown uniform, which I would get sometime before the second meeting. I couldn't wait—an official Brownie. The first step toward becoming a full-fledged Girl Scout—the campfires, the singing, the Saturday-morning cookie sales. Nirvana!

The troop met after school, and on the day I went, the Brownies were making plastic place mats for the cookout—*cookout!*—they were having in a few weeks. The mats were made by weaving rows of plastic strips, each a different color, into a large rectangle. I was invited to sit on the floor as part of the Brownies' circle and join in, my first semi-official act as a troop member. It wasn't selling cookies or sitting around a campfire. But that would come soon enough. And I'd have this cool placemat . . . this rainbow of a placemat . . . this awful, impossible-to-make placemat! Ugh! The plastic strips kept slipping and fell out of order. And when I pulled them tight, they'd break. My mat wasn't even close to the rectangular beauty on display by the troop leader. It was a lumpy mess! *Am I really Girl Scout material after all?* I wondered. Next to me, a girl with a pixie haircut and a button nose wove a perfect mat: smooth, not too tight, and flat as a pancake. *She'd* be ready for the cookout.

Pixie Girl must've felt me watching her because she turned a second later and looked down at the mass of twisted, snapped plastic strips on my lap.

"You're doing it all wrong," she said. It was really more of a whine. And then, "Your mat looks really dumb."

Dumb? This from a uniformed Brownie.

"Well. . . ." I mumbled. *What should I say?* I knew it had to be good. Then, it came to me: "You're a stupid asshole!"

The words flew from my mouth. Loud. Bold. Proud! They echoed through the room, and every hand stopped weaving. Plastic hung suspended in the air. Every Brownie froze. After a moment, Pixie Girl broke the silence.

"That girl called me a bad word. A really bad word!"

She pointed at me as she hollered, but she could've saved her breath. There wasn't a single person in that room, including the troop leader herself, who had missed the word "asshole" coming from the mouth of the struggling new recruit. I looked down at the green tiles of the floor, my face burning. *What would they do to me?* I was reminded of a few days earlier, Sunday, when my dad had been out on the lawn behind the house trying to fix the lawnmower. He had been cursing at the top of his lungs, calling the mower "a fucking lump of shit" and "a goddamn son of a bitch"—terms once reserved for the laboring VW bus. Suddenly, a man's voice, carried by the wind and through the trees near Connie and Doug Bradford's house: "Watch your stinking mouth, Hendra, or I'll have you arrested!"

Arrested? Is that what was going to happen? They'll haul me away and lock me in jail? Or would they just wash my mouth out with soap like I saw Connie do to Becky's brother Jeremy when he called her a "Fat Cootie?" Becky and I had peeked through the crack of the bathroom door and watched Connie pry open Jeremy's mouth and wedge half a bar of Ivory Soap between his jaws. It foamed as he gagged and spat. Connie added a bit of water and scrubbed her hand around his mouth. Finally she let him go and sent him to his room in tears. *Which was worse: prison or Ivory Soap?*

The troop leader made her way toward me, her pink face red, her lips trembling. Only her hair, frozen by hairspray, remained calm.

"Jessica Hendra, you will stand up and walk from this room immediately!" I did as I was told and abandoned my plastic mat then and there. "Go and wait outside for your mother to pick you up. You are *not* to come back," she told me.

And then, the worst words of all: "You will never be a Brownie!" In that one moment, the dreams of the cookouts, the cookies, and the campfires were over.

Banished . . . a punishment worse than soap or jail. A life without the uniform I so desperately wanted. I left the troop meeting disgraced—a Girl Scouts of America juvenile delinquent. Outside, I waited for Mom. The troop leader occasionally peeked out the window to make sure I remained planted on the bench, but I didn't have the energy to make any more trouble.

Finally, my mother arrived. She wore a cardigan over my favorite of her T-shirts, this one from the Pink Pussy Cat Boutique. It had a sly-looking cat on it and words that, just the other day, I had struggled to read: "Stroke Me and I'll Purr." Of course I didn't know that the Pink Pussy Cat Boutique was an infamous sex shop in the West Village. I just thought the cat was cute.

When I saw her, I started crying.

"What happened, Jessie?"

I told her the whole story, about the deformed plastic mats, about the pixie-haircut fiend, about the life sentence handed down by the troop leader.

"Oh well," she consoled. "Maybe they'll forget about it and let you back in."

But I knew that would never happen. We walked over to the class-room where Kathy remained in a Brownies meeting with a slightly older troop. I looked through the window. She was still in the weaving circle, and I could tell things had gone more smoothly for her. But she didn't look thrilled. She looked stoic, her glasses balanced on her nose, her brown hair hung straight and flat on her shoulders, her pudgy face tensed as she listened to the parting words of her troop leader.

When Kathy came outside, she walked apart from the other girls.

"How did it go?" my mother asked.

"Fine," Kathy said curtly.

"Do you want to go next week?"

"Yes," and that was it. When my sister didn't want to talk about something, there was no coaxing her. And my mother wasn't one to coax. I didn't feel like talking either, and we sat in silence in the back of the VW bus. But my father was home that night, and I told him what happened. Now that I would never be a Brownie, there seemed no reason not to.

"Screw 'em," he said. "It's an inane fascist organization. I can't imagine why you would ever want to be a part of that."

His reaction left me feeling better and worse. Better because he made me believe that the Girl Scouts were stupid anyway; worse because now, I felt stupid for wanting to be one in the first place. At the time, I didn't consider where his comments left Kathy, who was determined to struggle on in her troop. But then Kathy always had a kind of determination that I never did. She seemed almost immune to my father's pronouncements. There was a distance between him and her, a mutual distrust. And as I became increasingly obsessed with Daddy, she became increasingly private and emotionally contained. My mother saw the bond that had formed between Daddy and me. Though I thought I looked strange, with my drifting eye and blond hair, she reminds me today that I was charming and cheerful—and, as she puts it, "infinitely easier to get on with than Kathy." Perhaps so. I just remember how very afraid I was for Daddy, that something terrible might happen to him. I felt better and safer when I was with him, and feeling safe became my obsession. Even at six, I felt I had to always keep tabs on my father because my mother never did.

In the months that followed, he traveled more and more to New York. His work for the *Lampoon* seemed to be picking up. In part, that was because of the piece he had written late that summer. I can still remember how he came bounding into the house from his barn office, declaring proudly that he had something in mind for the magazine.

"It's called 'How to Cook Your Daughter,'" he told us.

Cook *your daughter?* I was beside myself. "Why do you want to cook us, Daddy?" I sobbed, my face crumbling.

Kathy never flinched. She announced that if my father was going to write about cooking her, then she was going to write about cooking *him.* "What a splendid idea!" my father said, and he encouraged her to write and draw a companion piece. "We'll call it, 'How to Cook Your *Father.'*" It was published in the *Lampoon* that September, on the page that faced Daddy's article. Of course, neither Kathy nor I understood the sexual overtones of my father's piece—why the daughter would be wearing "a bikini top, black velvet choker, (and) ankle socks" and rubbed with oil and liqueur. I was just jealous of the $50 Kathy got from the *Lampoon*'s publisher, Matty Simmons.

But I'll never forget the look on my father's face when he first told us the title. He said it with a slight challenge in his voice, almost as if he meant to upset us. I wonder why he told us at all? Why not just keep it to himself? We never would have known what he was writing up there.

Whatever our misgivings, the guys at the *Lampoon* must have liked it. By the time Christmas vacation arrived, my father had become more a part of the magazine's family than he was our own. Gone for days at a time, he'd bring back copies of the *Lampoon* and leave them lying around the house. The magazine seemed to understand him. In its pages, he could be his passionate and ironic self. For the *Lampoon*'s December issue, for instance, my father and another editor, Michael O'Donoghue, created a pair of satirical environmental "mini-posters for your den, study, or rumpus room . . . each pair carefully Protecto-packed in seventy-six layers of high impact, sixty-pound Dyna-Gloss paper wadding." Michael's presented a flower with greenback petals and, in a purple, childlike scrawl: "War is not unprofitable for poster-makers and other living things." My father's was of a shad-owy figure walking through a dense and magical forest. His caption: "This poster looked better as a tree."

My parents opposed cutting down trees—for Christmas or most any other reason. So my family bundled up a few days before the holi-day and trekked into the freezing cold to unearth one.

The morning we left L.A., I had wondered what the cold was like, and we got to know each other that first winter in New Jersey. Being able to play in the snow or go skating after school made up, in part, for the painfully long hours at Lebanon Township Jail. Connie and Doug Bradford proved great neighbors and helped my mother dig the VW out of a drift when my father was in New York. They loaned us candles when the power went out. Our stone house had a rickety furnace and radiators that spent more time clanging and banging than warming the room, so we passed our time inside huddled by the fireplace in the living room. Going upstairs to bed proved agonizing after sitting by the fire. Kathy and I would climb into our beds and scream as we slipped beneath the ice cold covers. Then we'd dance lying down, if only to get our blood going and the sheets a bit warmer.

But when we were outside skating on the nearby pond or hurtling down frozen driveways on a sled, the numbing cold seemed inconse-quential. Sometimes my father would come sledding with us. He was fearless, like that boy on the trike years before, ramming himself into the brick wall over and over and over again. My father plummeted down the steepest hill at top speed with Kathy and me taking turns sit-ting between his legs as he steered. We would shriek as we slid faster and faster, and Daddy would scream along with us. He took us skating and always made us wait on the frosty bank of the pond while he went out on the ice to test its safety. Before he left, he tucked his scarf into the multicolored sweater my grandma Georgina had knitted him from old bits of wool. It was knobby and oversized and smelled of cigar smoke—much like my father himself. But he had lost quite a lot of weight since we lived in L.A. and looked leaner and stronger that winter. He'd skate to the edge of the ice, his eyes sharp and clear, his cheeks bright with cold, and as I watched him glide to the center, my heart grew as still as I sat, as if worrying with me that the ice might not be thick enough. That it would crack beneath him. That he would be swept into the dark water. That the ice—like the cars in the city, like *Heroin*—might take away Daddy. But then I'd smile as he came skimming back to us, yelling that it was safe and then holding us up until we got our skater's legs.

On the afternoon that we went looking for our tree, the day had turned gray and damp, with the sort of dim sunlight that promised snow by nightfall. Kathy and I pulled our empty sled and followed my mom and dad, who carried a large, sharp spade. We headed about a quarter of a mile down the road to the icy driveway of Hall's Christmas Tree Farm. There, we knocked on the door of the farmhouse. Mrs. Hall answered, and the smell of cinnamon and hot chocolate wafted onto the porch. *Could it be?* I couldn't stop myself from wondering: *That's Santa's wife. Mrs. Claus. It* had *to be!* She smiled slightly at the sight of the sled and the spade, and when she heard my parents' request, she offered us the use of her handy chainsaw. No thank you, my father said, but might we have a garbage bag to wrap the roots in? Even if we were forbidden to *buy* garbage bags, we could, in good conscience, beg one for this cause. Mrs. Hall went into a kitchen drawer and handed my father the bag. Go ahead and take any tree, she told us. Free of charge.

"That's for being neighbors!" she said, handing Kathy and me each a gingerbread cookie, which made me *certain* she must be Santa's wife. After all, who else would reward *us* for being their neighbors?

We tramped up the hill and into the woods, in search of the perfect tree. The forest was stunning. Acres and acres of green pines in all shapes, heights and varieties. Snow blanketed their boughs as they swayed gently in the wind. We crunched from tree to tree, assessing the width and general beauty of each, and, of course, its height. That could be a problem in a house with low ceilings. I wanted a wide, furry tree. Kathy wanted something more stately. So Daddy helped us choose, going from this one to that, arguing merits and defects, imbuing each tree with a separate personality.

"This one is a real crazy," he'd say. "Look at those branches flying all over the place. Now here's more of the quiet type." He'd move on. "Reads Plato. . . ."

After a while, all of us were getting so cold that a decision had to be made. Kathy and I compromised: We'd take a Norwegian pine that was full but rather squat. It seemed, as my father put it, "jolly." We hopped and stamped our feet to keep warm as my dad worked up a sweat digging . . . and digging . . . and digging through the frozen ground with his spade. After more than an hour and a flurry of curses that I hoped Mrs. Claus couldn't hear, Daddy finally hefted the tree out of the earth, roots intact. My mom helped hoist it onto a sled that was far too short for the tree. Then my parents wrapped the garbage bag around the roots, and Daddy tied our tree to the sled with some twine he had stuffed in his pocket.

The sled proved too heavy for Kathy and me. So my dad and mom began pushing from behind, trying to do as little damage to the tree as possible. We made the journey back toward Mrs. Hall's house and then down her driveway. As we trudged along the road home, a station wagon appeared behind us, a cut tree strapped to its top. As it passed, the kids in the back looked through the window at our sled and dug-up pine. They seemed puzzled, but I was proud. I thought about how we would replant the tree after Christmas, how we had *saved* it. I knew it was grateful.

We brought the sled to the side of the house and opened the door as wide as we could. Kathy, my mom, and I cleared a spot in the corner of the living room. Then we helped my father fill a deep pan with dirt. He stood the tree in it and buried its roots. It was up to Kathy and me to water it, which we did diligently. Several days after Christmas, we helped my father replant the tree outside our house. We looked for the softest spot of earth, and found one that wasn't frozen solid, under the eaves of the old barn. There, it took root again.

Besides the Christmas posters my dad helped create, the December issue of the *Lampoon* carried a piece that, even at six and a half, made me curious about the complicated relationship my father had with the Catholic Church. It was a satire of the life of Jesus, but this time, the Messiah was a woman. The piece was called "Jessica Christ by FR. Tony Hendra," and Daddy took me aside to show it to me. "I thought you might like it, treasure, seeing that your name was in it," he said. The piece was done in simple comic book form, with large print and pictures of Jessica Christ doing good deeds. But Jessica wore robes with plunging neck lines, not to mention a Marilyn Monroe pin-up-style bathing suit when she walked on water. The language was simple, and I could read some of it. But like most of my father's humor, the jokes were lost on me.

" 'Take eat,' Jessica said, 'for this is My body."

" 'Hubbba Hubbba,' said the apostles."

The last picture showed Jessica nailed to the cross, her huge breasts exposed. Only a skimpy loin cloth dangled from her curvy hips. It terrified me. I told my daddy I wished he had used someone else's name instead. "Don't be silly," he said. But I had seen the small, devotional, black, wooden cross with a silver figure of Christ, the cross that my father kept carefully stowed in one of the drawers of his desk in his office. Not yet seven, I could just sense how Jessica Christ and the lovingly preserved silver figure contradicted each other. What I couldn't yet comprehend was how the viciousness with which my father went after religion seemed the flip side of the love that he had once felt for it. His venom made me nervous. It was, and remains, a rebellion beyond my depth.

I was left completely confused about Christianity. My dad told me that they had Kathy and me baptized "just in case." *In case of what?* When I asked him about the Easter Bunny, he told me it was "the risen Christ Vampire who comes to suck the blood of little children." Still, he would later take us to Midnight Mass in the city and make a point of reciting the responses in very loud Latin—over the English of the rest of the congregation. Why? Because, he explained, "real Catholics speak Latin."

I had a superstitious notion that my father's decision to use my name in his parody might bring the wrath of God upon me. And my father did little to allay my fears. In fact, he confirmed them just a few weeks later. When Daddy told me the *Lampoon* had a little recording job for me, I was ecstatic. I would have a line on a record they were putting together called *Radio Dinner*. Now I would finally have a chance to make $50, just as Kathy had done with her illustrated "How to Cook Your Father."

I also got a day off from school. Kathy, my mom, and I were to meet Daddy at the recording studio in the city. Instead of risking the trip in the VW—which seemed beyond terminal, its clutch having given out on the steepest hill in the neighborhood—Mom drove our "new" International Scout into Manhattan. The Scout, which Kathy and I dubbed "Flossie," had no back seats. Instead, we sat on narrow metal side-benches. Forget seatbelts; we clutched handrails that suspended from the Scout's ceiling. Too late, a neighbor told my parents what the used car dealer hadn't—that Flossie had been run into the ground by the local mailman. Jolting through the Midtown Tunnel, we met up with city traffic and discovered for ourselves what the neighbor meant. Flossie was not at her best in traffic. Like the VW van, she had a habit of stalling, and too often we sat frozen when red lights turned green. The honking gave me a headache.

Still, I was full of excitement when we finally walked out of the elevator and into the recording studio. Assorted members of the *Lampoon* were waiting for us, including Michael O'Donoghue, then one of my father's closest friends. The guys showed me around the sound booth, the colossal earphones, the warren of levers and buttons that controlled the volume, the mike that needed to be adjusted to accommodate my four-foot height. When the engineer said they were ready for me, I suddenly got shaky. My father had to feed me my line:

"What can you expect from a God who crucified his own son?"

I practiced it a few times with him, working to say it exactly on his hand signal. On the first take, I got the line wrong. On the second, I said it too fast. Finally, after a few more tries, I nailed it.

"That was perfect!" Daddy said, taking the headphones off my small, bright-red ears. I was elated. We stepped from the booth, and I held his hand as we stood with Michael, my mother, and Kathy. The engineer played back the cut. I was thrilled to listen to myself coming through the speakers, but after he heard it, my father looked down at me.

"Did you know you are going to hell for what you just said, Jessie?"

My stomach turned. I hadn't gone to church more than a handful of times, but I had heard all about hell from my dad—the burning bodies, the devil, and the red-hot pokers stuck in your eyes for ever and ever. Jessica Christ had worried me. But now, I had said something bad about God. My worst fears were coming true, and it was my own fault. "But you told me to say that, Daddy!" I blurted. "You told me to say that!"

"It doesn't matter," he said calmly. "You are still going to hell. In fact, Jessie, now we are *both* going to hell."

"But Daddy, what if I say I'm sorry?" I was desperate.

"It's too late for that," he said. "God listens to records."

Maybe everyone in the room laughed. All I remember is that no one reassured me that I was not, in fact, destined for eternal damnation. It might not have made much of an impression if they had. I always believed my father.

I got my $50 and went off to spend it in wonderland—the gigantic FAO Schwartz on Fifth Avenue. But I felt sick as I looked at the doll house furniture, stuffed animals, toy cars, and roller skates. Yes, they could be mine. But all I could think about was what awaited me. Hell.

God listens to records. And there was nothing I could do about it.

A few months later, my father lay naked on the ice of the frozen riverbed outside our house, curled in a fetal position. Above him, my mom brandished a blood-specked baseball bat. He was freezing to death. He had to be. After all, it must have been close to zero outside. And he lay there shivering, in a pool of blood—until the *Lampoon's* art director told him he could get up. Kathy and I watched from the shore.

Christmas had passed, and whatever thoughts I had of going to hell had abated, but my fears for my father remained. He still traveled into the city often, and when he might return never seemed certain. And so I was glad when he began bringing his work home with him— no matter how bizarre it turned out to be. At that time, the *Lampoon* had no budget for its photo spreads. Open the magazine, and you would see the editors modeling T-shirts or a naked Michael O'Donoghue as "Mr. Yum-Yum Cosmo, cutie of the month" in a *Cosmopolitan* parody. So when my dad decided to parody a burly hunter clubbing a baby seal for the *Lampoon*'s "Men" issue, he offered to shoot it in our backyard. Why not stage the shoot on the frozen river? And why not feature my mom as the club-wielding hunter? And have Daddy curl up on the ice naked, with Mom standing over him, brandishing a bat? And why not let Kathy and me watch? Of course we knew nothing about what the shoot would entail. No one had told us Daddy would be naked and lying in fake blood. Or that Mom would be pretending to kill him. All my parents had suggested was that Becky Bradford might not want to come to play that afternoon.

As Kathy and I stood by, my mother came down to the riverbank dressed in a long black skirt, boots, and a fur jacket courtesy of Anne Beatts, the issues editor. The *Lampoon*'s art director, Michael Gross, had been setting up to take the pictures, and when he was ready, my father strode from the house in a robe and some old shoes. Michael handed my mother a worn baseball bat, and then poured bright red liquid, almost fluorescent, over a section of the river that had frozen solid. Then my mother took her position on the ice and hoisted the bat high over a shoulder. "Everything's ready," Michael called out, and with that, my father stripped off his robe. Shivering and chattering, he flung himself, completely naked, on the ice and in the pool of blood.

Then he curled up at my mother's feet while she wielded the bat. Michael had to work quickly.

The full-page color picture appeared in the next issue with the caption "THIS MUST STOP!" My father looks pathetic and vulnerable, his white skin almost translucent. My mother towers over him — menacing, armed, ruthless, and in a position of power, a place she never claimed during their marriage. I suppose some kids might have been horrified by the image. Not me. I was just glad Daddy was home, and that he wasn't being hurt for real. No matter what might be happening around us, at least I knew where he was. For me, that was all that really mattered.

By that winter, the *Lampoon* had become a family affair — Mom in the baby seal picture, Kathy with her sketches for her "How to Cook Your Father" piece, and me for my damnation-earning portrayal of a truculent Christian on *Radio Dinner*, the record that God would be listening to soon. Daddy hadn't just brought his work home. He brought the staff along with it. Together they seemed to embolden each other in all the worst ways. They were playful and fun, but even their humor quickly turned dark and angry. They pushed each other to push the limits. And they brought into our already peculiar house, a lifestyle that seemed epitomized by the *Lampoon*'s January 1972 edition, an issue my father conceived. It was entitled, "Is Nothing Sacred?"

Not surprising, the answer for him and others on the staff was a resounding "no." The cover featured the favorite dorm poster of Che Guevara with a dripping cream pie in the face. Inside were child abuse and molestation jokes, a Son-of-God comic book, Martin Luther King on a target, and a Virgin Mary dildo. My father seemed especially proud of the edition. Like "How to Cook Your Daughter," he saw it as some of his best, most biting work.

Henry Beard was the first member of the *Lampoon* staff to come to the New Jersey house. Later, when I read *Catcher in the Rye*, I thought immediately of Henry, a grown-up version of Holden Caulfield with his black glasses, shabby docksiders, and rumpled yachting attire. Henry kept his dark hair short at a time when the other guys in his club were letting it down. Doug Kenney wore it shoulder length and occasionally in a pony tail. Michael O'Donoghue let his hair grow, as did Sean Kelly, my father, and everyone one else I can think of. In the *Lampoon's* midtown office, sitting behind his desk, Henry resembled a mad scientist overseeing a group of scraggly orderlies.

At twenty-four, Henry was already executive editor of the *Lampoon*. The magazine had become my father's sole source of income, though he was still just a contributing editor. So, for all its seeming lack of formality, Henry's visit was, for my mother, a version of the boss coming to dinner. When he stepped off the bus from New York, his pipe was already firmly entrenched in his mouth. Without comment, he took in the VW, the barren countryside, the house, and Kathy and me. Families, in any form, were an aberration at the *Lampoon*, and Henry did not seem to know quite what to make of us. Besides, he was at an age where having children seemed inconceivable.

He sat close to the fireplace to defend against the chill of the rest of the house. In the years to come, our winter visitors adopted the same strategy to stay warm — knocking themselves out through lack of oxygen, and falling asleep on the sofa. Henry, however, managed to stay awake, chatting with my dad and, of course, smoking his pipe. Kathy and I tiptoed in and out of the kitchen, where my mother was cooking a chicken, to take mute peeks at the visitor. Half an hour after the propane gas tank emptied, my mother pulled a perfectly half-done chicken from an oven that had gone cold.

Kathy and I watched as she tossed lit matches under the broiler plate, trying over and over again to relight the stove. "Oh shit!" she said, emerging from underneath the oven. I could see she was thinking. But what were her options, really? This was rural New Jersey, and it was 9:00 P.M. at night. Even if there had been somewhere to eat that was still open, we couldn't take the boss there, not even a boss like Henry.

Then it dawned on her. And really, it was the only option. She picked up the chicken pan and carried it into the living room. "The fuckers forgot to deliver the gas!" she explained. And with Elizabethan ingenuity, guest and hosts skewered the chicken with the poker and took turns holding it over the flames. Dinner was served promptly at 10:30 P.M. Kathy and I could barely keep our eyes open.

After that dinner, I always liked Henry. I'll never forget the image of him roasting a chicken on a poker over an open fire—the mad scientist goes camping. And I came to like him more as my family's life with the *Lampoon* progressed during the next few years. In large part that was because, as drugs became a fixture in everyone's life, Henry stuck to his pipe and filled it only with tobacco—at least on his visits to our house. Henry waited until spring to come again, and by then, my dad had been hired on full-time.

Even Michael O'Donoghue, who hated the cold, came to stay in New Jersey with his girlfriend, Amy. He spent the entire weekend huddled by the fireplace, complaining. In contrast, my father made a point of getting up in the morning and immediately heading out of the house. He tramped through the snow and chopped firewood, showing off his skills as an outdoorsman, though for whom wasn't clear until later. But on that Sunday afternoon, my father and Amy conspired to get Michael outside regardless. They grabbed him and, with my mother's help, hoisted him out of the warm refuge he had made for himself on the sofa. Grasping his arms and legs and deaf to his protestations, they carried him through the front door of the house and pitched him into the snow, laughing all the while. I laughed with them, but the scene seemed even more unnerving than seeing my naked father lying in a pool of fake blood. Michael was my father's good friend, so why were they ganging up on him like that? Of course, I couldn't understand the sexual tension that had surfaced between Michael, Amy, and my father—a tension that would soon ruin their relationship.

But Michael's humiliation added to the feeling I already had: To my father, the joke was *always* more important than the feelings that it hurt. I still loved him, maybe more desperately than ever. And that's why I didn't want him to leave the house that night in April—the night he crawled into bed with me and changed my life forever.

3.

PINKEYE

THAT'S WHAT PEOPLE DO WHEN THEY LOVE EACH other.

I needed to remind myself of that. To say those words over and over again—the words that Daddy had said the night before. At least he had stayed. At least I had kept him from going into the city and coming back who knew when.

My dad rested on a white wicker chair on the porch of the little house across the road from ours. We called the place the Forge because it had once been the workplace of the blacksmith who had built our home. When my parents bought our place, the man who had been my dad's comedy partner, Nick Ullett, bought the Forge. But Nick never used it, so we kept it up for him. Kathy and I loved the wide porch in back. It jutted over the river, and we could fish from it, not that we ever managed to catch anything. The Forge was to be rented out for the spring and summer to Daddy's boss, Henry Beard, and Daddy had taken me by the hand to help him sweep out the cobwebs of winter in preparation for Henry's arrival.

We didn't talk much while we cleaned. I didn't know what to say. And as the sun set and my dad rested, I looked over at him and thought about what he had told me last night while he lay next to me in bed: "That's what people do when they love each other."

And I did. I loved him so much. More than I loved anyone on earth. So why did I feel so scared? And so ashamed? I tried squeezing my eyes tight against the tears, willing them back. My lips started to quiver, and I pressed my mouth shut. My father must have noticed.

"Treasure, come over here and sit with me."

I looked at him and realized that, for the first time in my life, I didn't want to. For the first time, I didn't want to be on his lap, in his arms, against his chest. But as I had the night before, I did as he asked. I walked slowly across the porch and sat stiffly on his lap.

"I am an asshole, Jessie, a drunken asshole."

I looked into his eyes, and I could smell the cigars he smoked mixed with his sweat—just as I had last night. Then I burst into tears. Daddy said nothing more, and when I stopped crying, he took me by the hand and we walked back across the road.

What was he trying to tell me? That he was sorry about what happened? But why? Wasn't it what people did when they loved each other? Why should he be sorry then? My head spun. I didn't understand what we had done. And I couldn't figure out how I was supposed to feel about it. *Daddy* wasn't *an asshole. It must've been* my *fault. He must've seen me there crying and thought that maybe I didn't love him anymore.*

I didn't know what to think, how to feel. I just knew things had changed with my father. And the nightmares came for the first time soon after.

It's dark and I'm in the house alone, wearing the same nightgown he had made me take off the night before. Every room is dimly lit, as though the bulbs have been switched from 175 watts to fifteen. I look out the kitchen window and see a shape by the barn. It moves toward the house, toward me, and I know that it wants to hurt me. Maybe it's a man, but it seems like a monster, and I run to the kitchen door. I try to lock it, but the bolt won't budge. The door flies open and becomes so heavy that I can't push it shut. So I run into the empty living room and try to lock the side door. The old, rusty hinges break off, disintegrating in my hands, and I sense the monster coming closer. I run up the narrow stairs to my parents' room. The windows are wide open, and like the door downstairs, have become too heavy to shut. I look out their window and suddenly a bright spotlight falls on the figure. It's a man whose face I can't see. I'm petrified. The kitchen door is wide open. The hinges in the living room have fallen to dust. The windows won't budge. There's no way to keep the man out.

Or the other dream:

I'm stuck in a deep hole, a well maybe. I can just barely see the sky. The hole smells musty and damp, and it's so small I can't lie down. My knees are pressed to my chin; my arms are pinned to my sides. My hair covers my face, and I gasp for air. Then I hear voices. My mother! My sister, Kathy! They're looking for me, and I hear them walking around the hole calling, "Jessie! Jessie, where are you?" I try to call out to them: "I'm here! Look down! I'm right here in this hole! Help me! Please help me get out!" But when I open my mouth, no sound comes. I strain and strain, but I can only hear myself whisper. I know then that they will never hear me, that I'll be stuck in the hole forever.

I began sleepwalking. Some mornings, I woke to find objects tucked into the corner of my bed: a rolling pin from the kitchen, a bar of soap, a wooden duck figurine that had been on one of the shelves in the living room, the china eggs that went with it. I never understood why I had taken them. I was like a six-and-a-half-year-old Lady Macbeth.

Of course, I told no one. How could I? What would I tell them? That Daddy had made me do things I didn't understand? "That's what people do when they love each other," he had said. In my heart, I so desperately wanted to believe him. But my head seemed unwilling to let me. And that conflict, that irreconcilable conflict, began to take its toll.

I never liked Lebanon Township Jail, but now I felt terrified to go to school. And to the ballet class I had always loved. And of being outside at all. My ballet teacher tried everything to get me to come back to the dance studio, but I went into near hysterics at the idea. I clung to my mother and had to be carried sobbing back to the car. I didn't even understand why.

I grew attached to my mom, even though I never considered confiding in her. How would I explain something I didn't understand? I had always adored my father, and even if I had thought that what he'd done was wrong, I had no illusions about my mother standing up to him. So instead, I simply hid. When she took Kathy to school in the mornings, my shame kept me in the Scout. All of us had conjunctivitis that spring, and I had gotten a very bad case. I knew what pinkeye looked like, so I used it as a way to stay home. I'd wake up in the early morning darkness and sneak down the ladder of the bunk beds I shared with Kathy. Then I'd tiptoe into the bathroom off the landing, shut the door, and switch on the light. I was still too short to see my reflection in the mirror, so I'd position a stool to stand on. I'd lean toward the mirror and go to work on my eye. I chose the right eye because I could barely see out of it anyway. (Kathy and I had both inherited my father's astigmatism). First, I would tuck all my hair behind my ears. Then I'd use my index finger to rub all over the eye — on the lid and on the soft skin underneath. The rubbing burned, but I needed to look convincing. When it almost glowed red, when the white looked completely bloodshot and the skin around it raw, I would stop to inspect. Then I would spit on my hand and rub the saliva over the entire area. I hoped it would look like pus. Sometimes, if I had some of the little specks of sleep on my eyelashes, I would carefully collect them in the palm of my hand and press them into the corner of my eye to make it look crusty.

When I was satisfied, I would climb off the stool and head back to my bunk. Then I'd lie down very carefully, positioning my head just so on the pillow. It was critical that none of the crust I'd created fell off my eye. If it did, I might be sent to school.

When I heard my mom getting up in the next room, I would give my eye one final, careful rubbing just in case the redness had started to fade. She usually woke up alone; Daddy had begun spending entire weeks in the city.

"Mommy, my eye still hurts!" I'd tell her.

She would peer at me. "Well, it still looks bad." The fateful pause. Then: "You'd better stay home."

Relief.

I was always nervous that when we dropped Kathy off at school, one of the teachers might run out to the Scout, grab me, and force me into the building. I would hide as best I could, sometimes covering myself with my jacket. But no one ever came out. They had clearly given up on me.

Back home, without my dad around, I headed upstairs to my room to lose myself in a make-believe world — the sort I could control.

Inside the walls of my Victorian dollhouse sat delicate furniture from a store in New York. Each room was full of tiny replicas—plush nineteenth-century sofas, mahogany tables, and porcelain bathtubs with tiny claw feet. I had minute plates of food: iced cakes, loaves of bread, cheese boards, and whole chickens. I wanted nothing modern, especially the family that lived in the house. The mother wore a long Victorian dress, the mustachioed father a dark suit, the children black button shoes. They had a nursery with cozy brass beds, a rocking horse, and thumbnail-size copies of Kate Greenaway books. My house even had a nanny, bedecked with a black cap. I camped next to the house, sticking my face into their living room, admiring the straight-backed, red, velvet sofa, the tiny grandfather clock, and the fake wood burning in the fire place. The nurse became Mary Poppins and sent the little girl and boy up to their beds in the nursery. I pretended that she was tucking me in along with them, kissing me on the forehead. "Spit spot into bed," I made her say. And none of them had pinkeye.

My mother pried me away from that world long enough to take me to the doctor. If he thought my pinkeye was fake, he didn't let on. He prescribed drops that would cure conjunctivitis, but of course they wouldn't work on me. After weeks and weeks of the morning rubbing ritual, Mommy suspected I was making up my illness—mainly because my conjunctivitis always got mysteriously better on Saturday but worse on Monday. But she thought it simply had to do with how much I hated school, and she arranged for Kathy and me to transfer in the fall. I doubt she had the emotional energy to examine what was going on with me anyway. Looking back, I'm not sure she truly wanted to be a mother—not then, when she was surrounded by a group of creative singles looking to make their way in the world. Here she was, shuttling us to school and packing sack lunches. There they were, free to do as they pleased—and her husband ran with them. For her, just getting through the day had become a challenge.

I don't know if my mother knew of Daddy's many affairs, but everyone at the *Lampoon* did. The tryst my father had with Michael O'Donoghue's girlfriend plunged the office into chaos, and the rift between the two men quickly became public. It wasn't the first time Michael and my dad had shared a woman. It was just that this time, Michael was furious at what he saw as a betrayal. My father tried to smooth things over at first. In a letter he wrote to Michael that my mother showed me recently, he even came close to apologizing:

> Michael
>
> I have never done anything, at any time, for any reason that was intended to hurt you. There are few people I desire to hurt less. I never did and I never will.
>
> I have never tried to elbow you out of the magazine (sic) or the record or any other project, and I never will. It would be suicidal.
>
> I'm not enjoying all this one iota. It's sad, poisonous and terribly unfunny. So please, let's stop. I miss you.
>
> *Tony*

Even in trying to apologize, it was all about my father—how *he* wasn't enjoying the drama, how squeezing out Michael would've been suicidal for *him*. My mom believes Michael opened the letter, read it, and returned it without comment. Writing years later about the affair and subsequent falling-out, my father adopts a more indifferent tone: "Now in the hip-happening, going-too-far, nothing-is-sacred, dish-it-out world of the 1972 *Lampoon*, this sort of thing had happened once or twice before. . . . The line between loyalties and love were very in-distinct, and claims on people made no sense."

Maybe for him, but not for O'Donoghue, who demanded a complete, unequivocal apology from his former friend. "He seemed to be trying to will me to admit a wrong, a terrible wrong, an immeasurably terrible wrong and then die," my father wrote later.

Michael should have known what I have come to accept: Admitting terrible wrongs is far beyond my father.

The situation escalated, the *Lampoon* offices divided, the adversaries avoided each other until, finally, a confrontation. According to my dad, Michael's last words to him were: "You're slime, Hendra. I hate you! You're scum, you hear? Nothing but scum, slime!" My mother, however, was never one for showdowns. The affair, and in fact all the affairs, must have hurt her deeply. But she dealt with my father's behavior by avoiding it. She didn't want to know. She didn't want to see. She didn't want to hear. While the *Lampoon* offices were filled with high emotion, Mom stayed silent and absorbed the blows, as if she were on the seal's end of that *Lampoon* photo shoot. My not wanting to go to school occupied the tiniest corner of her mind. So I remained inside my dollhouse and missed the last month and a half of first grade.

Kathy found my "illness" irritating. "You're always getting to stay home, and I have to go to stupid school!" she yelled at me one evening as we fought over who got to sit closest to the tiny black-and-white television that my parents, with reservations, had finally purchased. They were, I suppose, ambivalent about television. My mother wasn't interested in it, and my father regarded it as emblematic of the stupidity of American culture (perhaps because he had had no success writing for it). Once we had one, however, he got sucked in too. An insomniac, he often spent long nights glued to the tube. As a family, we watched *Monty Python's Flying Circus*. Mom and Daddy had gone to Cambridge with almost the entire cast, and my father naturally had a professional interest in what was probably the most innovative comedy on television. Still, he couldn't help but warn us of the terrible "brain rot" we would get from watching too much. And like many things my father said, suddenly this thing, this "brain rot," concerned me. After an hour of Saturday morning cartoons, I worried I had caught it. When my mother read Kathy and me *Charlie and the Chocolate Factory*, I was astounded to hear a whole song devoted to the ills of watching television.

I asked Mom if Daddy had written the book. "No," she answered, "but I wish he had."

Jockeying for the best spot on the bed to watch TV was just one of the squabbles Kathy and I had that spring. My special stay-at-home privileges did nothing to improve the already competitive relationship I had with my sister. We were so close in age that some fighting was inevitable. But it became more than just the normal sisterly button pushing. When we fought, I sensed that Kathy truly disliked me. She did all the things that siblings might do, twisting my wrist to give me an "Indian burn" or digging her nails into my arm until little reds marks appeared. But she did it with a gusto that made me think her anger was deeper than any mark she left. Kathy saw me as prettier, even though I always felt too awkward to be pretty, with my floating eye and pigeon toes. But to Kathy, thin defined pretty, and thin I was. She, however, was chubby, and my father made sure she knew it. When he wasn't calling her "Thunder Thighs," he made jokes about her "extra tires," grinding her self-esteem to dust. Weight had always been a tremendous issue with my father, and the *Lampoon* years were his thin time. But he would go on and off diets and (when he wasn't too hung over) made a point of working out. He equated fat to weakness, and despite her smarts and determination, Kathy was simply a fat kid to my dad. She assumed he preferred me because I wasn't, and perhaps she was right. In the end, her weight might have been her best protection. Yes, she resented me. But she never knew the consequences of being Daddy's girl.

When Henry Beard took over the Forge, he brought with him something that came to symbolize all that was wrong in my household: a croquet set. My parents and their friends saw it as a chance to exact revenge. It wasn't so much about going from hoop to hoop. Instead, it became about the opportunity to smash another player's ball far off into the bushes. And so rivalries, jealousies, and personal vendettas played out on our lawn.

Members of the *Lampoon* staff (and their assorted significant others) came to get away from the sweltering city and took full advantage of the nastiness of Henry's croquet set. Kathy and I looked on while the adults became monsters. Matches routinely ended in cursing and tears. Forget what they taught us in school: that it didn't matter whether you won or lost. For my parents and their friends, winning *was* everything, but how they won—and who they hurt along the way—meant even more.

I had seen this kind of game-playing before. Michael O'Donoghue had started it by bringing his Monopoly set to our house during the winter. He, my father, my mom, and sometimes one of Michael's girlfriends used to sit up all night playing and smoking grass. Even from my room, I could hear the gleeful shouts as someone cleared someone else out. Sometimes they would get too tired or too stoned to play any longer, and they'd leave the game lying there, in mid-play. Kathy and I knew better than to disturb the Monopoly board in the morning.

But Michael no longer came to the house, given his feud with my father, and warm weather and croquet supplanted cold nights and Community Chest. If Kathy and I joined in a game, we were treated with some mercy, but only if it wasn't too late in the afternoon. By evening, everyone was so drunk or so high that no one cared whose ball was sent skimming out in to the far reaches of the garden.

One evening, the croquet had gone on even later than usual. Lunch was a distant memory and dinner nowhere in sight. All the adults had been drinking since three in the afternoon, and the mood had grown nasty. Sean Kelly, a *Lampoon* editor, had brought his soft-spoken girlfriend, Valerie, to our house for the weekend. And in proper Hendra form, she was welcomed by becoming the croquet target of the afternoon. After her ball was sent off the course one too many times, Valerie finally crumbled.

Wielding her croquet mallet over her head, she ran toward the barn and began pounding it over and over again as tears of rage poured from her eyes. I watched Valerie's delicate arms, as though in slow motion, swing the wooden mallet toward the wall with all her might, letting out the repressed frustrations amassed during a weekend with these ruthless satirists—men for whom a show of emotion was cause for ridicule, for whom the joke was always the most important thing.

I was fascinated by what she was doing. I fantasized that I was there next to her, banging my mallet against the barn, screaming and crying too. I didn't know exactly why, what it was I wanted to scream out of my body, but I knew I felt something there. Now, of course, I realize it was confusion over what had happened with my father. I no longer felt safe. And I had begun to feel angry. I had just turned seven,

but there wasn't an adult around me who cared that I was a kid—
or who had any idea that it mattered. But I didn't run over and join
Valerie. I knew that if I did everyone would only laugh at me, just like
they were laughing at her.

That summer, for the first time since *Heroin* killed my parents'
friend, I became very aware of drugs. Sure, there had always been
drugs around my family, but I began to make a real connection
between what the grown-ups put into their bodies and the behavior
that came out. I started to notice when the rolling paper appeared. Or
when the coke was lined up on a mirror with a razor blade. The
grown-ups would come and hover over whoever was setting up the
drugs. The look in their eyes—the anticipation—reminded me of
the look my father had showed me the night that he crawled into bed
with me. And I would grow nervous. *Why did they look like that? Why
did it mean so much to them to pull smoke so deeply into their throats?
And why were they sniffing white powder up their noses?*

After the smoking and the snorting, the music would switch from
Brahms to the Beatles, and the volume would rise. Meals were put on
hold. Often, the group would gather along the river, where everyone
would strip and plunge in naked. Kathy and I never did. We would
stay behind in the house, running upstairs to change into our swim-
suits before joining everyone by the water. No one told us to put on
our suits; we just preferred it that way. In fact, we wanted everyone to
wear one. Nude adults were supremely embarrassing, even to kids like
Kathy and me, who had grown accustomed to having their parents
walk around naked. In this upside-down world, my sister and I were
the uptight and responsible ones, the square, boring guests who sat in
the corner of the sofa while the hip people partied.

During these skinny-dipping sessions, I was especially concerned that our neighbors might walk by. It was easy to see the stream from the road. Just a few low trees and bushes could obscure a direct view of the Hendras and their pals—and all their private parts—from the eyes of anyone taking an afternoon stroll. It wasn't as if the stoned and naked grownups were quiet, either. They splashed and giggled and cursed almost as much as they did while playing croquet.

I sat on a rock one afternoon, watching the red glow on the end of the joint that was making its way around the group, when I heard the familiar voices of Becky and Jeremy Bradford. They were closing on us fast, so I knew they must be on their bikes. I scurried up the river bank and looked down the road. To my horror, they weren't alone. Walking behind the bikes were their mom and dad! Doug wore a white T-shirt and jeans, Connie a sleeveless, blue shirt and matching Bermuda shorts. They had clothes on and just plain old regular cigarettes between their fingers. And every step brought them closer to the spot where they would be able to see my parents sprawled out on the river rocks—naked, naked, *naked* with all their naked, naked friends. The bright summer sunshine streamed down like a spotlight, highlighting the sets of protruding breasts, the shocks of pubic hair, and—most disturbing to me—the dangling penises. They would see it all. There was no way they would just walk by. How could they with all the racket going on? Inside my head I was screaming, *Shut up! Shut up! All of you shut up!* But the splashing and cursing only seemed to grow louder. I began to pray: *Please, Lord, don't let the Bradfords see us. Please, oh please, don't let the Bradfords see us. . . .*

4.

LEMMINGS

GOD MUST HAVE LISTENED TO *RADIO DINNER* BECAUSE he did me no favors that day.

Becky and Jeremy saw them first. They stopped dead in their bicycle tracks, frozen, staring across the bank at the scene on the river rocks. I hid in the bushes, an instinctive but pointless reaction because, of course, my neighborhood friends knew that these were my parents. Doug and Connie came alongside their stunned children and followed their stares. Not knowing that anyone was on the road, my father, in a moment of terrible synchronicity, stood up on one of the rocks and unwittingly modeled every inch of his nude body to the Bradford audience. Without a word, Connie grabbed Becky's bike, yanked it around, and started pushing it back up the road as fast as she could, Becky still on it. Doug followed his wife, lugging Jeremy and his bike.

I stayed hidden in the bushes for most of the afternoon, wondering how I could ever show my face at the Bradford house again. I never told my parents that our neighbors strolled down the road that day. Why bother? They would have thought it was hysterical or that I was being too uptight. The Bradfords never said a word about what they had seen, at least not to me. In fact, the next evening, Connie called to very kindly ask Kathy and me if we would like to go with them to the Dairy Queen. My mother had never heard of the place but said we could go if we liked. We did, and it was heaven.

Even Henry Beard, a relative conservative among the *Lampoon* crowd, succumbed to the spirit of treating Red Mill Road as a small nudist colony. He shocked the passengers of a passing car one morning by walking casually from the Forge to our house in nothing but loafers. He arrived at our door, borrowed a book, and lay down on the lawn to read and smoke his pipe, like a professor on holiday.

While everyone was experimenting with taking off their clothes, Kathy and I were busy putting them on. Our craze that summer was dressing up. And like my obsession with the Victorian dollhouse, dressing up in long party dresses and playing prince and princesses became a way to escape. While the drugs and drink flowed freely downstairs, we wore white gloves and set up tea parties on the second floor. Despite the scene her parents had witnessed, Becky Bradford was still allowed over and joined in the tea parties too. We even held our dog, Freckles, prisoner, stuffing his front legs through the sleeves of dresses and tying bonnets on him. He tried to walk around our bedroom with his back legs completely bound in a gold, 1950s prom gown and a flowered hat rigged to his head with yarn.

Freckles was a stray who had wandered on to the New Jersey property when we were in Los Angeles. When we returned from California to reclaim the house, Freckles was part of the package. He was a medium-size mutt, with a white face, a mostly black body, and two-toned legs. The little black dots on his snout were what earned him his name. My dad considered Freckles a reincarnation of his own father. "When he looks at me with those eyes, I know he's really dad," he once told us. I wasn't sure exactly what that meant. I just knew Freckles was a good ol' country dog and a frenzied guide. If you went for a walk, he'd follow for a time, then take off running ahead before running back to urge you onward, panting and wiggling all the while. He also kept a sharp eye on his territory, barking wildly and chasing every car that drove by the house until his legs gave out.

And as he had done with the rest of us, my father wanted to use Freckles for a piece in the *Lampoon*. The cover, no less. The concept was simple, my dad explained (though I don't think he bothered to tell Freckles, reincarnated father or not): Freckles would be pictured, his tongue hanging out, with a gun to his head. The caption? "Buy This Magazine or We'll Kill This Dog." Freckles, however, was no professional, and the *Lampoon*'s art director wouldn't even give him the chance to audition. Of course, we still loved him, and we thought the art director was wrong. After all, he submitted to being dressed up without so much as a whimper, unlike the cat that scratched and clawed whenever we tried to dress her in doll clothes and put her in a baby carriage.

Our dress up clothes came from a junk shop about a mile up the road. It was owned by Mrs. Kruger, who stood out in my mind as the neighbor who, by comparison, made my family look good. Not normal. Just better. She seemed a bit like Granny on *The Beverly Hillbillies*—about sixty with wire-rimmed glasses and rotting teeth. She lived next to the junkyard, in a shack that no longer aspired to be a house, with her twenty-something boyfriend and a girl she had all but adopted. Yes, her boyfriend was more than three decades younger, and yes, he was about as much of a wreck as the shack where they lived. But Mrs. Kruger was friendly and let Kathy and me have discarded New Jersey debutante attire for a quarter a bag. She might have done well saving some of it for herself. I never saw Mrs. Kruger in anything other than jeans. And Missy, the girl who lived with her, sported cutoffs, flannel shirts, and an array of baseball caps. The outfit seemed about right for Missy, though. In the woods, she shot anything that moved and was often seen carrying something dead—a rabbit, a woodchuck, sometimes a raccoon. Once, Kathy and I met her with a lead-filled squirrel in her hands. She told us about the fresh squirrel pie she had made for dinner the night before and seemed a little insulted when we refused the slice she had left in the kitchen.

Dressing up proved an escape from the adult world that frightened me, but the other games we played were imitations of things I had seen and experienced. I had walked in on my parents having sex and had seen guests sneak off into the woods or lie on top of each other in the grass. And, of course, I had seen plenty of nakedness. So I began playing "Lady and Man" with the daughter of one of the few New Jersey friends my mother had. I was the man, she was the lady, and we went off to the Forge, unused during the week, and lay in one of the guest beds. I would tell her to take off her clothes. Then I would touch her body all over and give her hugs and kisses. I knew I was bad, that I shouldn't be touching her "privates." But I still invited her to come over to the Forge with me. By the end of the summer, we had stopped playing the game—mainly because my friend didn't want to anymore. But my simultaneous fascination with and horror of anything sexual continued.

I began to feel like I had asked for what happened with Daddy, as if my interest in sex had encouraged him. One day while playing

Barbies at Becky's house, I put Barbie and Jeremy's Batman figure in bed together with Batman on top. I poured through my father's R. Crumb comic books staring at the exaggerated breasts and genitalia. The *Lampoon* issues that lay around the house had "Photo Funny" sections with naked people in bed. I wanted to look but felt guilty when I did. I couldn't talk to my mom because I was sure that I already knew too much for a seven-year-old. And I couldn't talk to Daddy. I was scared that if I did, it might happen again.

In the fall, Kathy and I started at a new community school. It was much more progressive than Lebanon Township, and the teachers took the time to coax me into class. Not finishing first grade had taken its toll. I was behind in reading and math and needed extra help to catch up. But at least I consented to go.

The situation between my father and Michael O'Donoghue was making it hard for the *Lampoon* to function properly. Michael made it clear that any friend of my father's was no friend of his. People found themselves having to sneak around so as not to be seen as allying themselves with one side or the other. My father's office was moved away from Michael's.

The *Lampoon*'s first recording, *Radio Dinner*, had done very well, and the magazine's publisher, Matty Simmons, thought it would be good to put together another album. *Radio Dinner* had been produced by my dad and Michael, but they clearly were not going to be working together again. O'Donoghue had gone so far as to suggest that Daddy be fired, or at least that his work and my father's not appear in the same issue of the magazine. Henry, probably sick to death of the whole thing, told him not to be ridiculous. Everyone was uncomfortable with Michael and my dad being in the same building. It seemed to Matty Simmons that it would be an excellent idea to separate them, and so he put the recording project in my father's hands.

The new project would be a musical called *Lemmings*, and it was conceived as a parody of Woodstock, taking on such rock icons as Joe Cocker, Bob Dylan; John Denver; Crosby, Stills, and Nash; and James Taylor. My father, Sean Kelly, Paul Jacobs, and Christopher Guest would write most of the lyrics, and I listened as they gathered in the New Jersey living room to hash out the John Denver parody:

> Oh, Colorado's calling me
> From her hillsides and her rivers and
> Her mesas and her trees,
> When blizzards snap the power lines
> And all the toilets freeze,
> In December in the Colorado Rockies . . .

I sang along to most of the lyrics of "Colorado," but I always skipped one part:

> The baby didn't die until we'd burned
> Up all our wood.
> Considering we ate her raw
> She tasted pretty good.

I had had enough of eating kids with "How to Cook Your Daughter."

Lemmings opened in New York on January 25, 1973, and it seemed a big event in my life—mainly because we got to stay overnight at the Roosevelt Hotel in New York. My father cursed

Matty Simmons for being cheap. But I was incredibly impressed by the Roosevelt. I stood on the red carpet in the lobby and didn't mind that it was threadbare. And when we left for the theater, we took a wonderfully bumpy cab ride down to the Village Gate on Bleecker Street, a no-frills venue that seemed less theater and more enormous basement.

In true *Lampoon* style, *Lemmings* was packed with "bad" words and overt references to sex, drugs, and rock'n'roll. But it was much too late to protect us from any of that. Not that anyone suggested we should have been left at home. Instead, Kathy and I sat drinking Shirley Temples and watching the show. I had a wonderful time. Although every joke and parody flew over my head, I responded to the energy of the show and to the obvious enjoyment of the adults watching it. Besides, the music was fun. I liked when Chris Guest put on a hat and played the harmonica in a Dylan parody. I giggled watching Chevy Chase act crazy in a motorcycle jacket. And, along with most of the audience, I fell in love with a fat, bearded guy named John Belushi. He threw himself around the stage and made noise with an energy that I related to—more like a kid than an adult. He stumbled and screamed his way through a Joe Cocker imitation, falling down and springing up again like an insane jack-in-the-box. I had heard the real Joe Cocker many times, coming out of the speakers of my parents' stereo. But I didn't recognize that John was doing satire. I just thought he was adorable as he stood there and yelled into the mike:

And I think of days
Of purple haze and Freon,
Smokin', jokin',
Doin' Coke with Leon.

I made no connection between "doin' coke" and the white powder I had seen around my house.

During the next few months, Kathy and I became child groupies of the show and begged to see it as often as we could. I learned all the words to songs I couldn't hope to understand. We scampered backstage, star struck, but recognized none of the problems brewing—the predictable squabbles between actors and Belushi's increasing drug use. All that winter and spring, I listened to the *Lemmings* soundtrack and sang along as if the songs were from *The Little Mermaid*.

The success of *Lemmings* meant that my father was working much less at the magazine. And though I loved the show, I missed the Saturday visits Kathy and I used to make to the *Lampoon* offices, when we'd drive into New York with him, so he could finish some project there. Kathy and I would roam the empty hallways, testing out the chairs and desks. I liked Matty Simmons' chair best. It was big and soft, and I sat at his desk and drew on spare scraps of typing paper.

On one of those Saturday trips, months before their friendship came to a terrible end, my father took us to Michael O'Donoghue's loft on Spring Street. I was startled to find that he didn't have a bathroom. Not in his place anyway. You had to go all the way down the hallway and look for a closet that had a toilet in it. The loft was dark and crowded, and Michael had a bizarre collection of ragtag toys littering his home. I shrieked as I sat on the severed leg of a mannequin he had tossed on a chair. Kathy and I haltingly inspected scores of decrepit dolls. Their stuffing oozed from ripped bodies. Tattered and dirty stuffed animals seemed to leer from the loft's dark corners. It felt as though the loft were a toy graveyard, full of the former friends of children who had, willingly or otherwise, abandoned their dolls and animals to Michael. *Where did he get this stuff?* It felt so creepy, as though there was some story, some message in this apartment of misfit toys. *Maybe Michael doesn't like children. . . . I'll bet that's it! And if Michael doesn't like children . . . and he and Daddy are friends . . . and Daddy sleeps here . . . then maybe* Daddy *doesn't like children either!* I was stunned. But then it started making more sense.

Many of the pictures of children I had seen in the *Lampoon* made me feel this way, especially the ones in Michael's stories. I poured over his parody of Eloise looking for clues. There she was, this incorrigible little girl, who didn't live at the Plaza but in a downtown fleabag full of junkies, transvestites, and dirty, old men. Then I found his *Vietnamese Baby Book* with its sentimental illustrations of a baby in a diaper with missing arms and stumps for legs. And his *Children's Letters to the Gestapo*. It seemed as if Michael made a point of going after childhood the same way my father went after Catholicism. It sometimes scared me: These were the people in charge; these were the adults. *They'd better like me. They just* had *to!* I looked around the loft again, at the rotting toys that didn't look happy. I just wanted to go home. Instead, I sat quietly, watching my father and Michael smoke a joint that seemed to burn forever.

The *Lemmings* cast was far less sinister. They joked and laughed with Kathy and me, and during the long *Lemmings* run, many became regulars at the country house—especially John Belushi and his fiancée, Judy. Of all the New Jersey visitors, John was the most fun. He would hoist me up on to his wide, padded shoulders and carry me around the garden while I laughed and tottered about. Once I giggled so hard that I fell backward. John caught my feet just before I would have tumbled to the hard ground below. He played games of tag with Kathy and me that invariably ended with him collapsing on the ground in mock death. And I became to him what Freckles was to me.

I followed him wherever he went. I sat next to him at meals, witnessing an appetite that truly was extraordinary. In his biography of Belushi, Bob Woodward describes John in the *Lemmings* era as a "menacing teddy bear." It was precisely that quality I found so attractive about him: He seemed cuddly, yet slightly dangerous.

On the nights we had guests, my father (and whoever was out at our house) carried a long, wooden picnic table and benches down to a stone barbeque we had inherited. Our high-tech, outdoor sound system consisted of the electrical cords of two stereo speakers stretched as far as possible toward the side door of the living room, which was left open to let music fill the garden and beyond. Daddy turned up the volume as high as it would go, and the Rolling Stones, Linda Ronstadt, the Grateful Dead, and the Beatles blared out into rural New Jersey. Its only competition? Our neighbor Doug's chainsaw. At night, after Doug put away his power tools and lawn mower, the music had the place to itself, and the reviews from our neighbors would come in the form of phone calls and bitter gossip: "Goddamn those Hendras. Worst thing that ever happened to Glen Gardner. That music! And all those hippie bums turning up at their house! Can't wait 'til they go back to wherever the hell they came from!"

And what did the house think, the majestic old house? Its stone walls vibrated with guitar riffs. The smell of pot and hash penetrated its weathered beams. It had been the only witness to what had happened between my father and me, and I couldn't help but wonder: *Did it want us to go too?* I still loved the house, no matter what had happened in the darkness of my bedroom. And I was sure that the house was not only alive, but that it, more than anyone else inside it, would protect me.

That feeling was only slightly shaken by the visit from the witch who came one night to investigate the spirits my father said lived there. The witch was named Janet, and she brought her Ouija board, along with a man named Tom. They were friends of a friend of my parents, and after a few minutes, I could tell they weren't part of the usual *Lampoon* crowd. These people were different. They were nice—and sarcasm-free. And Janet was very clear about her "powers." She called herself a "sorceress." Of course, her ability to contact the spirits lurking in the dark corners of Fifty-five Red Mill Road became easier when all the adults smoked grass and dropped acid before the séance.

The Ouija board came out after dinner, just as Kathy and I headed to bed. My mother took us upstairs while everyone else gathered in the living room, ready to bridge the gap between the living and the dead. In the morning, my father told us what had happened. Kathy and I shivered as he recounted the message from the Ouija board: "This is a dead house," it had spelled out over and over again. He told us how the table had tipped and rattled as the words came forth. But he said he swore he could feel Tom pushing against the table, causing it to shake.

He thought the Ouija-board message was a fake, but Daddy also told us he was certain that he *had* seen a ghost in the window of his bedroom. He said he had gone upstairs to get something while the others were still downstairs. Suddenly, a face had appeared outside. At first he thought it was Tom playing another prank. Then he realized that there was no way Tom could have gotten up one flight to the window.

"Was it a mean ghost, Daddy?" I asked, not sure if I wanted an answer.

"What did it look like Daddy?" Kathy wondered.

"It was a white face, girls . . . a thin, white face. It was the ghost spirit of this house. It did not look mean or vicious," he said, "just terribly, terribly sad."

There was something in the way Daddy said it that made me feel he really *had* seen something. I had always thought the house had a spirit. Now I knew for certain what I had always suspected. It *didn't* want us here. And I knew something else—or at least came to understand it later. My father feared the ghost's sadness because he feared his own death and what lay after.

He was a bit of a hypochondriac. I remembered in California when he had a terrible flu and got himself in such a state about his impending death that my mother asked a neighbor, conveniently both a physician and a psychiatrist, to come over. I heard Daddy ask if the doctor thought it was time to send for a priest. I wasn't sure if he was just being dramatic or whether he truly thought he was about to die. As always, it was hard to separate sarcasm from authenticity. I also remember one night when he must have been tripping or stoned, screaming that he was dead and lying in his coffin. He had the lapsed Catholic's fear of the hereafter: He no longer believed in heaven, but he was guilty enough to imagine he would end up in hell.

Daddy pondered his sighting for a moment and then began telling us about the other ghost—the one that lived in the study. His name was Fred Without a Head, and Daddy talked about how Fred roamed the house at night, holding his head in his hands. Unlike the sad face he'd seen hovering outside his bedroom window, we could tell he was making up headless Fred. Even so, I often thought about Fred and didn't like being alone in the house at night.

Perhaps that's part of the reason I loved the late-night dinners by the barbecue. Setting up was always fun. Kathy and I were the busboys and carried the plates and silverware down to the table. We had contests to see who could carry the most without dropping anything. It was beautiful in the late evenings, when the darkness held off until just before nine. When it fell, Kathy and I got to light the candles. But after a while, when the wine was gone and the guests chose hashish and acid for dessert, I began to feel anxious. I was losing the grown-ups to the goodies on the table, and the guests and my parents got noisier and more restless.

Most of the drugs produced elation, at least among this crowd, and the chatter and laughter grew accordingly. There seemed to be few bad reactions to anything, except, of course, until the next day, when hangovers roamed the house like headless Fred. But sometimes, things went awry. One night, when a guest brought something particularly exotic and many strong-smelling joints circulated, I watched as my mother slipped momentarily under the dinner table, overcome, by her account, by the fear that she was buried alive in the black hole that had suddenly opened beneath her. Sean Kelly leaned down and announced, rather dramatically: "A woman seems to have disappeared under this table!" At least he showed some concern, sarcastic or not. I noticed that Mom passed on the joints thereafter and took it easy on the drugs in general after that night.

In his biography of Belushi, Bob Woodward describes the cocaine use at *Lemmings* rehearsals and suggests that my father introduced John to the drug. Woodward also says that my father often had to get drugs for the cast in order to keep the show running smoothly. I was too young to really be aware of all this. I saw some coke use at the time, but actually less than in the years to come, when my father's own coke habit grew (as John's obviously did as well). The drugs of choice in New Jersey were more hallucinogenic than speed or coke. But I do remember the flurries of phone calls later in the *Lemmings* run, which I now realize were probably to find the drugs needed to get Belushi on stage. By then, John was coming out to the country less often. And as he became more difficult to handle, my father's relationship with him understandably cooled. Still, in the early months of the summer, everyone from the cast still seemed relatively united.

Because of Fred Without a Head or anything else that might be lurking in the dark house, Kathy and I hated to go back inside alone, especially with all the grown-ups down at the bottom of the garden. If I were tired, I lay down on one of the benches and put my head in my mother's lap or begged someone to put us to bed and sit outside the bedroom. Once or twice John's fiancée, Judy, would sit in the window seat on the upstairs landing, waiting for Kathy and me to fall asleep. Sometimes, I woke up at two or three in the morning and looked out the bedroom window to see the candlelight still flickering at the end of the lawn. I went out onto the landing to find that whichever adult had come with us into the house had long since abandoned the post. I'd walk down the dark stairs and stand by the kitchen door, listening to the faint sound of laughter coming from the table. I wanted to check that everyone—anyone—was still there and hadn't driven off while Kathy and I slept.

The day after those parties, the guests—some of whom had been sent to one of the bedrooms in the Forge—wouldn't appear at our house until late. Often, they might say their good-byes while my parents worked around the house, gardening, chopping wood, or mowing the lawn. My mother tended vegetables and made almost every meal from scratch. My father did most of the household chores. But of course, that didn't stop him from having fun. That summer of 1973, the *Lemmings* summer, my father, competitive as ever, took a stout rope and an old tire and rigged up a bone-crushing swing that tretched from the Forge over the river and into the trees on the other bank. The trick was to take a running leap at the tire so that it—and you—went as fast across the river as possible. Kathy and I tried, but it proved too frightening. I smacked into a tree and almost broke my nose. But John and my father took turns battling it out to see who could swing the highest and fastest, yelling in exhilaration as they flew across the rocks, their feet wedged into the tire, their hands clutching the rope. They were better at being kids than Kathy and me.

One scorching afternoon, my dad set up a slow-walking contest on the hot asphalt of the road by the Forge. Kathy, Becky, and I were the contestants. Whoever could walk the slowest on the burning tar would be the winner. The prize: a check from my father for $50. I walked slowly, the sticky asphalt searing the bottoms of my feet. Kathy and Becky quickly folded and ran across the road. I had won! As I hopped toward my dad, he wrote out the check with a flourish and handed it to me. I smiled as I read pay to the order of. And there was my name, Jessica Hendra. Then I saw how my father had signed the check: "Mickey Mouse." "Never do anything just for money, Jessie," he lectured. I simply stared at the check, my cheeks burning. He had embarrassed me, and I felt angry—but it wasn't just because of the check. It was not that I disagreed with him, but I was beginning to sense the hypocrisy of his moral code. He was not Robin Hood. And I had come to understand that, despite what my father had told me, what he had done to me was wrong—on that road and in my bed months before. I knew the way he teased Kathy was cruel. I knew the way he disregarded my mother was unfair and hurtful. Now, here he was, watching his daughter burn her feet on the steaming road, all to teach me about important values? I heard him rant and rave about the misdeeds of those in power, and I know he castigated them in the *Lampoon*. But I never once saw him look at the wreck he had made of his own family and hold himself accountable, as he held Nixon accountable for ruining the country.

One night toward the end of that summer, deep into one of the barbeques, one of Glen Gardner's finest dropped by for a visit. The feast had been set up as usual down at the barbecue. I remember John was there with Judy, and Sean Kelly with Valerie. Dinner had been served particularly late, and after just a few bites, I had slipped onto my mother's lap in exhaustion. Before I went to bed, I heard John say that he had brought something "really special." I had no idea he meant acid. Mom took Kathy and me to the house and tucked us into bed.

I woke up a few hours later. Finding the landing empty, I ventured downstairs to do my usual check on the grown-ups. I stood by the kitchen door looking for the candlelight when I noticed a short figure with an enormous flashlight crossing the lawn, heading toward the dinner table. He looked like a policeman from the outline of his nightstick and gun. The feast was still in full swing, and I was scared. I'd been brought up in a post-Kent-State-and-Watts-riots household, where police were "the pigs." The Brownies and the safeties at Lebanon Township School may have been fascists, but there was no question about the police. And I still remembered what my dad had said that night in Los Angeles, when the California Highway Patrol office stopped him for speeding: *They always take the children to jail first, you know, girls.*

I didn't know at the time that my parents and their guests were about to come perilously close to getting locked up for at least several years; there were enough drugs of different shapes and sizes sitting out in the New Jersey moonlight. Anxiously, I ventured out the kitchen door and stood on the lawn. My father had seen the officer, too. He rose quickly and strode across the bridge to divert Sergeant Pig before he got too close to the table. Then I heard him speaking to the officer in a plummy British accent, as if this unexpected turn of events had changed him into a character from a P. G. Wodehouse story. "So sorry, dear fellow . . . yes, yes, music too loud, disturbing the neighbors . . . how dreadful . . . happy to turn it down, my good man . . . frightfully sorry and all that . . . hope we haven't inconvenienced you . . ."

He chatted on as he deftly led the policeman back across the lawn, toward the house, and away from the incriminating table. Luckily for my parents and their guests, my father's act was convincing. Sergeant Pig was young and must not have been the suspicious type, a Glen Gardner bumbler who had no clue what was really going on at the bottom of the Hendra garden. And my father didn't seem the type of chap that did drugs—not with that accent. The call to the police station had been a complaint about loud music, and Sergeant Pig seemed content to handle that matter and no other. Satisfied, he returned to his car, my father still chattering at his elbow, and drove off. I ran down to the dinner table to ask someone to put me to bed. The grown-ups still looked nervously in the direction that my father had headed with Sergeant Pig, and they appeared incredibly relieved when Daddy came back alone. Everyone congratulated him on his brilliant maneuver, and the next day, my father sealed the deception. He carefully composed and sent a letter to the officer in charge of the three-man Glen Gardner police department. The letter commended Sergeant Pig on his tact in handling the situation and added a note of general praise for the work of the township police. What he did not say was that everyone who had been at our house that night was eternally grateful.

My mother has since called that dinner the "Last Supper." To her, it marked the end of the *Lemmings* era. It also turned out to be the beginning of an entirely different—and unpredictable—life, one that seemed only to grow darker and darker for me.

PART II

JUNE 2004

BY THE TIME I GOT HOME WITH *FATHER JOE*, I WAS IN a hurry to read it. Frantic, almost. I needed to know where things stood, and I kept hoping I would find something in it that would make me feel better. I read it all day, peeking at it when I was supposed to be playing "Polly Pocket" dolls, laying it on the floor and reading while I was folding laundry, skimming a sentence or two at a red light. I finished late that evening. And nothing in it—nothing—made me feel any better. There was no hint that this book was anything other than the abridged story of my father's "sinful" life.

I'm not a Catholic theologian, and I'm out of my depth when it comes to a discussion of what, in religious terms, constitutes "confession." But I cannot believe it is anything like the one my father makes in *Father Joe*. He admits to having committed "crimes." He asks Father Joe if he should give details; Joe, he writes, tells him it isn't necessary.

Not necessary? Of course details are necessary. Details are everything. Because the details my father won't mention . . . those are the details that everyone my father hurt lives and breathes. And some of us remain there, emotionally damaged. I know them. My mother, for one. My sister, I suspect. And me. Stranded. And as he walks away on the path to eternal life, he declares himself forgiven and absolved of these generalized sins, specifics spared to protect himself. And, of course, to sell books.

Would anyone buy a book—*would anyone publish it?*—if he talked about what he did to his not-yet-seven-year-old daughter that night in New Jersey?

Then there was the dedication. My sister and I—and our children—are included in it, as is our mother. But his depiction of my mother is rather sketchy. His dedication gives the impression of a reconciled family, one that has forgiven and forgotten and gathers for the holidays to remember old times. Perhaps my father thought it would flatter us to silence, the same way a sucker keeps a kid from crying.

Yes, I was angry. But I also wasn't blind to the merits of the book. Like his readers, I responded to the depiction of Joe, to the humor and the insight into how terrible it is to lose your faith and how wonderful it is to find it again. The belief that God's love transcends all is wonderful. And the fact that my father created this book spoke volumes to his talents. He was and remains in my eyes a genius. Yet simply knowing what I knew about Dad made accepting what he wrote impossible. It was a horrible lie. A con. Maybe the book was, in fact, a parody. And maybe, like many of my father's best works, only he and a handful of others would ever get the joke.

After I had turned the final page, I walked through my silent, dark house to the living room. I reached up to put *Father Joe* on our bookshelf, the spine turned so I couldn't see the title. But when morning came, the bookshelf seemed to have grown a glow-in-the-dark arrow just above *Father Joe*. What should I do? What *could* I do? Was it better to forget it or do something? *Could* I forget it? And what could I do anyway? He had written a history of his life, of his sins. How could he have taken on such a project knowing that he could never tell the truth of what he had done to me, what I hoped was his most egregious transgression? But, as always, I found myself back in that complicated place, and, as always, I wanted to give him another chance.

I Googled every review and all the interviews about the book my father had given. And I hoped I would see it. Perhaps he'd say it this way: "For the sake of my family's privacy, I have not given the whole story." Or maybe: "I really can't accept your praise without a caveat." Something, *anything* to make me think that the book was not about evading what he had done, not about minimizing the harm to the point where it no longer existed, not about making it seem as if it never even happened. I found nothing, no indication whatsoever that my father carried any guilt about the sins he omitted from his "painfully honest" book. Instead what I read was Don Imus touting it for Father's Day.

I turned off the computer and sat staring at the screen, still unsure of what to do next. So I did what a lot of women do in the midst of uncertainty: I called my mother.

She was just getting up in the Topanga Canyon house where she lives with her second husband, and I asked if she had seen the review in the *Times*. She had, she said, and she also told me that her friends in New York had been calling to find out how she felt about *Father Joe*. She called the dedication of the book "absurd."

Everyone who knew my family knew that my parents' twenty-year marriage didn't end well. That my father had left my mother for a much younger woman and then made the divorce proceedings as nasty as possible. My parents had barely said more than two or three words to each other at family occasions since 1985.

The time had come to tell her what had happened that night in New Jersey. Not because I wanted to upset her but because I wanted her to understand *exactly* what my father left out. I had alluded to something years before but had never discussed it with her in depth. With her, I had treated what happened just as my father had treated his sins in his book.

"I have to tell you exactly what I am talking about," I began. There was no other way to do it but to tell her straight out. When I finished, I just kept talking. "It makes me sick to say it," I told her, still not giving her a chance to respond. "It makes me want to throw up just like I made myself throw up all those years to get that taste out of my mouth."

My mother caught her breath as if she'd been punched in the stomach. Then: "Oh Jessica!" Then, the question so many others have asked: "How could you have him in your life after what he did?"

"I don't know, Ma, I don't know." I *didn't* know, but by now, I should've had a better answer than that. "I just kept hoping he might apologize. I kept hoping it could be made right somehow. I just kept hoping that he'd finally say it was his fault. *All* his fault." It was as though I was trying to convince myself that my reasons made sense. "Now I see from this book that it never meant anything to him."

Mom suggested that I sue him or try to get him prosecuted. "That wasn't molestation, Jessica. That was rape," she told me. And I was angry enough to consider it. Neither of us knew if this were still a possibility, so I decided to call my therapist (although I stopped seeing

him regularly once my anorexia was under control, we remain close).
I wanted to find out what he knew about my legal position.

I took the girls to school. When I got home, I dialed his number.
He had seen the book review and had anticipated my reaction. Yes, it
was "infuriating" to see my father being held up as a saved man, but he
doubted there was any legal action I could take. Not now. He also
wondered: Would getting involved in a legal battle be good for me
emotionally? But he understood my outrage and my sense that, this
time, I had to stand up for myself.

I had tried to do it before. But as he had throughout my childhood, my father simply overwhelmed me. Standing up to him had
never worked before. Why would it now?

I pulled out the Yellow Pages and looked under L. Laundry
Equipment . . . Lawn and Garden . . . Lawnmowers . . . and then . . .
twelve pages devoted to Lawyers . . . *Did I even have a case?*

*But which of them do I call? Just any lawyer? What about family
law? Maybe. A daughter sues her father. That seems like family law.*

"Oh no, no . . . you need a criminal lawyer for that kind of thing,"
the receptionist at the family law firm told me. *So I did need a criminal
lawyer.*

"Here's the number for the bar," she said. "They'll give you a refer-
ral."

A criminal lawyer . . . So it wasn't just a crime in *my* eyes. Other
people thought so too. And it wasn't just other people. It was people
who knew the law. Of course I already understood that. I'm sure I had
for years. But to be giving "the names of the parties involved" to a criminal lawyer thirty-two years after the worst of it . . . it just felt surreal.

"Who was the perpetrator?" the voice on the other end asked.

"Tony Hendra," I said, my heart thumping.

"Victim?"

"Myself, Jessica Hendra."

"Relationship?"

"I am his daughter." Nervously, I added: "He is my father."

After I finished giving the lawyer the details of what happened, he asked me when I had first told someone about it. "I told my best friend when I was about twelve," I said. And I had talked about it with a few other friends as a teenager. Ten years ago, I had finally told a professional—a psychiatrist I was seeing. And I remember how he had told me then that I could press charges. I had decided against it.

The lawyer listened to all of this. Then he told me what I had suspected. I no longer had a case. The statute of limitations was one year after "disclosure." That was the situation for both a criminal prosecution and a civil suit. "I'm very sorry," he said, "but I can't help you."

I was more relieved than disappointed. It was an option that had felt wrong to me from the moment the psychiatrist offered it years before. I couldn't imagine suing my father. For what? I didn't want money. I didn't want to see him in jail. I just wanted him to own up to what he had done.

The next night I went to a meeting at Charlotte's preschool. In a classroom, little yellow chairs, the kind kids sat on to eat their lunches, had been placed in a circle. Parents drifted in, chatting and laughing, and then tried to balance their bodies on seats made for toddlers. I hovered around the classroom, my mind elsewhere. A dad that I knew came and stood beside me.

"Hey, Jessica. Your last name is Hendra, right?" I turned. "Is your dad Tony Hendra?"

Oh God! I couldn't deny it this time, not as I had in the bookstore. Other people at the school knew my father from the *Lampoon* or from his portrayal of a band manager in *This Is Spinal Tap.* They were well aware that I was his daughter.

"Yes," I said coolly, hoping it would end there.

"I was just listening to an interview with him on the way over here. It was on NPR. You know that show *Fresh Air?*"

I nodded my head. It suddenly felt heavy.

"He was talking about his new book. It sounds fantastic! What a life! A really cool dad. And now he's written this book, admitted all his dark stuff. You must be so proud of him."

I tried to hold them back. But the tears began welling in my eyes and sliding down my cheeks. The poor dad looked horrified. "Are you okay? Did I say something wrong? I am so sorry. . . ."

"No, it's not your fault." My voice trembled. "I just . . . I just have a lot on my mind. . . ."

"I am so sorry."

"Really, it's fine." I tried to gather myself, but I couldn't. So much for being an actress. I might be able to pretend I'm someone I'm not, but I couldn't escape who I was. "I'll be right back. Tell them to start without me."

I retreated to the director's office, the only parentless corner of the entire preschool. I closed the door and collapsed in a chair, this one adult-size.

Maybe Daddy was right all along. Maybe it is my fault that I can't get over what happened. Maybe something is wrong with me. Is it that I'm so self-involved that I can't see things clearly? Should I just forget about this stupid fucking book and pretend my dad is a great guy?

But I knew that I couldn't. My anger had nothing to do with the fact that my father's book was a raging success. It was the hypocrisy of what he had done and the hubris it took to do it.

I looked out the window onto the small yard where my little girls had spent so much time playing and thought about a Saturday morning not long ago, when Julia and Charlotte woke up with an overwhelming desire to splash in the ocean. Kurt was out of town, and I'd spent three hours preparing that morning—making snacks, pulling out and putting on bathing suits, and loading the car—before we headed north on the Pacific Coast Highway. We passed the crowds in Santa Monica, the Pacific Palisades, and Malibu before parking at a secluded spot just north of Zuma.

As soon as we stopped, the girls leaped from the car, and Julia, at six-and-a-half, flew down the sand and began jumping the waves as they rolled ashore. Charlotte, younger by three years and not as sure of the water, hung back but finally ventured down to the shoreline, where she began squeezing the wet sand between her toes and rubbing it all over herself. Within minutes, her bathing suit filled with sand, and lumps sprouted when she stood to walk into the surf toward her sister. They held each other up as the waves crashed around them. For a couple of hours, I hovered at the shoreline, just a few feet from them, yelling "Not so far in . . . not so far in, girls!" And each time a wave approached, I caught my breath.

When they finally retreated, the sun had begun to set, and the beach had almost emptied. The sounds of music and screaming kids had given way to the pounding of the ocean. "Mommy, does that noise ever stop?" Julia was sitting on my lap.

"What noise?"

"That noise. That noise the waves make. When I leave the beach at nighttime, doesn't nature turn that noise off?" She asked it the same way she might ask if the checkout lady sleeps at the supermarket . . . or, sadly, why I had lied at the bookstore about being related to my dad.

"No honey, nature never turns that noise off," I told her. "Not even when you go to sleep. The sea goes on and on forever."

She looked up at me, her blue-green eyes slightly scrunched.

"You mean we don't tell nature what to do?"

"Not really," I said. "Nature just does pretty much what it wants."

She was quiet for a moment. "Mommy, who are nature's parents?"

A tough question. "Umm . . . I don't think nature really has parents."

She looked up at me again. "If nature has no parents, how does nature know stuff? How does nature take care of itself? Who took care of nature when it was a baby? How did nature grow up?"

I felt out of my depth.

"I don't know, honey. Maybe nature just figured it all out on its own, maybe it had to."

Charlotte continued to play in the sand, nonplussed by the conversation. Julia went on. "I think nature has parents," she said, "but you've just never seen them."

I looked toward the horizon while I considered her theory.

"That makes sense," I told her. And with that, the world seemed right to Julia, who snuggled back down in my lap and started asking about getting ice cream.

Now, as I sat in the director's office, wondering what to do, I couldn't help but think of that moment and how Julia's grand questions made me consider who I was and what I had become.

I thought about how I had once looked to my parents for answers. More than that, I had looked to them to make me safe, to protect me. One day sooner than I knew, Julia and Charlotte would be grown women. The time when I meant everything to them would have long passed. I only hoped that I could do better by them, much better, than my parents had done by me. I knew they would do what I did—what every adult does, either in nostalgia or remorse: They would look back to their youth, reliving the memories of when life was so much simpler. And that day on the beach, I had promised myself to do everything I could to give them their childhoods.

Did that mean I should simply say nothing about what my father had done to me? What would I tell Julia and Charlotte to do if they ever found themselves in this kind of situation? I would say speak out. Do what you feel is right. And years and years from now, when I tell them about this, what do I want them to hear? That their mother was too scared to tell her story? Or that she was a person who valued the truth enough to take the risk of coming forward? One thought kept repeating itself: *I want them to be proud of me. I want to be a role model for them. As a mom. And as a woman.*

The next morning I called Rudy Maxa in Washington. I remembered his offer.

"Rudy, you said I might have something to say about the *Times* review. Well, I do. I have a *lot* to say about it."

5.

KRISZTINA

BY SEPTEMBER 1973, MY MOTHER HAD HAD IT WITH New Jersey—and of being isolated for much of the time with me and Kathy and a few neighbors with whom she had little in common.

For about a year, there had been a plan afloat for my parents to buy into a loft building in the still incredibly cheap SoHo area of New York with other members of the *Lampoon* staff. That plan had to be modified a bit when the friendship between my father and Michael O'Donoghue fell apart. He told my mother point blank that he might trade a word or two with her if they met by chance, but "I will never speak to your husband again in my life, Judy." So the plan was revised to include only Henry Beard and Sean Kelly. My mom, perhaps in her desperation to get out of New Jersey, traipsed around SoHo looking at places. But organizing a group of satirists to do anything, let alone buy an entire building, proved fruitless.

By the fall of 1973, my mother had abandoned the plan to buy in the city but not her efforts to escape Glen Gardner. She found a loft on East Fourth Street that she thought we could afford to rent. It was $300 a month for a 2,000-square-foot space that had been used as a glass-cutting factory only two years before. It was narrow and had twelve-foot-high ceilings and windows along the front and side walls. In those early days of loft living, anything with a bathroom and a semblance of a kitchen qualified as inhabitable. This loft had the added luxury of a "bedroom" in the front. It didn't have a door or anything other than a half wall, but it did have a water bed sunk into the floor. Kathy and I thought the water bed was one of the strangest things we had ever experienced. We went to check out the loft with my parents one day before we moved in and spent the entire time rolling around on it. I couldn't imagine anyone *sleeping* on such a thing. I got slightly seasick just lying on it for ten minutes.

I had mixed feelings about moving. On one hand, I knew that my family would definitely fit in better in the city. Everyone had long hair and wore jeans in the East Village; everyone looked like my parents. I would no longer be troubled by the fact that we were the weird Hendras. On the other hand, I loved living in the country and playing outside, and I was much happier at my new school. I didn't have a lot of friends, but the ones I had I'd grown used to. I was scared of all the things kids fear—changing schools, being the "new girl," having to make friends. But I didn't have a choice. The loft had been rented, and we were moving. The only good thing was that we were not going to sell the New Jersey house. We would keep it and use it on weekends and in the summer. My father promised we would hold on to Fifty-five Red Mill Road whatever might happen. It was like the scene in *Gone With the Wind* when Scarlett O'Hara's father tells her, in his Irish brogue, never to give up Tara. "Land, Scarlett O'Hara, land!" Never mind that our Tara was a fraction of the size of the

O'Hara spread. In the few short years we lived there, it had become our ancestral home.

My dad might have had a few misgivings about the whole family moving to the city. The fact that my mother, my sister, and I were out of the way in the country had made it easy for him to carry on with his extramarital affairs and drug and alcohol binges. Perhaps having a family to come home to would put a damper on all of that. As it turned out, he just carried on. He never felt compelled to offer explanations to any of us for his long absences, whether we lived in New Jersey or waited for him at the dinner table in the loft. If he was two or three hours late—or if he didn't come home at all—we just accepted it as part of our family life, no questions asked.

One clear problem with moving was our beloved dog, Freckles. At first, my mom and dad thought we would leave him in New Jersey during the week. A neighbor would feed him, at least until the weather got cold. Kathy and I hated the plan. But my parents were convinced that Freckles was a country mutt who would hate life in the city. The day we left, he chased our Scout down the road for as long and as far as he could until his lungs and legs finally gave out. Kathy and I watched from the back of the car, sobbing at the sight of poor Freckles chasing behind us, his tongue hanging out, his ears back, his black-and-white fur rippling in the wind. A few days later, we began getting phone calls from neighbors begging us to come home. Apparently, Freckles had limped back to the house, planted himself on the lawn, and howled long and loud for two days straight. We drove back to get him, and Kathy and I were delighted. Why wouldn't we be? After all, we weren't the ones who had to walk him, who had to hold him back as he tried to fight with the Doberman pinschers guarding the gas station on the corner. We weren't the ones who had to keep him from sniffing the homeless who slept on our street or restrain him from lapping up the vomit left in the gutter by one of the methadone addicts who visited the clinic a few blocks away. Those jobs were left to Mom.

The loft sat on East Fourth Street between Lafayette and the Bowery. When we arrived, it was one of only a few residential buildings in the area; many of the other spaces were still being used as factories or warehouses. Twenty-five East Fourth Street was a tall, gangly, slightly awkward eight-story building. Its front lobby was shabby with peeling paint, cracked dark green tile, and a worn linoleum floor. There were one or two mouse holes, and sometimes in the evening, a little creature would scurry past our feet. Facing the front door was a wide elevator doorway with a tarnished gold bell at the side. The bell served as the way to call the elevator to the first floor. But when it arrived, the real adventure began.

Using the elevator required learning a protocol so sophisticated that only those who lived in the building could truly appreciate it. Visitors never seemed to get the hang of it, and for the most part, were not supposed to "drive." The elevator was manually operated with a lever that had to be pushed to one side to make it move. It had sliding metal-cage gates, and it wouldn't budge unless they were shut correctly. Once you figured out how, you still had to master the timing of starting the elevator and letting go of the lever in order to stop at the right floor. The elevator opened directly into any of the eight floors of the building, and there was one large loft space per floor. But if you let go of the lever too late, whoever was getting off had to jump down into their loft. If you let go too early, passengers had to climb up to their door. This was complicated by the fact that if the operator let go of the lever too quickly, the elevator would short the electrical system. The elevator ran on twisted cables that looked ancient, and the contraption would sometimes groan, creak, and sway in the most horrible fashion. Because it required an operator, whoever had the elevator on his floor had to drive it down and pick up the passenger on the ground floor, who would, in turn, return the person who had come down for them to his floor and keep the elevator himself until someone else came in. It was a good way to get to know the neighbors. The old merchant marine who lived with his graphic-designer wife on the fourth floor used to run the elevator in his boxers, suspenders, and slippers. The artist on the seventh floor came down in paint-covered clothes and wild hair; the woman on the sixth floor opened the elevator door with an oven mitt on her hand. Often, guests would want to try running the elevator. The desperate shouts—"Help, help, get us out of this fucking box!"—told us of their failures. I preferred the five flights of the dusty stairwell.

The only walls that divided our loft enclosed the small bathroom and separated the front room that held the water bed. To create a bedroom for Kathy and me, my dad got some six-foot slabs of sheet rock that stood exactly half way to the ceilings. He made big box rooms out of them, forming what he called our "holding pens." Our mattresses went on the floor, and we didn't have money to decorate, so Daddy made much of the furniture. Kathy and I liked accompanying him to the lumber store to buy wood for the kitchen counters. He loved to create. Once, he fashioned a table from one side of a huge wooden spool that had been used to coil electrical wire. He "borrowed it," he told us, from Con Edison by going downstairs late one night and hefting it off the street and into the elevator (which seemed completely overwhelmed by its weight and creaked even more than usual). Then he cut off one side, sanded it by hand, and stained it, propping it up with metal legs. It became our kitchen and dining room table.

New York proved an adventure. The second floor loft was used as a studio by a masseuse who specialized in Rolfing. At night, she held primal scream therapy and rebirthing sessions. Kathy and I looked at each other in amazement as we listened to the screaming adults: "Help me mommy!" Or: "I don't want to come out!" It was as though they were just outside our door.

Then there were the huge cockroaches to contend with. Some days it seemed like they were everywhere, crawling out of the bathroom, lying dead in the sugar bowl, whizzing around beneath the bed. Daddy made up stories about how they came out at night in hordes to play loud cockroach music and dance, sing, and party in the sink, feasting on crumbs and spilled juice. When I woke up in the middle of the night, I imagined going into the kitchen to find the big black bugs standing on their hind legs, spinning and dipping, rotating their cockroach bodies in an ecstatic frenzy.

If you walked out the front door of our building, you were sure to come across the locals—stocking-capped sailors with the names of girls tattooed on their arms who sat on the Bowery asking for change. There was a men's shelter down the street, and many of them slept there at night and hung out on the block during the day, trying to get drunk. I had one favorite: a black guy with wild eyes and a crazy laugh who held a sign that read, "Forget the whales. Save the winos!" My family, which had always seemed so different, was now just a part of this hodge-podge of people who had only one thing in common: They were all New Yorkers.

Having a washing machine of your own was the luxury of luxuries in New York. Most apartment buildings had laundry rooms in the basement but few loft buildings did. The basement of Twenty-five East Fourth Street had cobwebs and some rats but nothing else. So once a week, Kathy and I helped my mom gather all our dirty clothes, stuff them into pillow cases, and cart them off to the Laundromat on Second Avenue. It was the only one in the neighborhood. The couple who ran the place chain-smoked and ate sardine sandwiches with tomatoes and garlic as they ran their fluff-and-fold service. The place reeked. Once, my mother got fed up with sitting around for hours and gave the fluff-and-fold service a try. The clothes came back stinking of salty fish and Marlboros, and with a few new grease stains to boot.

The city screamed. Sirens wailed. Garbage trucks stalked the streets in the early morning, rumbling and making a terrible racket as they crunched up the trash. The Hell's Angels kept their headquarters a few blocks away, and they often rode up and down our street gunning their motors all night. My father made a habit of leaning out the huge window in the front room to implore them to "Shut the fuck up!" To which they sometimes yelled back that they were going to frigging kill him if he didn't mind his own goddamn frigging business. Once, one of them even tried lobbing a brick up to our floor. I worried that my father would tumble out the window, that the Hell's Angels would pounce on him and finish him off. But he reassured me that he could protect himself. He rode his bicycle everywhere and always slung an enormously thick metal chain around his neck to lock the bike up—or fend off attackers and punish the taxis that cut him off. As always, I couldn't help but be scared that something might happen to Daddy. At breakfast, he might assure me he was coming home early, but by 10:00 P.M. he'd be nowhere in sight. Living in the city made my fears worse. His frequent absences were more apparent, and now I saw firsthand the frightening world into which he would disappear.

"Mommy, when will Daddy be home?" I would ask as she sat reading George Eliot on our makeshift brown sofa. Silence.

"Mommy, where's Daddy?"

Louder this time. My sister and I were accustomed to having to repeat questions two or three times before we would get a response from my mom. It was as if we needed to call her back from some other place, perhaps nineteenth-century England or her own dark imaginings about where her husband might be.

"I don't know, Jessie. I'm sure he'll be home soon."

Then I would lose her again. *Home soon.* I began to know what that meant. My mother had no idea where my father was, whom he was with, whether he would even come home that night or just show up again in the next few days.

Still, she went to bed each night seemingly unperturbed. I learned only years later that Mom wasn't indifferent at all. She just realized what took me years to learn: No one could control my father, and there was simply no point in trying. I, however, couldn't sleep and stayed up for hours, listening for the creak of the stairwell door (there was no calling the elevator after eleven), the loud plunk of the bicycle chain tossed on the wooden floor, the sound of rummaging in the fridge for seltzer water. And when and if he did come home, I was filled with relief and anxiety. He was safe, yes, but was he drunk or stoned? I didn't know exactly what those terms meant, but I knew the behavior that went along with them. I knew the glint in my father's eye when he was stoned, a kind of "fuck you" look. I knew the sniffing and the tiny flecks of white powder around his nose. And if he were drunk, I knew he could be argumentative and then suddenly maudlin. He had told me that what happened between us was because he was "a drunken asshole," and I was scared that when he was drunk or stoned, it might happen again. But despite everything, I still adored my daddy. Even now, I don't understand precisely why.

There were times when my father put us all in terrible peril. On Friday nights we often drove out to New Jersey for the weekend. We might wait for him for hours, and I'd pray that the plan to go to New Jersey would be abandoned when he came home drunk or stoned. Driving with him then was terrifying. But even if my mother summoned the courage to suggest we postpone leaving until the morning or that perhaps she should take the wheel, he would always insist that he was "fine to drive" and be pissed that anyone had intimated he couldn't hold his liquor. Once, when he got us all in the car at around 10:00 or 11:00 P.M., he tore down Sixth Avenue and into the Holland Tunnel, changing lanes, swerving and careening off the guard rails. Kathy and I screamed and sobbed, and even my usually stoic mother was hysterical. In New Jersey, we stopped for gas, and Daddy reversed the car into a lamp post.

If he were sober, however, the rides to New Jersey were great. He told us stories of the "Tunnelkins," creatures who had a wheel rather than legs and spent their days rolling from place to place, hiding behind the metal doors that line the sides of the tunnel. Of course, there was an evil ruler of the Tunnelkins, who was forever torturing his subjects.

There had always been much after-hours socializing among the *Lampoon* staff. A lot of it involved drinking together, a component that my father insisted was vital to the creative engine of the magazine. One of the favorite hangouts was the Coral Café, a bar in a hotel across the street from the *Lampoon*. Kathy and I went there once— very briefly. I remember finding it pretty swank at the time. In truth, it was a complete dive. The conversations that took place there were, in my father's words, "extreme. Sometimes, the talk was of dead babies. Sometimes it was about Nixon. The level of verbal sparring was such that if you did not hold your end up you were discarded," he said years later. Being eight at the time, I failed the test. Kathy and I were duly discarded and did not go again. Nor was my mother welcome at these cutthroat sessions. Few women ever were present, except perhaps Anne Beatts, who, as far as I know, was the *Lampoon*'s only female editor. The Coral Café became a kind of *Lampoon* boys club where, in the tradition of all good boys clubs, the only women were the ones serving the drinks or getting fucked on the side. The alcohol itself was cheap, and, as my father wrote, "The drinks cost the same as subway fare, so there was no point in going home." Especially if you had no particular interest in spending the evening with your family.

But my dad is a complicated man. He often felt guilty about the drinking, the drugs, the affairs, the betrayals. One night, I went into the kitchen and found him lurching around the loft. He flung himself down on the sofa and started to sob. I offered to sing him a song—the only thing I could think of to make him feel better. And so we sat on the sofa, and I sang him all the lullabies I could remember while he sniffed and wiped his eyes and eventually feel asleep. But the guilt didn't stop him from replaying the same scene the next night. My father's feelings of regret drove him to try harder to cover up his chemical abuse, and his shame became just another part of his drug and alcohol problems.

That's why I tried to stop him from going out at all. Despite what had happened in New Jersey, I still felt compelled to keep *him* safe. When I heard my father opening the stairwell door after everyone had already gone to bed, I flew off my mattress and ran to him. I just couldn't bear the anxiety of wondering all night where he had gone—and if he were safe.

"Daddy, please don't go out now, please!" I was almost crying, and I quickly slipped between him and the door.

"I'm just going out to get some cigars, treasure. I'll be back soon," he promised. I refused to budge. I had heard the cigar line before.

"Jessie, I promise. I am just going out to get some cigars. I will come right home." I relented and moved away from the door. What could I do? He went past me down the dim stairwell, and I stood there, listening to his footfalls until they went silent. I shut and locked the door, then tried to stay awake. Finally I abandoned my vigil and, like all the times before, swore never to believe the cigar story again.

The mornings after a binge were the worst. My father was in a horrible mood, and, if he had been doing a lot of coke the night before, the sniffing, snorting, coughing, and spitting were deafening and nonstop. And there was always the morning weigh in, a ritual more usual than the yawn-and-stretch. Daddy would stand naked in the middle of the kitchen on an old postmaster's scale. I feared the weigh-ins. The results would either produce elation or, more often, a black fit that included screaming, throwing things, and, on occasion, bashing holes in the bathroom wall. At those moments, the thin wafer crackers came out, food logs were kept, and Daddy officially began a diet again. Watching my father's rage if he gained weight reinforced the sense I already had that being fat was a terrible, terrible thing. Poor Kathy. She had become a target of my father's *because* she was chubby. Even at eight, I grew very self-conscious about my body, especially after what had happened with my dad. I instinctively wanted to hide myself, to stay small, to never grow. I felt awkward and clumsy and went into a panic one day when I overheard my mother telling a friend that I had "a swimmer's build." To me, that meant I was getting fat. And if I got too heavy, I knew Daddy would despise me.

Predictably, I had a lot of anxiety about my first day in the New York City public school system. Kathy and I were going to go to P.S. 41

in the West Village. There were so few kids in our immediate neighborhood that we didn't have a local public school, so even though we were technically in the East Village, the West Village schools were ours too. Not that the school wanted us. My mother had to shout to make her point heard the day we signed up. The school officer muttered something about the perils of letting us in and was so rude that a teacher who had overheard the exchange afterward apologized to my mother. Kathy, my mom, and I walked over to Greenwich Avenue on the first day of class. I was sick to my stomach at the idea of new kids and new teachers. Miss Mole never looked so good.

My mother left us at the gate. I sniveled; Kathy looked grim. I have no memory of my teacher, just of another new girl who would become my closest confidant for years to come. Her name was Krisztina. Our early connection was perhaps prophetic if only because it signaled to Krisztina that I had some pretty deep anxieties.

Right after our snack time on that first day, I felt nauseated. I asked to be excused and chose Krisztina to be my bathroom buddy. She stood outside the stall door listening to me throw up milk and cookies. The next day, the same: first, the snack, then right to the bathroom. The entire first week we repeated the routine. Once or twice, I went to see the nurse. But there seemed to be nothing wrong with me, just new-school nerves.

Krisztina was bigger and stronger than me, and she became protective after our trips to the bathroom together. We could not have looked more different. Krisztina's face was round and full, her skin almost olive, her hair rich and dark. She seemed sturdy; I looked frail and edgy, as if I might break. But we complemented each other, and even when we weren't in the same class, we stayed friends.

My mother wasn't very happy with the school, which smacked a bit of the conservative Lebanon Township. And Kathy was even more miserable than I was. She hated her new teacher and didn't like any of the kids in her class. So my mom decided to look into another public school, also in the West Village. P.S. 3 was an experimental school with an inspirational principal, but the classes, which combined several grades in the then-fashionable open classroom system, were hit or miss. Kathy lucked out and got a wonderful teacher who really had a handle on the classroom. In my class, a mixture of kids from the third grade and above, a day was successful if everyone sat down for at least thirty seconds. Some of the kids were truly intimidating, especially the ones who had been left back a few times and now towered over my little eight-year-old frame. Ironically, the toughest girls in my class were named Hope, Charity, and Faith, and my still-noticeable cross eye drew their attention. They flung at me all the usual insults, as well as a few new ones, such as "crossed-eyed bitch" and "fucking four eyes" if I dared to wear my glasses. There also was the occasional violence at P.S. 3, but I never saw a gun—mostly just a lot of punching. Then there was the fabled day when a kid brought his knife to school and went after another kid's foot. And the time when a boy managed to climb up on the roof and began tossing broken tiles into the yard below. Hearing of all this, my mother volunteered to help supervise during recess. Within minutes, she felt overwhelmed when a boy grabbed a girl's long earring and tore it straight from her ear.

To up enrollment, quite a few kids were bused in from Harlem—an idea conceived with the best of intentions, but one that also created a lot of racial tension. Fights between white and black kids were almost everyday occurrences, and everyone would gather in a circle around the dueling pair. One side would chant: "A fight, a fight, a nigger and a white. If the nigger don't win, we'll jump in!" And then the other: "A fight, a fight, a nigger and a white. If whitey don't win, we'll jump in!" Kathy and I were too intimidated to stick around to watch the fights, which were held in the street after school.

The lunchroom also featured plenty of action. Kathy had a boy in her class, Sidney, who liked to wear to school the bras of his sister, Big Susan. Not only was Susan busty for her age, but she also held the coveted position as the leader of the girls' gang. At lunch one afternoon, Sidney jumped atop one of the tables and began to rip off his shirt. There it was, Big Susan's bra draped across his scrawny, nine-year-old chest. Sidney spun the T-shirt over his head in true stripper fashion before flinging it into the lunchroom crowd. Then, just as he began to unbutton his fly, a teacher yanked him off the table.

A few months after school started, I was dragged into a corner of the playground. A group of ten- and eleven-year-old girls decided it was time to tell me, the new kid, the facts of life. "You know all that shit about the stork and finding you under a cabbage patch? Well guess what, Cross Eyes? That's a load of crap. . . ." I don't remember exactly what they said, but I didn't bother to tell them that I'd never had the pleasure of believing in the stork anyway. Neither did I mention that the Easter Bunny was, according to my father, "the risen Christ vampire." I had seen a lot, and I already knew far more than I should. But I looked so innocent, so awkward, so small, and so shy that no one would have guessed my secrets.

Later that fall, my father had a building fit and made some new "rooms" for Kathy and me. In truth, we stayed in the same room, but my dad raised my bed above Kathy's and attached a wooden ladder so I could climb up. My new "room" was so high that, from my bed, I could see right over the six-foot wall that blocked the back of the loft from the living room area. That meant I could hear every word spoken in the kitchen. Usually there wasn't much eavesdropping to do; the re-markable thing about my parents' relationship was how little they fought, given how much they had to fight about. In fact, I don't re-member ever hearing my mother raise her voice to my father, no mat-ter his behavior. But one night I awoke to what seemed like a serious discussion.

"She's pregnant," I heard my father say. And for once, he actually sounded guilty.

6.

PUNK

"WELL, WHAT ARE YOU GOING TO DO ABOUT IT?" MY mom seemed more exasperated than surprised.

"I don't know, Jude. I don't know." My dad sometimes called my mother Jude.

"She'll have to get an abortion, I suppose." *Why wasn't she angry?*

Daddy kept silent, and I sat straight up in bed, straining to hear more. I had no idea what an "abortion" was, but I did know what it took to get pregnant, especially after my facts-of-life session at school. Maybe if I went down the ladder and stood by the living room wall, I could catch what else they were saying.

In the dim light, I made my way down from my loft. I realized too late that I had forgotten to navigate around the punching bag my father had hung from the ceiling; I was used to waking up to the sounds of him sparring. My parents were pacifists, save for the punching bag and the Two-by-Four List—a running tally kept by my father of all the people, mainly right-wing politicians and sanctimonious Hollywood stars, whom he wanted to hit with a two-by-four (among them: Nixon, Agnew, Jane Fonda, and Barbra Streisand). In the darkness of the loft, I walked smack into the punching bag and felt it sway ever so slightly, creaking as the chain that held it up swung back and forth. I looked across to where my sister slept. She hadn't stirred. But my parents remained silent. I decided to head back up the ladder to bed, and that night, the pregnant woman appeared in my dreams in the form of a tall, blond woman with a large, pink hat covering her face. I never dared ask my mom or dad about what I had heard, but it made me feel even more deeply that my family was a mess.

Even though we were now at different schools, Krisztina and I continued to grow closer. We saw each other almost every day, and she often came to the country with us on the weekends. If Daddy came home stoned or drunk, I had the superstitious and totally irrational idea that if Krisztina were with us, nothing terrible would happen. The house suffered in our absence, especially in the winter when we might arrive from the city on Friday night to find the pipes frozen solid. But we girls thought these domestic crises were fun. Kathy and I were passionately reading the *Little House in the Big Woods* books. We took to calling our mother "Ma" and felt like Laura and Mary Ingalls as we bounded down to the river in the early morning with pans and buckets to get water for washing and cooking. We even took to dressing up to do our household chores, donning the long skirts we had from Mrs. Kruger's junk shop.

Often, I went over to Krisztina's house for sleepovers. Her parents had met in a communist prison camp in Hungary before the revolution, and they managed a daring and romantic escape to Paris, eventually settling in New York. When I met Krisztina, they had recently divorced. Her father, an artist, was a quiet man who never really embraced American life the way Krisztina's mother had. Perhaps this was one of the problems that had ended their marriage. Krisztina's mother, Olga, supported herself as a textile designer. To me, she seemed a glamorous woman, a Central European Audrey Hepburn. I say Central European because many of the Hungarians I came to know through Krisztina became enraged at my assumption that they were Slavic or even Eastern European. I once got an earful from Olga for presuming that Hungarian and Bulgarian had the same linguistic roots. Olga wore thin black eyeliner on her wide brown eyes, her hair pulled back in a chignon, and a hand-painted, brilliantly colored scarf tied fashionably around her neck. She smoked long Benson and Hedges cigarettes and spoke in a throaty accent that was much more exotic than my parents' British ones. Her bathroom held pots of pink cold cream, lipsticks in wonderful cases and colors, and perfumes from Paris—the sort of things that were never part of my mother's liberal 1970s style. If Krisztina and I wanted to play with makeup or pretend to file our nails with emery boards, we went to Olga's apartment on Fourteenth Street.

Being glamorous and newly single, Olga had a busy social schedule. Often, she would leave Krisztina and me in the apartment at night. "Be good, girls," she would say in her Zsa Zsa Gabor voice, and before she had even left the building, we were pulling clothes from her closet, trying on dresses, and taking turns zipping each other up. The scarves and high heels were the last pieces in our transformation. I became "Fanny Radcliff" and Krisztina "Jackie Clifton." We lit candles and pretended we were in a fancy restaurant eating Cap'n Crunch cereal with crunch berries out of Olga's best bowls and drinking vintage grape juice from her thin-stemmed, crystal wine glasses.

Krisztina liked being with my family, given her parents' split, but I liked it at her house better because there were never any drugs. My father's coke use had grown heavier, and he often did lines on the kitchen table. Once, I found some in the fridge, and thinking it was confectioner's sugar, put my finger in it and took a taste. I winced, and suddenly, my gums became numb, and I felt like my head were about to explode.

I don't really know who dealt to my father; I do know there were certain bars he used to frequent regularly. Sometimes I was with him when he stopped in for a drink (a soda on my end), and I saw some very warm handshakes with the bartender and a little white packet slipped into Daddy's pocket. I also recall picking up the phone one night in the loft and having a rather bizarre conversation with a man who was looking for him.

"Hello?" I said.

"Hey man, is Tony there?" A slow, slurred voice could barely get out the words.

"No."

"Who are you, man? This is Brie. I mean, I *think* that's who I am, but none of us really knows, you know? You think you are who you are, but you just don't know."

"Yeah," I said, completely confused.

"Who do you think *you* are?" the voice asked again.

I wasn't up to an existential conversation with a stoned stranger. "Daddy's not here," I said and put down the phone quickly.

More and more often, Daddy had "colds" in the morning and would sniff and splutter like crazy. Exercise became his one relief for his massive hangovers. It seemed a form of confession for him during the years that he didn't set foot in a church. He was a good runner, and often Kathy and I would get on our bikes and ride alongside him for miles. If we were in the country, we went along the roads around the house. If we were in the city, we rode across town and followed a bike path that ran along the West Side Highway. Daddy would joke that we were his trainers. We played along. "Get your knees up, Hendra!" we'd shout. Or "Come on, you can do it!" as we raced ahead. The punching bag had inspired him to take up boxing again, and he joked that his fight name was "The Game Cornish Hen," a play on his Cornish ancestry. When I look back, it amazes me that despite all the terrible things he was doing to his body, my dad managed to stay in pretty good shape. But all through the long rides he would snort, sniff, and spit huge globs of thick, green saliva into the street.

Things were going well at the magazine in 1974 and 1975, years that many consider the heyday of the *Lampoon*. My dad was firmly established as "in," and the man who had been his closest friend and then his fiercest enemy, Michael O'Donoghue, was out. My father later wrote that the day Michael quit was "somber," but he also admitted that he was "not a passive party. . . . I did my best to cut him out. And I did—I drove him out." Professionally my father was at the top of his career and devoted himself to the magazine. My mother once told me that the times my father was most confident were also the times he was most dangerous. By that she meant that his behavior had no boundaries. When his confidence was high, he became omnipotent and felt morally untouchable. He had more affairs, he drank more, he did more drugs and behaved with a "fuck you" arrogance that put him above everyone else. Perhaps that's why, around this time, after almost three years with no repeat of what had happened in New Jersey, my father touched me again.

It was in the bathroom of the loft, the only room in the place with walls and a lock. I had gone into the bathroom to chat with my dad while he bathed, something I did quite often. After all, seeing him naked was nothing new. The bathtub was right next to the toilet, and Daddy often used a shower attachment to clean his hair and back. I sat talking to him while he washed. But unlike all the other times, when he left the bath this time, he had an erection. I didn't really know what it was, but I could tell that his penis looked different than it usually did. He stood next to me in his towel as I got up from the toilet. I must have been wearing a nightgown or a dress because I remember he reached into my underwear. I simply looked up at him. He put his fingers in my vagina as he had in New Jersey that night years before. And again he said those words: "You're too small." Then he asked me to touch his penis. Unlike the incident two years before in New Jersey, I don't remember what happened after that. Except that, like that first night, I did whatever he asked.

This time, there were no signs of trauma, no rubbing of my eye or refusing to go to school. Again, it never occurred to me to tell my mother. She couldn't stand up for herself with him, let alone for me. And so I went to school the next day, continuing to feel awkward and shy, nervous around boys and worried about my body. About a year later, Dad touched me in the bathroom again.

It was not until about two years after that I finally told someone all that had happened with Dad. Of course, my confidant was Krisztina, my best and only true friend. I must have been around eleven or twelve.

We had steadily grown closer and closer as the years passed, and Krisztina had become almost a part of our family. But for some reason, she hadn't been able to join Kathy and me dressing up as young hookers for a photo shoot that included other children whose names I've since forgotten.

It was for the June 1977 issue. The "joke" was that we were being given a special award for making the most money during the summer. The picture shows us sitting on a suburban lawn somewhere (we might have driven to Connecticut), dressed in true 1970s "Super Fly Boutique" clothes that had to be pinned on and shrunk by the stylist to fit us. I was given a long cigarette holder and huge white boots with a purple fire design up the sides. The boots had platform heels, and I remember the extraordinary feeling of walking in them, as if I were floating. I had on a pink miniskirt and top and white sunglasses. Kathy had cut-off shorts, heels, and a bright orange boa. The boys were dressed in pimp suits with tall, black hats. None of us understood the humor of the picture, but the *Lampoon* crew found it hilarious. All of us got the usual pay from the magazine, $50, but I also got to keep the boots, which became part of our dress-up collection.

We were on a sugar high when I told Krisztina about Daddy. Kathy was out somewhere, so we were sitting down by her bed in the loft. We liked to sit down there, especially if we wanted privacy. My "room," being on top, was easily seen from the rest of the loft.

We had just brought home a stash of Twinkies from the deli on Broadway and Eighth Street, and as we ate them, we began on the subject of how fun it was to sleep together. We could talk and laugh as late as we wanted. And for some reason, that reminded me of the night in New Jersey. I cringed inside. I was getting old enough to understand a little more clearly what had happened that night, and my shame about it was growing. Suddenly, I blurted out: "Daddy touched me in weird ways one night." She put her Twinkie down and looked at me. "What do you mean?" I said very little else—just that he had touched me in places he shouldn't have and that I didn't like how I felt—then or now. I told her he made me touch him back. Then

Krisztina confided in me. A teenage boy had done "experiments" on her when she was eight, she said. He had touched her and had her touch him back. He had even put his thing inside her. We never thought of going to any grown-ups with our stories. What was the point?

Krisztina and I grew more daring during our sleepovers at Olga's. We never stayed at Krisztina's dad's apartment because he didn't keep Olga's social schedule. The older we got, the longer she left us alone, once or twice for the whole night. Krisztina and I moved up from grape juice and tried Olga's real wine. We even snuck a few of her Benson and Hedges.

We learned that with heels and a bit of lipstick we looked older and could get into see movies by ourselves. Not one ticket taker ever blinked as we passed over our money. Krisztina was usually the buyer. She already looked like a teenager even without the makeup. We walked over to the movie house on Seventh Avenue and saw *Rocky* at least four or five times and *The Spy Who Loved Me* even more. We figured out that there was a back door that could be opened just after the movie started, so if we were short on money, we only had to buy one ticket. Usually Krisztina orchestrated the maneuver, and I dawdled in the alley, waiting for her to quietly crack open the back door. It worked countless times until one night when Krisztina emerged from the front entrance of the theater with devastating news. An usher with a large flashlight had come to check out why she was standing by the back door of the theater. If only Krisztina had the diplomatic skills of my father! After that, we both bought tickets.

I liked dressing up and looking like a sixteen-year-old. But at the same time, I was worried about my impending curves and the whole idea of becoming a woman. I felt squeamish about getting my period or wearing a bra, both of which, I knew, were in my near future. What had happened to me, and all the nudity I had seen as a child, left me ashamed and embarrassed about my own body. In fact it was Olga who told me point blank that it was about time I start wearing a bra. She terrorized me with stories of what might happen to my "figure" if I ignored her. Instead of taking the subject up with my mother, I begged Krisztina to let me have one of her bras. I remember the first day I wore it. I felt none of the adolescent pride that I knew some girls had when they came to school with those telltale lines under their shirts. I took to wearing baggy tops.

Olga sometimes sent us off to the supermarket next to the apartment to do her grocery shopping. Usually we enjoyed it because we could sneak some treats for ourselves. But one afternoon, we saw to our horror that Olga had written "Tampax" on her grocery list. Krisztina and I were maybe twelve at the time—it never bothered us to get Olga's cigarettes, something we could get away with in 1977. But tampons! It was crucial that no one in the supermarket see us get them. Or if they did, that everyone knew that the Tampax wasn't for either of us. First we had to scope the aisles. We weren't exactly sure where the tampons might be, and we certainly weren't going to ask. We found them, not surprisingly, in the toiletries aisle, under the alarming heading of "Feminine Protection." *Protection against what?* I wondered.

The brand Olga wanted sat high up on the shelf, and bringing home the wrong ones just wasn't an option. Olga would have taken one look at them and sent us right back to the supermarket to exchange them, a thought even more mortifying than fetching the Tampax. But how to get the Tampax down. . . . Clearly we weren't going to ask one of the young male supermarket clerks for help. Krisztina's solution: I give her a leg up. It seemed like a good idea at the time. Krisztina was a bit heavier than me, but she also was braver. Much braver. I looked up and down the aisle. Empty. And so I made a step with my hands and hoisted her up.

Everything seemed fine—for a moment. But just as she reached for the box of Tampax, my hands slipped. With a cry that rang through the supermarket, Krisztina grabbed the shelf for support—and in the process, brought every box of tampons (along with a few packets of Over Night Pads, Light Days Pads, and even a box or two of douches) tumbling down with her to the yellow linoleum floor. Not just one but five young male clerks came running to see if we were okay. As one of them helped Krisztina up, I gathered my wits and said, as loudly as I could: "I wish your *mother* had never asked us to get *her* things for her!"

With the "things" buried under the milk in our shopping cart, we squirmed out of the chaos we had created in the toiletries section as fast as possible and made our way to the checkout. Despite—or maybe because of—the ruckus, we still weren't particularly comfortable with our selections. So we waited an extra ten or fifteen minutes until a female checker came on duty.

Others noticed my body was changing. One of my father's friends, a man I had known most of my life, called the loft one night. He must've been pretty messed up. "Jessie, hey, what are you wearing?" he asked me out of the blue. I jokingly told my father about it, and he flew into a rage. But then when Dad and I would go somewhere together, he'd make jokes about me being his "girlfriend." I became more and more self-conscious and started worrying about my weight. I thought if I stayed thin I could fend off puberty. I took to sneaking onto the scale in the kitchen and weighing myself. And I wasn't alone in doing so.

My sister was weighing herself; my father was weighing himself. Only my mother wasn't obsessed with her weight.

A few years later, I understood just how tormented my sister felt. In an open letter to the family, Kathy seemed to echo my feelings:

> When I was little, I felt horrible a lot of the time. I had glasses, straggly brown hair, a dumpy expression, and fat thighs. Daddy said the only reason I was fat was because I ate too many candies—but I never felt that he said much else. I loved him at the same time, but I always felt he did not want me around. . . . I found out that when I tried I could lose weight well. I had control. I did not have to be ugly. . . . By eating more I just feel like I am satisfying Daddy: that sneer he has can be so annoying. There's something so condescending about the "see I'm right" expression.

I suspect some at the *Lampoon* had grown just as tired of it. The magazine as it was when my father started there in 1971 had all but vanished. Michael O'Donoghue had gone to *Saturday Night Live*. Henry Beard and Doug Kenny sold their share of the magazine in 1975. And now, in 1978, my father was losing the magazine to his nemesis, P. J. O'Rourke. The *Lampoon* was moving in a direction that rankled Dad. He never was a big fan of the teenage-sex-and-gross-out jokes that made *Animal House* such a big hit. His humor was more biting, more wicked, more dark. The publisher, Matty Simmons, and P. J. felt that the new brand of humor would sell the magazine, just as it sold *Animal House*. I woke up to more and more violent and curse-filled rounds with the punching bag, and when I got out of bed, Daddy would tell me in between punches that the bag was either P. J. or Matty, depending on who was aggravating him that week. With my dad, more frustration meant more drinking and drugs. His cravings flared when he felt good but also when he felt down. Sadly, staying steady seemed almost impossible for him—and by extension, for all of us too. He took to coming home later and less often and doing more coke than ever. When he was home, the drugs were apparent. Even when we were in New Jersey, they followed us. My father had one or two friends with whom getting high seemed to be his only connection. One guy, supposedly an English nobleman who had fallen on hard times and now lived with his junkie girlfriend on the Lower East Side, we called Lord Michael. He stood small and balding, wore a large gold ring, and walked with a cane, but only for pretense. I knew he always carried a lot of drugs, and for that reason—knowing what they did to my dad—I didn't like him. Even so, he used to come out to New Jersey with us regularly. I remember one morning when Kathy and I set off for a horseback riding lesson on our bikes, leaving my father and Lord Michael chopping up a black block of raw hash with kitchen knifes in preparation for the evening's entertainment.

Kathy and I had taken different approaches to escaping the loft and the craziness my father brought home. For me, it was hanging out with Krisztina. For Kathy, it was school work and horseback riding, an endeavor that seemed to rile Dad. He told Kathy she looked like the "She-Wolf of Dachau" in her high boots and jodhpurs. And he added, as if for emphasis and with a sarcasm so dry that it cracked, "I left England to get away from people like you." But Kathy managed to tune him out or so it seemed. She graduated from Village Community School (VCS) and went on to the best public high school in New York: Stuyvesant. I continued at VCS for another year and managed to get into the second-best public high school in New York, Bronx Science. But something happened to me during the summer in between.

I started a diary when I was twelve, and one of my first entries seems telling: "TONY HENDRA IS NOT GOD!!!" I wrote it in huge letters across the page, but the meaning was even bigger. When my dad used to tell me that some song I liked was stupid or that the book I was reading was trash, I accepted his views as the unquestionable truth. Now, I was beginning to wonder if my father really was right all the time. It had finally dawned on me: this man who happened to be my father had dominated my life, had manipulated me in ways that suited him, had broken me down without ever building me up. I had always assumed that my father's words were gospel, that his opinions should be my opinions; he delivered them so forcefully. But suddenly, on the eve of my thirteenth birthday, it was as if a thunderbolt had struck. Maybe Krisztina had emboldened me. Maybe I finally began to understand what he had done to me and how truly wrong it was. But writing those words were my first real rebellion against my dad. After that moment, my attitude toward everything changed. I graduated from being a shy, awkward, and diligent girl to a troubled, angry teen.

Krisztina joined me there, and we started looking for ways to piss off our parents, particularly my father and her mother. The punk world of the late 1970s and early 1980s fit the bill perfectly. It embodied a tremendous amount of angry energy that was expressed in the way people dressed, wore their hair, and played music. Like a lot of kids in New York in 1979, our first exposure to this underground culture was the ritual of going to *The Rocky Horror Picture Show*. On Friday nights, the Eighth Street Playhouse filled with teenagers dressed as characters from the movie. Krisztina and I could barely hear the dialogue; everyone in the audience was screaming out each word. Walking home down Bleecker Street, we smoked clove cigarettes and decided in our snotty Manhattan way that the crowd had been "way too bridge and tunnel" ("bridge" meaning Brooklyn kids who had come across the Brooklyn or Manhattan Bridge, and "tunnel" meaning the Jersey crowd who came through the Lincoln or Holland Tunnel). For us, New York was divided into the chosen, those with a 212 area code, and those destined to spend eternity in one of the four other boroughs. We decided to head east in search of a better scene.

The first night that Krisztina and I ventured out to see a local band at CBGB night club on the Bowery, we spent hours preparing. We chose my house because Olga would have had a fit seeing us dressing as we did. My mother made no effort to dissuade us. But she demanded that we turn down the blaring Sex Pistols, "God Save the Queen," and "Anarchy in the UK." Then she fled altogether on the pretext of "some errands." After she'd left, I asked Krisztina to cut my hair. She had already cut her own in a short, slightly uneven bob. My hair was long, blond, and shiny—much too healthy and feminine-looking for a night at CBGB. We moved to the kitchen so the hair could be swept up more easily, and Krisztina began the job with a pair of large scissors. Then I noticed it—one of my father's carving knifes on the counter.

"Cut it with that knife, Krisztina!"

"With a knife?"

"Yeah, just pick it up and cut it all off, just chop through it. It will look so punk!"

Krisztina grabbed the knife and began her mission. It wasn't as easy as I thought it would be. Krisztina had to saw through my hair a handful at a time, and the choppings fell around me in long, uneven clumps. That left short, jagged clumps sticking from my scalp. It looked unbelievably bad, like a lawn mower had run amuck on my head, but we were much too pumped to admit our stupidity. The next step: to dye the mess platinum blond with some dye we had shoplifted from the drug store down the street. Krisztina's new shade was "midnight black." We left the dye on my hair so long that it became slightly green. All the better!

We pulled on black ski pants and ripped T-shirts, and Krisztina had on a bright blue, tattered coat that looked more like a rug. Our wardrobes had come from a hole-in-the-wall thrift store on First Avenue, where the clothes had been dumped in a huge pile that filled the place from floor to ceiling. To find what you wanted, you had to stand in the pile and dig. The woman who owned the place seemed thrilled to make a buck for stuff she probably got off the street anyway.

The final steps: thick streaks of black eyeliner, cheap bright red lipstick, and safety pins. It seemed much too tame to put the safety pins in the earring holes Krisztina and I had gotten for our eleventh birthdays. So she suggested that we should stick the safety pins all the way up our ears. We took the precaution of "sterilizing" the pins by holding a lit match to the sharp point and wiping some vodka on them. Then we took turns shoving four or five safety pins directly into our ear lobes and up toward the top. The top ones were harder and more painful, the cartilage there being so much thicker, but we carried on anyway, wincing and crying but not giving up until we both had rows of slightly bloody safety pins all the way up our tattered ears. Just as we finished, my mother came home. She screamed when she saw me.

"Jessie, what have you done to your hair!" She was close to tears over what remained of my once-enviable mop and furious with the both of us. We took it as affirmation. I had managed to upset even my stoic mother.

At 9:00 P.M., Krisztina and I went to pick up our friend Iana from her loft on Seventeenth Street. Iana's parents were Bulgarian, and like

Krisztina's, had left their country because of the Russian occupation. In their case, they hadn't fled but were exiled for antigovernment activities. Her dad was an artist, a wonderfully eccentric man who was always up to some project or other—going to Kenya and casting sleeping elephants in plaster or blowing up sculptures in a project called "The Big Bang." Her mother was elegant, sophisticated, and unusual in a more quiet way than her husband. Neither of Iana's parents said a word about how Krisztina and I looked. Her father simply smiled his squinty, mischievous smile, and her mother bid us a polite good evening in her strongly accented English. She did add something in Bulgarian to Iana, which might just as easily have been "God, those two look absolutely dreadful!" as "Don't come home too late, sweetie." But we had no idea which, and Iana wasn't telling. We envied Iana, if only for her parents. They let her do exactly as she wanted, and if she came in at four in the morning, they never said a word.

Iana herself was petite and pretty with long, wavy, brown hair and brown eyes. She had also put on black ski pants and eyeliner, but she had preserved her hair, and she wore tiny, pearl earrings, not safety pins. Her lipstick was Clinique. Iana always knew where to draw the fashion line and had enough self-respect not to do any permanent, or at least semipermanent, damage to herself. She exuded an icy self-confidence that left everyone who knew her in a sort of cowed awe.

Krisztina and I hoped we were shocking everyone we passed as we walked down Broadway and then over to the Bowery to CBGB. We tried desperately to look older than our fourteen years and to impress with our scowls. But it's hard to impress New Yorkers, and I'm sure most of them saw us for what we were—two young, insecure girls who were trying too hard. Iana knew she didn't have to look shocking to make an impression. She carried herself with her usual sophistication.

CBGB was a small club, and even from blocks away, we could see people spilling out of the doorway and onto the sidewalk. The street lamps highlighted purple Mohawks; blue, spiky coifs; leather jackets; chains; plaid plants; and fishnet stockings. The music coming from the building was loud enough to fill the neighborhood, but in those days, few people lived on the Bowery. I don't remember which band was playing, just that it sounded fast and angry. I had a twinge of fear when we went up to the door to pay our $5 because the three of us were very underage. But the huge bouncer at the door stepped aside and let us pass. Then someone stamped our hands, and we had arrived.

The club was packed, filled with cigarette smoke, sweat from crazed dancers, and an overwhelming smell of hairspray that rose from spiked, stiff heads. We were desperate to know these cool kids around us, desperate for even a word from one of Them. By two in the morning, I was elated because some guy with a homemade Clash T-shirt asked me for a light. I walked home on air to the sound of his voice: "Hey, you have a light?" I saw him in my mind's eye, covered with sweat from dancing so hard, black, spiky hair slipping over his forehead. I even got a "thanks" after my shaking fingers lit a match for him. I was too overwhelmed to do anything other than mumble "you're welcome" before he disappeared into the crowded dance floor. But one of Them had spoken to me.

The next weekend we went to CBGB again. After that, we braved other clubs, Tier 3 in TriBeca, the Mudd Club on White Street, Max's Kansas City near Fourteenth Street. We went anywhere and everywhere punk music played. We met other kids, most of them older than us. We met bands and became privy to the word-of-mouth grapevine that fueled where to go. Soon, Iana, Krisztina, and I became one of Them too. And when the "bridge and tunnel" crowd turned up at the current hot spot, we simply moved somewhere else. I made my room into a mini version of the First Avenue thrift store and left all my ripped clothes in a huge heap next to my bed. On the way home from clubs, we would peel street posters announcing concerts by our favorite bands off buildings and lamp posts. Then I'd re-paste them to my six-foot walls. All around my room the posters screamed: "THE BUZZCOCKS—HOTEL DIPLOMAT, THE CLASH—LIVE AT THE PALLADIUM, THE STIMULATORS—TIER 3, THE BAD BRAINS—CBGB." Every inch was covered. My mother said nothing; my father was livid. He told me I "looked like a dead rat" and that he found me insufferable. We fought endlessly about trips to the clubs, and he set curfews that he was seldom home to enforce. He would say things like "You need to be home for family dinner tonight, Jessie," which I found absurd considering that my father never bothered to come home unless it suited him. He thought the English bands I idolized were a "bunch of whining gits" and were precisely the reason he never wanted to live in England again.

Now, I realize he was angry because he was losing me. I suddenly had a group of heroes, and none was him. And I wonder if he also knew that I was finally understanding the impact of what he had done. I know how irritating I must have been at that age—full of attitude, dedicated to being a bored teenager when I was with my parents, pouting and playing with the safety pins in my ears during the rare occasions when all of us sat at the dinner table. But my father never acknowledged the role he played in making me what I was then. I had watched his "bad behavior" for years, and now, I was giving it back.

I thought I was rebelling against my parents, but the idea that I could outdo my father—either in wit or bad behavior—was folly. I remember walking into Max's Kansas City one night and seeing him chatting at the bar with Debbie Harry of Blondie. He wasn't *trying* to be cool, as I was. My dad *was* cool. I fled the club and went somewhere else, suddenly feeling terribly embarrassed about all the efforts I had made to look and act punk. I didn't realize that the true rebel of the family was my sister, slaving away at her books, saving money to buy a horse, dreaming of becoming a doctor, and quietly plotting her escape from the world of Tony Hendra. She also, as all of us began to notice, had gone from Thunder Thighs to a thin teenager well on her way to Twiggy. Her steely personality gave her the resolve to lose weight. And my father taunting her as a child gave her added incentive. I was having my own food issues. But I had none of Kathy's fortitude. Instead, I followed my father's pattern. I went on and off starvation diets. I berated myself for "cheating." When I cheated, I hated myself, and when I hated myself, I cheated more. Instead of coke, I popped Dexatrim or speed. The Black Beauties came from a friend of Krisztina's and were cheap. I took them in an effort to cut my appetite, but that never helped for long. Often, I swallowed five or six times the regular dosage of laxatives in an effort to purge myself. I almost enjoyed the gut-wrenching cramps and the hours in the bathroom. I saw them as punishment for my being "bad."

I envied the ninety-pound Kathy and thought, *Why can't I be like her? Why can't I live on half a cup of cottage cheese, an apple, a carrot, and a plain salad the whole day? Why am I so weak?* Then I heard about a new method of dieting. A friend who was already a compulsive overeater and bulimic told me you could "eat all you want and then just throw it all up." She made it sound so simple, and when you're a teenager, you don't think about the consequences of things that sound so simple. You don't know that if you make yourself throw up, your teeth begin to rot. That your throat gets sore. That your stomach aches all the time from the bingeing and purging. That bulimia is one endless cycle of self-hatred that simply takes over your life.

To me, vomiting sounded like a good way to eat all I wanted and never gain weight. But I found it more difficult than it sounded. My friend's instructions were simple: "Just stick your finger down your throat, and that's it." But it wasn't that clean or that simple. You had to stick your finger so deep down your throat that it hurt. You had to lock yourself in the bathroom with your head over the toilet trying again and again to get your finger down far enough so that something came up. You've already binged on all the food you found in the house, so there's no turning back. And if you managed to puke, you felt dizzy and sick and were left with sour breath and cramps. Sickeningly, as with my laxative agonies, I actually got satisfaction from the pain.

It was a full-time job to keep up-to-date on all the hip places and happenings in New York. Classes just got in the way. In early September, I went way uptown to 205th Street to my new school, the Bronx High School of Science. I walked into the massive building; stared down the loud hallways; heard the clang and clutter of lockers opened and slammed; took one look at the eager, hardworking student body; and walked right out of the building. I never went back. I had no notion of the consequences, of permanent school records, of upsetting my parents, of ruining my academic life. I thought I was making some kind of important antiestablishment statement by getting on the downtown subway and abandoning my first day of high school. They were all, as my dad might have said, fascists anyway. In truth I was scared, confused, and in pain. I thought I was angry about unemployment in England or wanted "Anarchy in the UK" (worthy worries if I were an underprivileged Londoner). But what was really on my mind was trying to figure out why I was so drawn to the destructive behavior that had begun to consume me. School got in the way of clubs and hanging out, so I decided not to go. I left the house each morning to preserve the illusion that I was attending classes. Some days, I rode the subway for hours. Other times, I wandered the few blocks to Stuyvesant High School and hung around outside, sitting on parked cars, drinking coffee, smoking cigarettes, and talking to the kids I knew, including Iana, although she only occasionally cut class to sit with me. She thought school was beneath her and that most of the teachers were "idiotic." But she had too much sense to trash her academic career. Krisztina, like me, wasn't thinking beyond the night to come and which club we would hit. She often met up with me outside Stuyvesant rather than attending the High School of Music and Art.

I was deluded enough to imagine that no one noticed my absence from Bronx Science. After a few weeks, I learned otherwise. I came home one afternoon to find the mail lying by the front door of Twenty-five East Fourth Street. Looking up at me was an envelope with the school letterhead addressed to Mr. and Mrs. Anthony Hendra. At first I simply stared at it, thinking how odd it was to see my parents so formally addressed. Who were these people, Mr. and Mrs. Anthony Hendra? Certainly not the people I lived with. They never seemed like Mr. and Mrs. anything. Then, I tore open the letter.

7.

THE FIRE ESCAPE

I WAS BEING SNITCHED ON:

"Dear Mr. and Mrs. Hendra," it read.

"It has come to our attention that your daughter, Jessica Hendra, has been absent from our institution for the last consecutive three weeks. . . ."

Busted . . . if my parents saw it. But the good news was, I found the letter first. That made it all the easier to toss it in the trashcan that stood by the front of our building. Then I paused, pulled it out, and looked at it again. It was serious. I could tell. And I wish I could say that I was having second thoughts. Instead, I ripped it to shreds, stuffed it at the bottom of the garbage and headed upstairs feeling guilty—just not guilty enough to tell my mother the truth. But the Board of Education doesn't give up. After another week without me, the assistant principal of the school called the loft. I wasn't there to intercept this time, and when I came home that day, I found my mother in the kitchen with an unusually stern look on her face.

"Jessica, I got a call from Bronx Science this morning. The principal said you have not been in school one day this entire term!"

What could I say?

"I'm sorry, Ma," I stammered.

My mother, the Queen of Stoicism, had finally reached her limit. She had tolerated the transformation of her youngest daughter from a pretty, quiet girl into a terrible teen. The knife-cut hair, the attitude, the safety pins, the loud music, the room that looked like a junk heap, the refereeing of the fights between my father and me. The phone call from the school proved more than she could handle.

"My idea of hell is being with you as a teenager for all eternity!"

I stood silent, shocked to hear this kind of emotion from my mother. She hadn't exactly yelled. And it wasn't even close to . . . say, my father screaming at the TV. But it had served its purpose. I stood in front of her feeling stupid and ashamed, and realizing, perhaps for the first time, that my mother wasn't impervious to her surroundings. Her outburst rightfully was directed at me, but I could sense the pain, the real pain, of my father's affairs, his drinking and drug habit, of Kathy's increasingly obvious issues with food, of me destroying my future. It almost made a serious and lasting impression—but not quite.

My father, of course, was furious, ranting and raving about my "fucking idiotic behavior" and threatening me with military school. I said I was sorry, more out of fear than remorse, and he countered by telling me I was "grounded," which I thought was an unbelievably 1950s Americana term for my dad to use. The idea of military school didn't appear his style either. Hadn't he warned me against the evils of militarism and patriotism all my life? What about safeties and not raising my hand for the Pledge of Allegiance? What about the Brownies being Hitler Youth? Hadn't he always encouraged me to resist authority? But faced with the messed-up product of his utterly confusing parenting, I suspect he thought the military sounded like a good idea. Not being grounded himself, Dad left in a passion and didn't return until the early hours of the morning. By then, he was irredeemably stoned and refused my mother's pleas to go with her to the Bronx, even though the letter from the school requested both of them present. So Mom and I trekked uptown without him to plead my case in front of "The Gang of Four," as my mom dubbed the principal and his associates. My father, as far as they knew, was "out of town." The Gang of Four took one look at my hair and accessories and suspended me. My career at the Bronx High School of Science ended before it began.

The next stop on my educational path was our local high school, Seward Park. My mother and I walked over one afternoon to sign me up. I thought I was now a street-smart fourteen-year-old punk rocker, but I shook in my combat boots when I saw the kids at Seward. They were tougher than my classmates at P.S. 3 and were much, much bigger. I knew I would never make it through a single day there. My mom knew it too, but private school exceeded our budget. My father didn't care if I got the shit kicked out of me. He thought it would do me some good and was nothing less than I deserved for "fucking up" such a wonderful opportunity as Bronx Science. Maybe he was right. As it was, I ended up getting accepted to a public school on Seventy-first Street that had a "gifted" program. I wasn't feeling the least bit gifted, but Krisztina, who had been kicked out of Music and Art for truancy, was going there, so it seemed as good a place as any. And I went, at least a few times a week, and congratulated myself in my diary: ". . . I suffered through a whole day of school today," I wrote. "Actually it wasn't that bad; you just have to get used to it. I'm going to try to go a whole month without missing a day. Not much of an accomplishment for the average person, but for me. . . ."

One afternoon, Krisztina and I were sitting out on my fire escape, smoking. It was okay for Dad to smoke cigars and pot in the loft, but he had a fit if he smelled cigarette smoke. It didn't matter. We sort of liked the fire escape. It was narrow and rickety, and the black paint was peeling, but for us it served as a private back porch. We took pillows out there and sat for hours, talking and smoking countless Marlboro Lights. Next door was a parking lot, and Krisztina and I could see right down onto the roof, spying on drug deals and guys taking a piss on the cars.

It was cold, and we were huddled in our coats, having the typical conversation of that year: "Madness is playing at Irving Plaza tonight. Do you think we can copy the stamp? I don't have any dough," Krisztina said.

"I can't go anyway. Daddy had a fucking attack when I asked if I could go out tonight. God I wish we lived alone, just the two of us. Then we could do whatever the fuck we wanted."

"Jessie, I was looking out my window the other day. (Krisztina and Olga had moved to an apartment on East End Avenue.) It's only three stories high. I know I could climb down out the window. Or maybe I could get a really long rope and get down that way."

"What are you talking about?"

"I mean I can leave whenever I want, and my mother never has to know."

I just looked at her.

"Okay, listen. I did it last night, and it worked. I climbed down and went to Tier 3. She never found out."

"You snuck out of your house and went to Tier 3 without me? You bitch!" I punched her shoulder lightly.

"I'm sorry. But there has to be a way for you to get out too. I mean where does this fire escape go? Nowhere at the bottom, but it goes up to the roof, right?"

"Yeah."

"Well, can't you get up the stairwell to the roof?"

"But the door to the stairwell is locked from the inside."

"Yeah, but I can get out of my house, come down here, open the front door with a key, walk up the stairwell, and unlock the door."

"Then we can both go down the stairs and out the front door. Do you think it might work?"

We decided to try. I gave Krisztina my key. And while she went back through the loft and up the building stairs to the roof, I climbed three flights up the fire escape. It didn't feel at all sturdy, and looking down through the iron slats made me dizzy. I looked across at where the Lower East Side met the gray sky of early winter. I hoped it wouldn't be too dark if I tried this at night, but if I could find a way to sneak out, it was worth it. I walked across the tarpaper roof, and passed the water tower, opened the stairwell door, and found a smiling Krisztina waiting for me. "It works!"

Krisztina and I agreed to try it for real that night. The problem was timing. We had no idea what hour Olga might go to sleep, so Krisztina could sneak out her window undetected. And I had to wait for her to open the roof door before I could get out. It was too risky to rely on it staying unlocked all evening considering that the artist and part-time drug dealer who lived on the eighth floor checked it each night. I would just have to get ready to go out and sit by the fire escape until I heard Krisztina coming. The plan called for her to knock on the fire escape door when she'd made it in. It would be safer if my parents were asleep, but it was impossible to know when, or if, my father was coming home. We reasoned that because the loft was so long and my parents' bedroom was on the opposite end from the fire escape door, no one would hear us sneak off even if they were awake. If Kathy found out, we felt certain she could be trusted to keep quiet. Maybe we might even get her to sneak out with us one night.

That night I "went to bed" early—meaning I went to my room, got dressed in a ripped plaid dress and fishnets, and waited in bed for my mother to go into the front room to read. Having told me to be home that night, Daddy was still out. We ran an enormous risk of meeting him coming home, either in the stairwell or on the street, but I decided not to think about it. At around 11:30 P.M., I heard my mom leave the living room. I made a "body" out of pillows and blankets, so the bed looked occupied. Then I quietly stole to the fire escape door. I sat by it, wrapped in my long, black coat to protect against the draft that came through the cracks. After what seemed like years, I heard a tentative tapping. I unlocked it and peeked out. Krisztina's eyes, defined in black, met mine in the flood light from the parking lot. We had a whispered conference.

"Was your mom asleep?" I asked.

"Yeah, but I almost fell out of the stupid window. I hope no one saw me!"

"My dad's still out."

"Shit, what if we meet him on the street?"

"I don't know. Let's just get down the stairwell. If we hear him coming up, we'll hide. Once we're out on the street, we can make a run for it."

The wind felt sharp as we began our ascent to the roof. I went second and felt, even more than I had on our test run, that I might plummet off the side of the fire escape or that it might fall away from the building entirely. *Oh, well, it's too late now.* In a few minutes, I would either plunge to my death sprawled atop a Chevy in the parking lot, or I'd be on my way to see one of my favorite bands. The fire escape held. We made it over the roof.

As we crept down the stairs, we listened but didn't hear my father's footfalls. Krisztina did a "Tony check" of the street from the front door and found it all clear. Into the freezing night we scurried, pulling our coats over our heads in an imagined disguise. We ran all the way to Irving Plaza. There, we searched the crowd outside for someone we knew who had a hand stamp from the club. Then Krisztina took out the black pen she always carried and deftly copied the stamp onto her hand and mine, and we made it in for the last few songs. At about four in the morning, I slinked back into the loft from the fire escape and got into bed. My parents never knew.

The Great Loft Escape became our almost-nightly routine. Considering we slept about two or three hours most nights, it's not surprising that we fell behind in classes. But I had found a way to escape without battling my father, and I was going to take full advantage. Once I had a near miss when I was walking up Fourth Street at five-thirty in the morning and Dad was letting himself into the building. I hid behind a car in the parking lot until he had plenty of time to get upstairs. Another morning as I headed to school, I heard Krisztina calling softly to me from the basement. She had arrived home to find that her mother had gotten up in the night and bolted the front door. She couldn't sneak back in her house, so she came downtown on the subway at dawn and spent a few hours among the mouse traps and discarded furniture.

Sneaking out could be avoided if I could wrangle permission to stay at Iana's. Her parents never watched the clock, and 3:30 A.M. was our usual ETA at their Seventeenth Street loft. Iana and I were now very close. In my diary, dated February 9, 1980, I wrote, "What tonight really turned out to be was 'talk' night. First off Iana and I had the greatest conversation. . . . she told me her 'deepest darkest secret' [whom she had a crush on at the time, which was not the kind of thing Iana usually revealed]. Well I told her my secret, about Daddy."

My two closest friends, Krisztina and Iana, knew. Still, I never mentioned a word to any adult. I saw no point to it. What had happened happened, I reasoned, and talking about it wasn't going to change anything. But it *had*, to some degree. Telling my friends *had* made me feel better. It seemed to relieve some of the pressure that had built. And they still liked and accepted me regardless.

Miraculously, given that we were fourteen or fifteen, none of us got raped, mugged, or murdered. I had a radar for avoiding scary people—or, at least, scary men—and if I ever grew wary of someone coming toward me on a dark night, I dodged down another street or hid until he passed. The three of us all knew never to accept an invitation to get into a car, and cars weren't really part of our world anyway. Not when we lived in Manhattan. The subway made me more than a little nervous. It seemed so easy to get trapped by some nut case. One night I came home with a friend who had dreamt up a unique defense against predatory men. She acted as though she were schizophrenic. She even kept an Alka-Seltzer or two in her pocket. In real emergencies, she'd break open a packet and put one under her tongue to create the illusion of rabid drool. We noticed a guy following us into one of the subway cars, and almost immediately, she started talking to herself, kicking and screaming at imaginary assailants. The guy got off at the next stop. I was glad she hadn't pulled out the antacids. I felt too timid to try any of this myself and once had to escape a stalker by jumping off the subway and sprinting through the Times Square subway station until I lost him. It never occurred to me to find a cop. They might wonder what I was doing out at three in the morning. Krisztina had skipped one of our clandestine dates because she jumped a turnstile and was arrested by the transit police. Olga had a near collapse when she had to go down to the station and bail her out. The police were not our friends. I preferred to walk rather than get on the subway. But the most frightening trip I ever had was in a taxi.

I had been at a club on Avenue A with a friend who was also named Jessica. When she and I were slouching around late-night Manhattan, she had an effortless, unpretentious cool that I could never achieve. For one, she really *was* English and had the accent to prove it. I had to live with the fact that, despite my parentage, I was just a New Yorker. She also was elegant, lovely, and hip all in one go. Her hair was short, reddish, and hennaed. Her skin was the perfect sort of pale. It accentuated her vivid red lips and slightly slanted green eyes (her grandmother had been Chinese). Besides, she was tall, exotic and—what really got me—naturally slim. I spent many afternoons with Jessica in one of the Ukrainian coffee shops that filled the East Village, watching her eat grilled cheese sandwiches or pierogies with never a care in the world. Meantime, I sat drinking bad coffee and wishing I could take just a single, guiltless bite. I also shared "my secret about Daddy" with Jessica, just as I had with Iana and my other close friends. But none of us ever thought of going to an adult. Perhaps they didn't know what I should do any better than I did.

Jessica scorned purses and carried her essentials in a small brown paper bag. She wore a 1960s Mod black-and-white checked skirt and a Rude-Boy porkpie hat. I tried to walk like her, talk like her, and even smell like her, making a pilgrimage to the Kiehl's Pharmacy on

Thirteenth Street and Third Avenue to buy the rose talc that she used. Nothing worked. I just became a rose-smelling version of me, clutching a crumpled brown bag.

We left the club at two-thirty that morning, and because it was raining hard, we decided to treat ourselves to a cab ride home. The first stop was Jessica's mother's loft on Crosby Street. After five or ten minutes, a Checker finally came down the slick avenue. Even as I was saying, "Great, a cab!" a guy a block or so up ran out of a bar and flagged the cabbie. The Checker slowed, but the driver must have seen us because the cab abruptly sped on just as the guy reached for the door handle. It stopped in front of us. Jessica and I were much too wet and tired to care about taxi etiquette, and we opened the door and flopped onto the dry black seats. I heard a loud *click*, and I sat up with a start. The driver had locked the back doors. Then I looked up front and saw her. The cabbie was huge. She took up the entire front seat, and the steering wheel wedged between her massive bosom and her stomach. Long, and not recently washed, brown hair snaked from under a soiled Yankees cap. And when she turned around, I could see that her front tooth was chipped and a mole hid itself in the many folds of her fleshy face.

"Where do you two cutie, little things think you're going?"

Jessica and I exchanged a glance. "Oh no, a loony!" I whispered.

"We're going to Crosby and Broome, please," Jessica said in her best Be-Nice-to-Crazy-People voice. The cabbie let out a long snort.

"I don't think we're going to Crosby and Broome, honey. I don't like Crosby and Broome. I'm gonna decide where this cab's goin'. And I think we're gonna run every light from here to 168th Street. I think I'm gonna have some fun with you girls, introduce you to my whip collection. When I'm done with you sweet things, I'm gonna run you right up to the Bronx and sell you on the white slave market!"

She cackled and floored the gas pedal, speeding up Avenue A at maybe forty or fifty. To me it seemed like at least a hundred. I looked at Jessica and began fumbling madly with the door. The lock wouldn't budge.

"Forget that, baby cakes. I've got this cab all locked up, sugar tits!"

Jessica and I began screaming, and though Big Momma had locked the doors, I could still open the window on my side. "Roll your window down!" I yelled to Jessica, who looked like she might vomit. We hung our heads out, screaming into a rainy and profoundly empty Manhattan. Big Momma just kept driving, running every red light as promised. *This is it! This is actually it!* I thought as the streets flew by. Then a guardian angel—a big black guy with a leather jacket—crossed Avenue A and Fourteenth Street. Big Momma thought better of adding manslaughter to her growing rap sheet, and she slowed down. That was all we needed. I thrust myself out the open window, pulling Jessica along with me. We landed hard on the street, and I cut my hand on a broken bottle. Jessica turned her ankle coming down. At least we were free. The Checker screeched to a halt, but Big Momma's bulk was in our favor. She struggled to extract her gigantic body from the front seat, and Jessica and I took off running, our guardian angel standing on the other side of Fourteenth Street, looking on in amazement as we fled. I turned back and saw Big Momma lifting her leg out of the car, waving her flabby arms at us and shouting, "Come on back, sweethearts. It was only a joke! It was only a joke, honey pies!"

We never thought to take her license plate number. We just got out of there fast. I didn't get into a Checker cab again for at least a year. But I never really moderated my behavior. I couldn't. After all, I was a bona fide "groupie" for certain bands—mostly of the British persuasion. And being out late at night was the only way to see them.

I was thrilled when a guitar player or singer I worshiped gave me a look—any look, really—or invited me into the dressing room after the show. Still, I always froze when he asked the inevitable question: "How about coming back to the hotel, luv?" I went through the back-stage drink. Then the first kiss routine. But I never went "all the way" with anyone in any of the bands. I must have pissed off a lot of horny English rockers.

For months, I had a huge crush on a great-looking black guy name HR, the lead singer of an underground band the Bad Brains. The group had come from Washington, D.C., and HR had incredible stage energy and wowed everyone by doing back flips in the middle of songs. I got girlish goose bumps when he called me "from the road" but was too nervous to do more than heavy kissing in the back room at CBGB. He never knew how young I was.

He had been getting more and more heavily into the Rastafarian movement, growing dreadlocks, talking about *jah*, and making music that fused reggae with punk. I had always loved reggae and had started listening to it with my father, who was a Bob Marley fan. But that didn't mean I was ready for what HR wanted. Just before his set started, in a voice that indicated he was either incredibly serious or in-credibly stoned, he invited me to move "back" to Ethiopia with him and become one of his wives. That's when I revealed to him, after months of making out, that I was only fourteen, perhaps a tad young to accept such an offer.

On the way home, I asked Krisztina, "Do you think I should have said yes?"

"What? No! Are you crazy?" Krisztina was always more realistic and less star struck. "You're going to live in a shack in Ethiopia with HR and his seven other wives, having babies and grinding wheat? Jesus."

In the end, HR did not go to Africa but stayed in Washington. The next time the band came to New York, I played it cool and so did he, maybe because he was put off by my status as a minor. Whatever the reason, HR never pressed his offer.

Even so, we were propositioned often, less because we were devastatingly attractive and more just because we were there. One night at the Palladium when the Clash was playing, Krisztina, Iana, and I hung around the back door figuring out a way to get in—the $15 entry fee was out of the question. One of the bouncers noticed. "Hey babe," he said to me. "You really want to get in? I can walk you right through if you give me some head backstage. I can get you right in easy if you came back here and jack me off a bit." In my diary I wrote quite primly, "Well, of course I said NO. I was very disgusted."

Still, I considered my virginity a burden. At fourteen, I thought it would be better to "just get it over with." Krisztina worked faster. One night, we snuck out to see the Specials, one of our favorite English ska bands, at an uptown club. We had no tickets or money, so we did our usual trick of copying the stamp. I managed to wedge myself right up against the stage and fixed my eyes on the bassist, who was unbelievably cute. The Specials were a two-tone band, decked out in silver suits and pork-pie hats with short haircuts, not the usual punky crew. I nearly had a groupie heart attack when, at the end of the set, the cute guitarist walked over to the edge of the stage and handed me a beer. *I'll keep this Heineken bottle forever!* I thought as the crowd dispersed and I ran to find Krisztina, clutching the cherished beer in my hand.

"Look, the guitar guy (I had only a very vague idea of the difference between a bass guitar and a lead guitar) gave me this." I thrust the Heineken at her. "He just walked right over and handed it to me! C'mon. Come with me! I really want to find him."

Hand in hand, we trolled around the club looking for the entrance to our backstage Mecca. We knew it was a very uncool to ask where the door was. If you had to ask, you didn't deserve to get in. When Krisztina and I found it, we just tried to act hip. We stood there smoking, pretending we had no idea where we were or that we were waiting for anyone. And of course, we swapped sips of the sacred beer. Finally, two roadies emerged carrying equipment. We saw roadies as the younger dukes to the band's royal family. Not princes—the musicians—and certainly not kings—the lead singers—but royalty all the same.

The roadies started chatting us up. Did we like the show? Where were we from? Did we want a drink? Did we have a smoke? Krisztina and I sat down on the equipment. After a few more questions, one of the guys asked me straight out: "Do you want to come back to the hotel?"

"Umm. . . ." I said.

He looked right at me. "You're a virgin, aren't you, darling?" he said in his East London accent.

I was struck by the way he said it. I should've been offended, I suppose, but the way he asked was so matter-of-fact. Like, "You're a New Yorker, aren't you darling?" or "You enjoy dancing, don't you?" Out of his mouth it became a question like any another, as if an answer either way was nothing to be ashamed of, as if the whole pick-up game ought to be played honestly and benefit both sides. It was the kind of shameless attitude toward sex that I knew I could never have. Of course I was way too young to be playing the game at all, but I imagined I was very sophisticated, and I'm sure the roadie, whose name was Rex, thought I was at least eighteen.

"Yes," I admitted. "Yes, I am a virgin."

"Well, if you want, I can help you out with that. If you don't, that's all right too." He sounded almost indifferent, but in a flattering way. "You're a beautiful girl, and you just decide whatever you want to do. It's all up to you."

The truth was it had never been all up to me. Whatever choices I might've had about sex and innocence disappeared before I turned seven, and the choice would never be mine again. If it had been up to me, maybe I wouldn't have been sitting there at four in the morning having this conversation at all. I might have had the self-respect to be staying in at night and studying for my math test the next morning, rather than stalking band members and holding their beers. But I couldn't tell Rex this. Instead, I begged off his invitation, and he took it no further. "That's all right," he told me and offered to get me a drink from the bar anyway.

While he fetched me a gin and tonic, Prince Heineken appeared. He took Rex's place and ran through the same questions, finally asking if I wanted to go back to the hotel. I liked him much less than Rex. But then, he *was* a prince. I bought some time. "Let me talk to my friend to see what she wants to do," I told him, but Krisztina had disappeared. She must have gone off with the other roadie without me noticing. Rex came back with my drink; the prince went to get his guitar; and Rex offered to help me find Krisztina.

I still was searching for her when the band loaded their stuff into a van and left without me. Finally I found Krisztina in the bathroom, looking disheveled and clearly preoccupied.

"Where the fuck have you been!" I accosted her. "I've been looking all over this fucking club for you! Those guys wanted me to come back to the hotel with them, and I didn't 'cause I was searching for you! Now they left!"

"Jessie, you're a big girl. If you wanted to go back to the hotel with them, you should have gone. Don't blame me because you're too scared to go by yourself."

I was pissed because I knew she was right.

We started walking home, me angry, Krisztina silent.

"Why did you just disappear like that? I know you were fooling around with that roadie. Why didn't you just tell me where you were going?" I said to the back of her head.

Krisztina turned.

"I went into a back room with him, and I got it over with. I fucked him if that's what you want to know."

I was shocked, not by her behavior but because now we were no longer equals. Ever since we had shared our secrets and learned that we both had been molested, I felt I knew and understood everything about her and that she felt the same about me. Now she had taken a step that I was afraid to take. She had left me behind. I felt hurt but sounded angry.

"God! I can't believe you did that. I can't believe you did it your first time in the back room of some shitty club. Not even at a hotel. Not even at someone's apartment! I just can't believe it."

We didn't talk again that night. And I was livid as I snuck back into the loft. I didn't have the confidence to do what Krisztina had done. I hated my body. She didn't hate hers. She exuded an open sexuality that got her into trouble. But I envied her freedom. And even as I saw that the molestation she had shared with me resulted in her promiscuity, I didn't see how what had happened to me left me the way that I was. All I knew is that I wished I could be like her. I spent the whole next day mooning over my Specials LP and thinking I should have taken the ride with Prince Heineken, even though I would have preferred Rex the Roadie.

I watched Krisztina's sexual adventures explode. Once she had started, it seemed she couldn't stop. It wasn't as though she enjoyed it much, either. Sex for Krisztina was like vomiting for me.

Olga caught her sneaking out one night, just as she was disappearing off the balcony with a rope around her waist. Understandably alarmed, Olga locked Krisztina in her room. To retaliate, Krisztina wrote a poster-sized sign and put it up to the window: "MY MOTHER HAS LOCKED ME IN MY ROOM PLEASE HELP!" It caused chaos among the neighbors, who knocked on the apartment door with questioning concern. Upon her release, Krisztina still managed to roam the city, sleeping with this guy or that, even showing up one day with whip marks on her back. She told me they had come from a lunatic on a street corner. I listened to her exploits with outward disapproval and secret envy (though the whipping was hard to embrace). And I worried about her. I went to clubs with her and made my way home alone after she went off with someone new. Once she even brought a guy to the roof of Twenty-five East Fourth Street, something I did myself a year later.

I became more and more determined to catch up with my best friend and "went for it" a few months later. He was a roommate of Krisztina's new and somewhat steady boyfriend, Steve. Steve seemed to be a stable, responsible guy and really loved Krisztina. He worked on Wall Street, standing on the stock exchange floor all day in a suit. After the market closed, he came back to his tiny downtown apartment, put on Doc Martens and torn jeans, and went clubbing. I'm positive Steve never knew her real age. I wasn't remotely in love with his roommate, Vinnie, but he seemed as good a person as any—and a relatively safe choice—for my first time. His only glamour in my eyes was his Britishness. Vinnie was a nice guy—and not bad looking, in a pallid English way.

I knew I needed to prepare for it. I remembered the conversation I had overheard between my parents regarding the anonymous woman in need of an abortion, and I had accompanied one irresponsible girlfriend no less than three times to an abortion clinic and heard the details of her "procedures." I knew Krisztina was "taking care" of herself, and I went to the Planned Parenthood Clinic on Third Avenue to get a diaphragm. I also had a conference with Krisztina the night before I expected it to happen.

"Tell me what to do. I feel so nervous. What if I mess up?"

"You won't mess up. You'll know what to do when it happens."

"I just feel so fat and disgusting."

"You're not fat," she reassured me. "You're perfect. Don't worry."

I tried to listen to her, but it was hard. I felt nervous when Vinnie and I got home early that night. The four of us been at a club, and Krisztina and Steve had insisted on staying, clearly part of the plan to leave Vinnie and me alone.

Sex was okay. Not good. Not awful. I was too uptight about my body and too ashamed about what had happened with my father to really enjoy it. But at least I had gotten it over with. I went out with Vinnie for a few more weeks and then decided to move on. After all, I was almost sixteen and no longer a virgin.

Besides plain luck, I figure there were two reasons I survived my adolescence. One, I hated drugs. Two, I was too ashamed to have much sex—at least compared to some of my friends. I have my childhood to thank for both. I had seen too many stoned and fucked-up adults to ever view drugs as anything but stupid. And the kids I hung out with were too poor to buy anything but some grass and maybe a little speed. I smoked pot once or twice but hated it. I got nothing but more paranoid than I already felt, and I walked home with my heart pounding. I spent the next two hours holed up in bed waiting for the experience to end. I still remembered seeing my mom slip under the New Jersey dinner table after too much hash, panicked as she cried, "I'm disappearing!" I figured I had inherited her tolerance for drugs rather than my father's. His beloved cocaine, the stuff I had mistaken for confectioner's sugar, had made me think I was going to explode. I wondered how my father could ingest so much of it without feeling as if he were going to rip his own head off. But this was the 1980s, when coke was the King of New York. My father suffered a heart attack when he was thirty-nine, a tremendous scare for him considering that his father, Robert, had died from heart failure when he was in his fifties. One of the doctors in the ER suggested that my dad might cut down on the coke if he didn't wish to die the next time. He followed the doctor's advice—for a week or two. If I had wanted to do coke, I could easily have pilfered it from his stash. I just wasn't interested.

There were always rich kids doing lines in the bathrooms of the more trendy clubs, and once I almost lost my life to a coked-out chick with purple hair and a nose ring because I bumped into her in the ladies' room and spilled her store. As I fled, a transvestite in high heels and a red wig, high as a kite, stopped me. "Now which bathroom do you think I should use?" Then he—or she—collapsed onto the filthy floor in hysterics. Most of the kids I knew stuck to cigarettes and drinking. I drank too, sometimes too much, but I drank more out of a feeling that I should than because I liked the sensation. As with drugs, I had too many bad associations with drunks to ever want to be one myself. What did I want to be? I had no idea. All I knew was that I was getting tired of clubs and cutting school but didn't really know how to get back on track. In the fall of 1980, I wrote this in my diary, already world-weary at fifteen:

> The first days of clubbing were good, everything was so new, it was all so exciting. Now going out, dressing punk, seeing bands, even cutting school, is more an obligation in a weird way. Sometimes I want it all to go away. I mean sometimes I want to never go to a club again, do well in school like I used to, dress totally normal, even dress kind of pretty.

I had come to identify myself with a certain life, and I was reluctant to change. Besides, my father would take credit for me straightening out. It would be like going back to him. It was as though I'd been saying to him, "You messed me up, and now I am going to mess up my own life to prove it!" If I got my act together, wouldn't that be like admitting that everything was okay when I knew it really wasn't? I had changed schools again, this time to a small liberal private school in Brooklyn Heights, and I began going to class more often. Krisztina's brother had gone there, and when she and I actually managed to graduate the ninth grade at our public school, we were offered places at St. Ann's. The fact that we managed to graduate shocked everyone, especially the principal, who told my mother in a conference that he was sure Krisztina and I were, and I quote, "dope addicts and no doubt shacking up with college boys," neither of which was technically true. The staff at St. Ann's was less fazed by our appearances. There were even a few other kids who looked like us, among them the Beastie Boys, who were already performing. I knew how much the tuition was;

my father berated me constantly about the bills. I also knew my mother (and Olga) had gone to considerable effort buttering up the principal to get us in. I spent a lot of time hanging around bars in Brooklyn playing pool instead of going to class. But because I was not completely, as Dad called me, "an overprivileged Manhattan teenage bitch," I made deals with myself. I never cut English or History and managed to get As on book reports and history tests. I could only cut French twice a month, science once, and math three times. I kept track of my eating habits just as rigorously, counting calories and how many times I vomited. And I discovered, simply by actually going to class more often, that St. Ann's had some cool kids.

Just as I had begun to emerge from my most reckless period, Dad seemed to be entering one of his, marked by the end of his tenure at the *Lampoon*. He and Sean Kelly left in 1978, disgusted with the effect of *Animal House* on the magazine. My father deplored both the movie and the gross-out jokes that had started to characterize the *Lampoon*. My dad was essentially ousted, and he took the rejection—of himself and his particular brand of humor—hard. The *Lampoon* had been more than a job; it had been, creatively and socially, his entire existence. My father is an intense man. To be satisfied, he must be passionately involved in something. When he was young, he had the Catholic Church and his quest to become a monk. That gave way to the world of satire, and I think he viewed the early *Lampoon* and its (almost exclusively male) members as a band of brothers fighting against social and political conservatism. Whatever terrible damage he did—to my sister, my mother, or me—was, as he has claimed, excusable in the face of his "precious mission to save the world through laughter." His weapon was the pen, and in his mind, it was always mightier than the sword. Now, he saw P. J. O'Rourke and the remade

Lampoon as instruments of Satan, bent on destroying what he had helped create.

My father always thought in terms of good and evil, black and white. Even during his self-imposed exile from the Catholic Church, he viewed the world that way: holy fathers (from the order of Saint Satire) versus devils (P. J. and fart jokes). Most of the brothers had already abandoned the *Lampoon*. When Henry Beard sold his founder's share, my dad was devastated by the ingratitude of Henry's exit line: "I have not felt this happy since the day I got out of the army." Doug Kenny walked off a cliff in Hawaii a few years after leaving. It was either a suicide or drug-induced fall. Michael O'Donoghue continued to score big with *Saturday Night Live*. And then there was my father, left alone with his satirical mission and his contempt for television, the medium that made the fortunes of many of his contemporaries. Stuck between drugs, affairs, and a few successful freelance projects, Dad thought about going back to the church. In 1981, he wrote a careful but desperate letter to his former spiritual mentor, Father Joe Warrilow, asking Joe to "get his faith back for him." I don't know if he ever sent it, but it wasn't enough to get him to Mass on Sundays.

Depression made my dad angry and temperamental, and it was then that I feared him most. But what did I fear exactly? Certainly not that he might hit me. My father hit me only once. I was eight, and it was a slap on the face. It shocked me more than it hurt. And he felt very remorseful, so much so that he brought me home a present the next day.

It seemed as if he felt more remorse over that slap than over the sexual incidents. But I'd still wonder, when he grew angry, whether he might try something sexual again. How could I not? When my father was livid, it seemed as if he took up the entire loft. And not just with his screaming. He became a veritable arsenal of weaponry. There seemed to be a rage that emanated from his body, like a glow of radiation that, if you got too close, might kill you. He was like a grenade ready to explode, his face red, his huge, blue eyes boring holes in his target. His words became bullets that flew from a sniper's rifle, chosen carefully and aimed to kill.

The simple truth was that Dad was always smarter than me—smarter than *anyone* I knew. That meant he could fight, using words anyway, with great precision and effect. Maybe he would employ some well-chosen phrase about the way I looked. Or he might mock my accent (American, not English, as his remained). Maybe he would ridicule my friends or confirm the fears I already had about myself—that I wasn't much good at anything but being a lazy bitch and would amount to nothing. And he was relentless, a pit bull that would lock its teeth on your throat until you simply stopped struggling. The only way to end a fight with my dad was to concede, absolutely and unconditionally.

That meant that Dad was never wrong, not even remotely. If you chose not to concede, he had two ways of ending a fight: He'd either storm from the house, or, if the fight were by phone, hang up. Countless times he'd say, "Just go away and think about it, Jessie. Go look at your navel and think about exactly what you have done to me!" And then a slam—either of the stairwell door or the phone. Usually, our fights dissolved into me going silent, and my dad going ballistic. An icy teenage stare was often my only (futile) defense against his verbal artillery.

Why did I care? Hadn't the damage he'd done been enough to make me never love or trust him again? I never saw it that way. Yes, I was trying to create an identity separate from his, trying to escape his suffocating influence and dominating opinions. But I still wanted him to love me. I *needed* him to love me. I was even hesitant to be angry with him, as I wrote in my diary:

> I am sorry, I mean I really don't want to feel this way, but Daddy is really starting to get short with me—temper-wise. Maybe I deserve it, but there are times when I really think I don't. He's such an ego-maniac. Total hot shit. I love Daddy and all, but sometimes he is very hard for me to stand. He's so self-centered. If anyone but him is in a crummy mood, it is always unjustified. Well, might as well turn the other cheek. I can never win a fight with him.

Not long after I wrote this, the fights would stop, and Daddy would be gone.

PART III

JUNE 2004

FOR THE NEXT FEW DAYS, I DID JUST AS RUDY SUG-gested: I wrote everything down—everything that came to mind as I read *Father Joe*. I told Kurt what I was doing. He agreed with Rudy. "Just get it all out on paper first," he said. Julia and Charlotte weren't happy. Their mom had locked herself in the office—their *playroom!*—to write or have intense, muffled phone conversations with friends. Charlotte didn't understand what was going on. But I overheard Julia say to Kurt, "Why is Mommy so upset about a stupid, old book?"

What could he say? I just thought back to that night at Charlotte's preschool, and how I had resolved right then that they would someday understand exactly why I was so upset.

"As a little girl I worshipped Tony Hendra, my father," I began.

He was—and still is—brilliant, funny, and charismatic, as demon-strated by his involvement with the *National Lampoon* and *Spy* magazines, as well as the cult movie *This Is Spinal Tap*. If I had not loved him as much as I did, what happened to me might never have happened. And I doubt that I would have kept silent for the past thirty-two years.

But with the recent, celebrated publication of my father's book, *Father Joe: The Man Who Saved My Soul*. I cannot remain mute. He has made sin and redemption his cause celebre, his raison d'être.

In his book—which a front-page review in the *Times'* Book Review anointed as belonging "in the first tier of spiritual memoirs"— my father confesses that, "No father could have been more selfish—treating his family like props, possessions, inconveniences, mostly forgetting them completely in his precious mission to save the world through laughter."

He writes that he was a "neglectful" and "terrible father," his self-indictment apparently the result of brutal honesty and self-examination encouraged by his relationship with his spiritual mentor, Father Joe Warrilow of Quarr Abbey in England.

But my father was so much more than terrible and neglectful. He was, in fact, criminal. And after reading his book, I decided I had to write the whole truth.

When I was seven, my mother, father, older sister, and I lived in rural New Jersey. My father worked for the *National Lampoon* magazine in New York City, living there part of the week. He also drank heavily and abused drugs, two habits he describes in *Father Joe*. He sometimes went on binges, driving into Manhattan and disappearing for hours or days, once returning home with head bandages after an unexplained pistol whipping landed him in an emergency room.

I grew up with a terrible fear that someday he might never come home. One night, as I was falling asleep in my bunk bed, my older sister fast asleep below me, my father entered my bedroom and told me in a whisper that he was going out for a bit. I asked him not to do that. He said he would come into my bunk and lie with me until I fell asleep.

He squeezed into my bed, and I snuggled into his arms. As I drifted off to sleep, he asked me to take off my underwear. . . .

I had thought for a long time how to tell what came next and finally decided to just write it matter-of-factly. What happened spoke for itself. It was why my father could not mention it in the book. No publisher would have touched it. I read through those paragraphs again and remembered how that night unfolded. After a few minutes, I continued reading:

For years, I never told anyone. Maybe I believed that *was* what people do when they love each other. Maybe I was afraid that my father would stop loving me. Maybe I believed he really would go to the city and never return. Because, as a child, what happened never made me stop loving him.

In retrospect, what followed wasn't surprising. For months I couldn't concentrate on anything. I didn't want to go to school. There were two other times when I was older—nine or ten—when my father told me to take a shower with him and again put his fingers inside me; both times, he pronounced me 'too small.' I kept my silence. As a teenager, I had truancy problems and became bulimic . . .

The letter continued for ten more paragraphs that traced my efforts to talk to my father and how he deflected each one. Then, this last page:

I appreciate that God's love transcends all, that sins can and should be forgiven, but somewhere in that message don't other people exist and isn't there some accountability? "The details" that Father Joe reportedly did not want to, or did not feel the need to, hear are the nexus where other human souls live and breathe in pain, emotionally mangled by my father.

Father Joe offered unconditional solace to my father, who appeared before him filled with torment. This was a great gift. Unfortunately, it's not a gift my father passed on. And that is what I find difficult to forgive. To read a book praised by reviewer Andrew Sullivan as having "spare[d] us no detail of his own iniquities as a parent," when I know Tony Hendra's writings are far from complete disclosure, seems to me a final act of disregard from a father.

In the last confessional scene, my father writes that he's afraid his misdeeds somehow resulted in the miscarriage of the unborn son he conceived with my stepmother. He also expresses guilt over my mother's miscarriage—though he left her months later and has never mentioned any remorse to her.

As I read the passage, it occurred to me that my father, apparently racked with guilt over what he has done to his unborn children, seems not to have come to grips with the sins he committed against his seven-year-old daughter. Or others, for that matter, though those stories are not mine to tell.

At the end of the book, my father walks away from Father Joe a free man, contrite, confessed, and apparently forgiven. But I feel certain that were Father Joe alive today, he would have lectured my father once again on the sin of selfishness. I don't think Father Joe would have been content just to know that only my father is healed.

It would have been extremely difficult for my father to have written about his sexual molestation of me. But to write a book about how he's come to terms with his sins—without having dealt with the victim of what I hope is the most serious he's ever committed—makes his book a fraud. In my book, my father hasn't earned the spiritual credits to tackle the subject of redemption. His is a facile book that should not have been written, and including me on the dedication page only made me an unwilling partner to his self-deception.

When I finished looking it over for what must have been the twentieth time, I took a deep breath and e-mailed it to Rudy. He called me a few hours later, crying. When I heard his tearful voice, I felt guilty.

"I'm sorry you had to read all that horrible stuff," I told him.

"Don't be silly, Jessica. No father could read this and not cry. The question is what do you want to do with this? I can get it into the right hands. But are you really up for what that will mean for you, for Kurt, for your mom? Are you up for thousands of people knowing this kind of thing about you? I am not saying don't do it, but if you do, all of you have to be prepared."

I paused. "Do you think my father might sue me for libel?" There was always the possibility, he said, but he didn't think my dad would be that stupid. But Rudy was right; this was a decision that was going to affect Kurt, my mom, my sister . . . all of us. Before I did anything more with what I had written, I needed to make some calls.

First, Kathy. She was at home, in Massachusetts, and I told her the whole story. As with my mother, I had alluded to things in the past. Now, I gave her the details. And like my mother, she asked the question that I couldn't answer: "How could you be in the same room with him after that?"

I said I didn't know.

Kathy seemed supportive but hesitant. As far as she was concerned, I should do whatever I thought best. Just leave her out of it.

My mother said I should go ahead and let Rudy send my letter out. She even discussed it with her husband, who agreed. If I got sued, he told my mother, the two of them would stand by me one hundred percent.

Kurt never equivocated. "If you think now is the time to finally stand up for yourself with respect to your father, then I say go ahead," he told me. "Do what helps you sleep at night."

He came with me to see my therapist, and the three of us sat in her office discussing the pros and cons of keeping silent or speaking out. After all, publicly denouncing your parent is, to put it mildly, an earthquake of a move. I might feel terribly guilty for doing such a thing, regret it deeply if I had not first tried every possible alternative. Just as the government practices diplomacy before declaring war. I didn't want to ambush my dad. I wanted to be straightforward with him. I wanted him to know where I stood.

When we got home, a package rested by the door. Inside was a copy of *Father Joe* sent to me by Random House at the request of my father. The card inside read "Compliments of the Author," and Dad had written an inscription on the title page "Show Julia and Charlotte the dedication. I bet this is the first time they have had a book dedicated to them, though it won't be the last."

Waiting for me were a few e-mails from my stepmother encouraging me to read the reviews of the book. I felt surrounded. But like every time before, I held out hope. I even fantasized that maybe, just knowing how I felt, Dad would consent to tell his readers what he had left out of his "confession." Maybe the book was a first step, not a last. Maybe a push from me was all he needed.

That night I wrote him a message. And, to my surprise, I sent it:

Daddy,

I got the copy of the book. In fact I had already bought and read the book when the copy from you arrived. I have not been in contact since reading it because I have been through such agonies trying to figure out how to tell you exactly how much this book hurt me and how angry it made me. You certainly have the right to write any book you want to, but in my opinion, you have no place writing a "confessional." The description of Father Joe was true and heartfelt, and the details of your childhood were funny and compelling, but your sins were confessed and dealt with in such sweeping generalities that it was very hard for me to take.

Either you confessed to Father Joe the sin you committed against me and understandably left that conversation out of your book, or you never confessed it to him and still remain with a dark stain on your "saved soul." If you did talk to him about it, you should have told me about it privately and given me the benefit of the solace he granted you. It is very hard for me not to feel outrage when I hear this book lauded as truthful. You know that it tells such a small portion of what really happened.

I could go on with this letter and tell you each and every emotion I had while reading *Father Joe*, but I don't see the point. I don't think you have ever wanted to acknowledge how much damage you did, and that was certainly clear in your ability to write this book and gloss over so much. I understand that you might feel that admitting you were "a terrible father" should be enough for me but it's not. You owe me more than that. What you did affected me so deeply that it has been my life's work trying to overcome it.

I had hoped that the relationship we have had over the last few years might continue. I have (we all have) appreciated both your and Carla's extensive hospitality and touching interest in the girls."

This all feels so useless, I thought as I reread the e-mail again. *I've gone to him before, during that awful Christmas at Aunt Celia's when I was in college. I* know *he remembers that. And what good did it do?*

I have tried twice already with confrontations (at Celia's) and letters (exchanged more than seven years ago) to make you accept that what you did was devastating. I have nothing left to say. Clearly not one thing I have said has penetrated your heart, or you would not have written the book you did and be able to accept the praise of having written a true and honest confessional.

I wish all of this could have turned out differently.

Jessie.

My father's response was typically confusing. I read it the same way I read *Father Joe*: at first glance, emotional and felt, at second, an artful dodge—much like the letter he had written to Michael O'Donoghue all those years ago.

"Jessie," it began . . .

I can't tell you how sad this makes me. I too thought that we had groped our way to some kind of *modus vivendi* and that you felt a measure of—an inadequate and clichéd word I know—closure. And of course I hoped and literally prayed that the subject of this book might help us further along that road. It is first and last about the love and forgiveness without which life is a relentless, mutually destructive, round of hatred and payback. That you have this reaction is beyond grief to me; tears keep welling up and have since I first read your message.

I'm so paralyzed with misery, it's as if Joe had died again.

This book isn't about us. It's not even ultimately about me. I'm a character in it and the reporter of it, but in the end it's about this extraordinary man I was lucky enough to know. I set out to write it—as I say in the prologue—to try to make him live again, because his loss was so numbingly painful to me, but also to try and bring his persona and wisdom to others. I owe Joe much more than that, but it's something. In a long and far from admirable life, I wanted to write one worthwhile thing before I died that might help people or inspire them or give them some relief from the horrors our supposed leaders and mentors inflict on them. It seems to be doing that. But it isn't me that's touching people. It's Joe. This is his book. Apropos Joe: I must correct you about [one] thing. I told you long ago that I had spoken to Father Joe, and you dismissed it as irrelevant; I even suggested that we go and see him together. You rejected that too.

You imply (with your mentions of "praise") that the book is about fame—and perhaps money. It's not. I've always been very uncomfortable with the first—what little I've experienced down the years—and never cared that much about the second. If the book makes money, it will mostly go to Quarr and to our local (quite poor) parish.

Of course you can bring all this crashing down if you wish, along with Joe's memory and much else. Does the finality of your last sentence mean that is your intention or is there some way to meet or talk and find a path once and for all out of this terrible place?

Dad

The message seemed full of high emotion and pathos. More than that, he neither denied what he had done nor accepted how I felt about it. As usual, I had simply misunderstood him and his work . . . just as he had told me in the past that I had misunderstood his "jokes." Just as he had said that I misunderstood what happened between us when I wasn't yet seven. The book, like that act, was really nothing to get so upset about. His message was clear: His book was about forgiveness—something that I, evidently, was incapable of. And so he had dodged me again.

I asked Kurt what he thought of the message. "I think he is a really good manipulator, Jess. That's what I think."

But I wasn't going to let go easily this time. I wrote back.

Dad,

I don't remember saying I would not see Joe. Or that your discussion with Joe was irrelevant. But be that as it may, what did he say? And how did you feel about writing a book about your relationship with him and the subject of forgiveness that did not include that discussion, that confession? Did the necessity of omitting that scene (for reasons that are obvious) give you any moment of questioning whether to write the book at all? Or did it not seem that important?

I received no answers. Only this.

> i just got your e-mail. can i call you? now? or today? or this
> weekend? give me a good time. i have a proposition for you.
>
> *dad*

Through e-mails, we set a time to talk, and I asked Kurt to take the
girls out, so I could have some privacy. I dreaded the moment it would
be time to call New York. Whenever I confronted my father, I started
out full of resolve and lost my nerve when I heard his voice. The call
began as all of them did: "Hi Jessie," my father said. His "proposition"
was for us to meet in New York, to talk "privately."

"Dad, I don't want to talk privately with you about this anymore. I
want someone else to be there. A shrink, a priest, anyone. I don't want
anymore secrets. We have talked privately. And you still wrote this
book the way you did."

"Just think about it, Jessie," he said calmly. "Think about it and
call me back."

Over the next few days, I looked into my heart and saw what was
there—and what was missing. What I really wanted from my father
was for him to understand me. To say he regretted what he had done
and that he should have come clean about it years ago. To acknowledge that he needed to do this, not only for me but in order to live with
himself. He did not, then or ever, really search for what it was in him
that allowed him to do such a thing.

I was a parent now. I knew the responsibility I had to my children.
I had sat up evenings regretting when I had lost my temper with them.

Worrying that something I said or did might have hurt them. Thinking that maybe it would be something they would never forget. Did my father ever feel that way, this man who seemed so insightful about so many things?

I e-mailed him the next day.

Dad,

I have thought long and hard about our talk the other day. I feel that meeting and talking is just more of what we have already done and honestly I can't see that those discussions made much of an impression on you. I don't want any more secrets. For me "closure" will only be gotten by getting this out in the open once and for all.

Jessica

I thought forever about that last line: *Out in the open? Once and for all? Was I really going through with it?*

I still wasn't sure what I planned to do.

Rudy had made some discreet inquiries into who would be the right person to see my letter. A friend had offered to put us in touch with David Shipley, the editor of the Op-Ed page at the *New York Times*. I had been planning a trip to New York with the girls and my mom in mid-June. If we decided to send the story to the *Times*, I would be available to see them when I was in the city. But I still hesitated to give Rudy the okay to contact Shipley.

Rudy advised me to talk to a lawyer friend of his in Washington. The lawyer was sympathetic but clear. "This could get out of hand very quickly if you go public," he warned. "Be prepared to hear things about yourself you might not like, to have every part of your life put under a microscope if you do this."

And another friend said: "If you do go public, Jessica, remember that Julia and Charlotte will some day read about it on the Internet. They will know everything. Do you really want that?"

I barely paused. "What happened to me happened. At some point I will have to tell them anyway. I would rather my children have an image of their mother as someone who spoke out. Not one who stayed silent. I would rather have to explain to them why I *did* do something than have to explain to them why I did not."

"Then Jess, you should send your story to the *Times*. Send it."

I put down the phone. *Would I ever respect myself again if I didn't?* The question had become rhetorical.

It was only a few days before we were set to leave for New York. But like Macbeth, I was "Letting 'I dare not' wait upon 'I would.'"

I needed a run. A long one. Miles and miles. And when I got back . . . when I got back, I was going to talk to Rudy and tell him to get the piece to David Shipley. Or I was going to delete every word and drop the subject forever.

I had ten miles to decide.

I got up early the next morning, around sunrise, and outside it felt cool and fresh. The best time to run, before the traffic takes over. On the street it was only me and a guy heaving copies of the *Los Angeles Times* through his car window, narrowly missing knocking me out at each reader's house.

I'm not a good runner. I plod. I don't bounce or glide, and there's absolutely no spring to my step. I run because I have to, because motion calms me like rocking soothes a colicky baby. And that morning, the pounding of my feet took on the rhythm of my thoughts.

Okay, why am I ready to give up on him forever? I picked up speed. Why? Why? I felt angry at myself for even asking. *Because I have given him chance after chance, that's why. I've told him how I feel.* I crossed a street and jumped back onto the sidewalk. *But he thinks so little of what he did, so little of me.* I ran faster, but I couldn't escape it. My dad simply never respected me. Not when I was almost seven, and never, ever after. I slowed a bit, as though deflated at the realization. That really had been it for him, I suspected. That night in my bed. In his mind, he had conquered me. And after that, I had never mattered, never *really* mattered.

For a moment, I felt like stopping, like giving up and giving in. And then I thought of his book, those reviews, and ran faster. *He learned nothing from Joe. Nothing! If he had, he would have been brave enough to face his actions.* I was panting. *It's not that I would have never forgiven him. I would have if he had just asked me to, if he had just admitted what he had done, that it was wrong. That it wasn't my fault.*

I pounded the pavement harder, with each word of each thought. *If . . . he . . . just . . . stopped . . . insisting . . . that . . . it . . . didn't . . . matter.*

The sweat poured down my face now, and even though the air felt cool, it couldn't chill my anger. *I asked for help. But he just . . . what's the word . . . he just belittled me, told me worse things had happened, told me to get over it.* There had never been a point of arguing with my father. It had always made me feel stupid. Worse than stupid, really. Idiotic. He had turned dismissiveness and hypocrisy into art forms. What he had done to me wasn't a big deal. But God forbid I tell a soul about it.

Maybe this was my only option? Somehow, that made me feel better. *Maybe telling the story publicly would shock him into seeing what years with Father Joe hadn't. Maybe, finally, he'd see the impact that his sins had had on others.*

But it was more than that, I knew. I had to stop seeing whatever I did in terms of my father. This wasn't about helping him. Who was I kidding?

My feet felt jammed into my running shoes. God, I hurt all over. I hadn't been sleeping. I always felt distracted, worried. But I had only gone a few miles, and I meant to finish this run.

I stopped to cross Olympic Boulevard. The previous Sunday, a cop had yelled at me for crossing on the red light. And when I thought about it now, I remembered back to when I was six, when the police pulled my father over, and Daddy turned to us and said, "They always take the children to jail first, you know, girls."

I crossed anyway and wondered, *What are people going to say if I do this? That I'm vicious? Envious? Petty? Self-involved?* A new word came with each step. *Will they think that I'm lying? Would* anyone *think that?*

The streets along my route had begun to come to life. Angelinos wandered from their houses in robes, picking up newspapers and letting their dogs out. I slowed a bit.

If I stay quiet this time, it will do me in. I'm sure of it. I'll end up doing what I've always done and turn the anger toward myself. And I'll hate myself even more than I already do. It's not just a book. It's a history of our family. And if I don't speak out, it will go down as the truth.

He thought I would never dare say anything. That I would accept the book because I have no voice of my own. Maybe we were past the apologies and the soul-searching. Maybe there was really nothing my father could say or do any more. Hadn't his book said it all? Hadn't his book told the world that he was the proud father of a saved soul?

By the time I reached mile ten, I had made my decision.

8.

PHEBE'S

BY SIXTEEN, I STARTED LOOKING FORWARD TO THE times Dad was away and the loft grew quiet. My mother, Kathy, and I were able to coexist without much friction. When he was away, I felt less compelled to sneak out. But food, for Kathy and for me, remained an issue.

Kathy had grown thinner and thinner. Her beautiful face was drawn and sunken; her eyes seemed hollow. Her skin looked as though it were turning yellow, as if she were jaundiced.

A doctor that she and my mother visited urged her to eat more. She tried. I watched her stirring chocolate mousse and butter cookies, sifting flour and whipping egg whites with her rail-thin arms—and not even licking the spoon. Knowing she was cooking made me anxious. How was I ever going to resist stuffing mousse into myself? What made me ever more anxious was what happened when she was finished. Eerily, Kathy loomed over anyone willing to try her concoctions, as if watching them eating was enough to sustain her. Every time I opened the refrigerator, I'd feel her eyes on me too. I was still bingeing and purging, and my sister made me edgy. And I made her nervous too, I could tell. We were both food watchers, interested in what everyone else was eating. I just had a harder time resisting than Kathy did. And just as she had once envied me for being my father's favorite, I now envied her for being so thin. I weighed a good forty pounds more.

But I was doing my best to catch her. I never ate meals, usually because I had either just pigged out, felt like starving myself that day, or had just thrown up after pigging out. The sibling rivalry flared whenever food was around. "Jessie, why aren't you eating?" was followed by: "Well, Kathy why aren't *you* eating?" We always had been competitive. To eat or not to eat was simply a new way of expressing ourselves. And she was winning. My dad took an interest in her unlike ever before. And even though I didn't particularly want to be the favorite anymore, I was still aware that she had taken my place. Thunder Thighs had finally been noticed.

Food aside, Kathy and I were getting along better, I suppose. I often invited her out with Iana (who had been her friend before mine), Krisztina, and me. Punk music had grown old faster than we were, and now, the really hip music was reggae, ska, and rap, which was making its way downtown from the Bronx. We hardly ever went to CBGB anymore but snuck out to the Reggae Lounge or clubs where the Sugar Hill Gang and other obscure rap artists played. Reggae and ska seemed dangerous politically and impossible not to dance to. The only bad thing about hanging out in reggae clubs was that I hated smoking pot. I turned down spliff after spliff from generous Rastafarians with heavy Jamaican accents. Their dreads bounced in piles high atop of their heads as they danced. I thought they were the coolest guys I'd ever seen—cooler even than the British punkers. And they were happy to have us there to flirt and dance with. Most were as laid back as their look. But some were a bit more aggressive. One night, a tall, long-limbed Rasta with a red, green, and gold hat and a lion of Judah on his shirt danced up to me. He grabbed my hand, took me in his arms and declared in a thick West Indian accent: "I and I am prince. I and I man, you woman. I and I have right!" I got the gist of what he said and tried not to be completely freaked. Krisztina finally rescued me, pulling me from the prince's strong grip. The wives and girl-friends of the Rastas wanted us to get our little white-girl asses out of their clubs, something they never hesitated to tell us.

Whenever Kathy agreed to join us, I was genuinely thrilled. There was no food involved, and it gave me a sense of companionship with her that I rarely felt. I adored showing her around a scene that seemed so "me." I wanted to share that with her, to be close to my sister, but it was hard for us to be intimate. So much remained unsaid. Part of me wanted to reach out to Kathy, to hug her, to hold her hand, to confide in her. But I just couldn't. I still felt as I had since we were kids: I wasn't sure my sister liked me. I suppose she had little reason to, really, especially when we were teenagers. I came off as self-important, igno-rant, and pretentious. I fancied myself a political activist because of the music I liked and the way that I dressed, invariably in black. I said I hated Reagan when, in fact, I was too apathetic to read the newspa-per or know anything about politics. In fact, I was barely making the grade at a private school where Kathy would have flourished; she slaved away at Stuyvesant. And then there was the fact that I had boyfriends. Kathy chose horses instead. After I shed my virginity, I had started dating aggressively. After all, I reasoned, I was sixteen and pretty much grown up. And what did I have to lose? Not my virginity. Not my innocence. So what the heck? Kathy must have known—not through some sibling telepathy as much as by her ears. We had had some renovations done in the loft; but sound still traveled.

In the new and improved loft, the kitchen now looked like a real kitchen, and full walls offered us some privacy. The architect we hired was imaginative but ended up doing more cocaine with my dad than carpentry. Kathy and I now had small but fully enclosed rooms in the back. Mine, serendipitously enough, was situated so that the fire escape door now opened directly into my room. How could I resist using it now that had my own private entrance and exit?

But like everything in my life at that time, I took it one step too far. At the time, I was dating a Haitian guy, Neville—a tall boy with sharp cheekbones, brown eyes, aristocratic features, and smooth, ebony skin. Dating is a euphemism for what we *really* were doing, which was hanging out in clubs and trying to find places to have sex. Neville was a little older than me, maybe eighteen, and it was not as if we or any of our friends lived alone. Once or twice we ended up on my roof—inspired by Krisztina's example—but it hardly felt cozy. Finally I decided to sneak Neville into my room. He was game.

It must have been around two in the morning when we made it down the fire escape and into my bedroom. My bed was small and narrow, and Neville was broad shouldered and stood about six-foot-three. Not that it really mattered. It was a bed, and we were teenagers. Compared to the roof, it felt like a luxury suite at the Four Seasons. We thought we were being quiet. Then I heard the footsteps. *Dad! He must have just come home.*

"Neville!" I whispered. "Oh God, it's my father!"

"Fucking hell!" Completely naked, Neville dove off the bed and looked frantically for a place to hide.

"Get in the closet!" I whispered. The footfalls sounded closer.

Neville ducked into the closet and crouched behind an old coat. I slid the door shut and threw myself back into bed, pulling the covers over me just as my father turned the door knob.

"What's going on, Jessie?" He peered into the room. "I heard something in here."

I pretended I had just woken up, no doubt overdoing the yawning and blinking. But I was thinking fast.

"Oh," I said and yawned again. "I just shut the window. It was getting cold." I think I might even have pulled the blankets up a bit more. Maybe I even shivered.

"Don't leave the window open at night. . . . that's just fucking crazy," he said. "Anyone could climb right up the fire escape and get in."

Dad leaned over to the window to make sure it was shut. Then he noticed the fire escape door.

"Are you out of your mind, leaving this door unlocked? What's wrong with you? Are you trying to get us robbed? Jesus."

Now I had to perk up. "I'm sorry, Daddy. Krisztina and I were out there this afternoon. We must have forgotten to shut it."

"Well, don't be so fucking irresponsible." Dad bolted the door. "Good night."

As soon as I heard him shut the door of my parents' bedroom, I went to the closet.

"It's okay," I whispered. "He's gone. You can come out now."

Neville looked as though he *had* broken in. He started searching for his clothes among the twisted sheets, as if he expected my father to storm back into the room at any moment. I tried to keep my voice down. "Why are you getting dressed? I mean he's gone! He's not going to come back. Look, I'll lock the door if it really makes you nervous." I moved toward the door.

"I'm going home."

"Why? He's gone!"

"Jessie, you are a blonde, white girl, and I'm black. If your father finds me in here, no one will blame him for shooting me. And if he doesn't kill me himself, he'll take me down to the precinct, and the cops will do it for him."

"Neville, this isn't the South. This is New York! What are you talking about!"

"It's all the same," he said, still searching for his shirt. "When a white man finds a naked black kid in his house, it's all the same."

I sat on the bed, sulking, and watched him get dressed. I didn't want him to be right, but I knew that he was. However much reggae or hip-hop I listened to, however many black kids I hung out with, I would never come close to understanding what it was to be black—not even if I had taken HR up on his offer and moved to Ethiopia. I didn't think my father would touch Neville, but he might have been pissed enough to take him to the local precinct. What we were doing might technically have been statutory rape. But I also thought how ironic it would be for Dad to turn in Neville when my father had done so much worse. I got up, unlocked the door, and watched Neville creep back out the fire escape. I thought I might never hear from him again. I was right.

After that, I didn't bring anyone else down the fire escape. But one night I woke up to soft knocking on the back door. I had made the mistake of telling a boy who had a crush on me about my system. Somehow he had managed to make his way into the building and down the fire escape to our place. I freaked out when I saw his pale face through the window and refused to open the door. I did, however, crack the window to tell him that I had no plans to let him in. He was way too intense, even for me. A poet of the Patti Smith school, he stuffed scribbled offerings in our mail slot. Kathy must have heard some of these whispered meetings, but she never said anything. The only person who knew all the details was Krisztina. I always told her everything.

My parents might have been oblivious to my life, but I wasn't to theirs, and I had some sense of the tight finances at home. I hated asking them for cash, so I worked odd jobs to make a buck. Sometimes it was babysitting (for those families that didn't think my appearance would forever traumatize their children) or putting up street posters for a friend who worked at a club. But I wanted something more substantial and landed my first steady after-school-and-weekend gig at a clothing store around the corner. The store sold "vintage" clothing, some of which truly *were* vintage and the rest of which were the sort of crappy stuff Mrs. Kruger sold back in New Jersey. After working there a week, I learned how the racket worked.

The owners bought most of the clothes from warehouses in Queens for a dollar a pound, then sold them at an incredible profit. I came on as sales girl, something for which I neither had the experience nor the aptitude. Supposedly, my job was to wander the floor, engaging the customers and sealing the deal. "That'd look great on you," I might say. Or, "Wow, I can't believe that's so cheap!" Instead, I'd hide in the racks straightening beaded sweaters and bowling shirts until some desperate shopper searched me out. Luckily we got paid by the hour and not on commission. I started on the main floor, but after a few weeks, the manager began to notice that I hardly ever sold anything. I was sure I was going to be fired. Instead she took pity on me. I was sent downstairs to the bargain basement, a place that was perfect for me because there were plenty of places to hide. Then the manager suggested that I might want to train as cashier. That sounded good until I realized I had to be able to count, add, and subtract—fast. My dyslexia got in the way, and I grew flushed and sweaty each time I had to make change. My line was always the longest and slowest. But they kept me on because, for the first time in my life, I was considered reliable.

My mother also had taken a job. She had done some book editing and began helping an eminent gynecologist with a book on child-birth. Neils Lauersen (Dr. L) was Danish, a hulk with shoulder-length blond hair, piercing blue eyes, a booming voice, and an even louder laugh. He was, by all appearances, a Viking in scrubs. My mom made her office in the kitchen of the loft, poring over theories on successful conception and ways to ease birthing pains. My father was predictably condescending. He never complained about the extra cash, but he did have a fit when he first saw Dr. L and his golden curls. When Mom went to meet Dr. L at his office, Dad made suggestive remarks about her "working late." One night, Dad actually beat her home. I had stayed in for the evening, taking refuge in P. G. Wodehouse and a summer day in the English countryside, where the worst that ever happens is Bertie Wooster mislaying his spats. Kathy was studying in her room, as usual, and when Dad came up in the elevator, I could tell he was drunk.

"You're actually here for once," he said by way of a greeting. "And where's Ma?"

"I don't know." I didn't really want to talk to him. "Still working with Neils I guess."

"I doubt she's doing any 'work' with that puffy, pompous prick."

I shrunk behind my paperback, and Dad must have realized I wasn't going to take the bait. He dropped the subject and trudged off to the front room. I tried to get back to Bertie and Jeeves but was too distracted. *Was Daddy jealous? But how could he be jealous of some-one he doesn't really love?* I was certain that he couldn't be in love with my mother. Not anymore. Not the way he treated her. I didn't think Mom was having an affair, but even if she were, how could he blame her? I almost hoped she *was* sleeping with Dr. L. Imagining my mother doing something like that cast her in a totally different light. It made her alive in a way she never had seemed to be.

In fact, my mom wasn't sleeping with the doctor. But something else even more surprising had happened. Mom was pregnant.

If my mother had managed to produce a son, my parents' marriage might have lasted. Dad always had a Henry VIII-type obsession with having a boy, presumably to carry on the sacred Hendra name. I knew he was deeply disappointed when I turned out to be a girl. But my mother wasn't destined to give birth to a boy. Her pregnancy, which might have been an accident or a plan to try to save their failing marriage, ended in a life-threatening miscarriage. She was forty by this time and had an ectopic pregnancy, and she was hospitalized and treated by the glorious Dr. L. My father called her room. He said he was sorry for what had happened, but it was simply too much for him to have to visit. She understood, didn't she? After all, she knew he hated hospitals. Instead, he went to a bar.

In the months that followed, my father embarked on a new venture, a satire of the *Wall Street Journal* that followed the formula of his successful 1978 project *Not the New York Times*. He had been around even less than usual and was back to disappearing overnight or for a day or two at a time. Then one night, he appeared at my bed. It was 12:28 A.M. At least that's the time my clock showed when I heard him. The smell of his favorite cigars mixed with a bottle or two of red wine wafted over me. Mom had long since gone to sleep. Her mood had neither gotten worse nor better since the miscarriage. She just continued to maintain the same façade that she'd built before I was born—emotionless, contained, the antithesis of Dad.

"Jessie," he said in a voice a bit louder than a whisper. "Get up. I need to have a chat."

"A chat?" Part of me was relieved. He hadn't touched me in years, but I could never be sure what he was thinking. *A chat? What was this about?* "Daddy, it's the middle of the night. I have to go to school in the morning."

"Oh screw that bunch of fascists. Come across the street to Phebe's. Have a drink with your old dad."

It was pointless to argue. It was *always* pointless to argue with my father. He had an amazing ability to make even the most bizarre proposition sound completely normal, to turn things around so that it seemed like *you* were the one with problem. Phebe's was the local hang out on the corner of Fourth and the Bowery, and it was open late. I pulled on the jeans that were lying by my bed and smoothed out the bright red T-shirt I'd worn to sleep. Then I followed my father through the silent heat of the loft to the stairwell door. My mother didn't stir.

Dad and I went down the five flights of dusty stairs and out the front door. The streets were still humming. Club O, the S and M place downstairs, remained open, and we could still hear the ear-piercing shrieks as we passed. Kathy and I missed the primal screamers who used to use the space. They were a timid-looking crowd compared to the S-and-Mers, who wore head-to-toe black leather outfits and toted bags that were no doubt filled with whips and other sex toys.

Dad and I walked briskly toward Phebe's, my father deftly whistling Mozart's "Jupiter Symphony." He took my hand as we crossed the Bowery and smiled as he opened the bar's door for me.

Phebe's had that sleazy dive smell—like someone had poured beer over the entire place and left it to rot. Cigarette smoke hung in the air, and large, thick men hunched over drinks at the bar. At least it was air conditioned. My father grabbed a place to sit, and as we waited for a waitress, I picked nervously at the vinyl-covered cushion. Someone had passed a weary night—perhaps waiting for a lover or a drug dealer—by burning cigarette holes all over the seat. Little patches of white foam poked through the black vinyl. I poked the foam back in as I waited to see what it was exactly that my father wanted to "chat" about. A tough-looking waitress in a Phebe's shirt finally came by.

"Hey Tony," she said. "What you drinkin'?"

My father smiled. "Two gin and tonics."

The waitress never hesitated. I'm not even sure she glanced at me. She just headed off to get our drinks. Dad looked across the table at me as he reached into his pocket and pulled out a thin cigar. He lit it and puffed, as if savoring my suspense.

"Well, Jessie," he began, slowly. "This isn't so bad, eh? It's not so bad to be out here having a drink?" *Compared to what?* I thought.

"No, Dad, it's nice," I said, not really meaning it. I would much rather have stayed in bed, though the air-conditioned rot at Phebe's wasn't all that bad.

"You want a puff?" He held out his cigar.

"No, thanks," I said, avoiding his gaze and still poking at my seat.

"You want a cigarette, don't you. Disgusting things. Fucking kill you, those will."

"Yeah."

"Well, treasure," he said, "I wanted you to be the first to know."

I looked up. "What, Daddy?"

The waitress came and plunked the drinks down on the table.

"Enjoy, Tony," she said as if I wasn't there.

My father picked up his gin and tonic and tossed out the tiny straw.

"Why do Americans put straws in everything?"

"I don't know, Daddy." Now I was nervous.

"Fucking everything. Straws in fucking everything."

Tell me, Dad! I felt like screaming.

"Anyway, treasure, I wanted to tell you first."

What? Tell me. Just tell me already.

He took a swig of his drink.

"I've met someone, a really lovely woman, and I am going to live with her." There. . . . there it was. I couldn't believe it: "I think everyone will be much happier if I move out of the loft." I barely heard the last part.

"What about Ma?"

"Jessie, listen, your mother and I have not been happy together for years."

Your mother! So she had already stopped being his wife, already stopped being Judy. Now she was *Your Mother*—my responsibility.

"We were never happy. A big mistake, the whole thing." He could've been talking about a bad first date, he seemed so casual. "We never should have gotten married in the first place."

No wonder he never went to see her in the hospital. He really had stopped caring for her. I sat there silently, head bowed, picking at the vinyl, harder, faster.

"Well?" I looked up. Part of me felt like crying, but I didn't. "Come on, Jessie. I wanted to tell you because I want you to understand why

I'm doing this. I thought a long time about this. About telling you. And now you're just going to pull this silent teenage bullshit?"

My father took a deep pull on his cigar and turned away.

"I just . . . it's just that I don't know what to say." I poked at the cushion some more. "I guess I'm just surprised. I mean . . . . I guess I'm just surprised."

"Well I was hoping you'd be *happy* for me. I thought if anyone could understand why I'm doing this, it would be you. I can't talk to your sister. No one can. She's too busy becoming a Republican."

He wants me to give this my endorsement? That's what he wants. He wants to not feel guilty.

"Dad, I'm just surprised. I mean. . . ." *I need to get out of here, to get away from him, from this conversation.* "Maybe you're right, but I don't know . . . maybe it is better this way but. . . ."

"Absolutely it is." As always, he seized on the part of the conversation that suited his agenda. "And believe me, it's better for your mother too."

He drank again and drew on his cigar. I looked around the room.

"I want you to meet my friend, Jessie."

His friend? I dropped my head and winced.

"I really want you to meet her," he went on, oblivious. "She knows how special you are to me, and she wants to meet you too." *Special?* "Maybe Saturday night. You could meet her then. There's a party Saturday night. Meet her then."

Not a question. More like a command. I sat there silently, sensing his eyes as I stared down at the carved-up table in front of me. I felt my seat for the cigarette holes and poked at them. "Jessica," he said finally, "*say* something."

I thought of what this woman might look like. Dark? Blonde? Tall? Short? Then I imagined talking to her: "Nice to meet you." *Would I say that? Would I really say that? Or maybe I'd say,* "I understand from my father that you guys are lovers." *Then I'd have to come home to my mother. How could I face her?* I saw her as she had been only hours ago, reading on the brown sectional, unaware of what was about to happen. All the nineteenth-century novels in the world could not protect her from the reality that was about to hit.

"Daddy, I can't," I said finally. "I have some stuff planned for this weekend." It was the best I could come up with. I should've known better than to try to fool Tony Hendra.

"Don't tell me you have some fucking band you have to see." He launched into me without a moment's hesitation. "Some bunch of out-of-work morons."

"No, but I promised some friends . . ." I kept on.

"Jesus Christ, Jessie. This is a little more important than spending the night smoking cigarettes with a bunch of screaming idiots."

I looked down at my father's hand as it lay on the table. He was drumming his fingers on the fake wood. I remembered how much I had loved my father's hands. How much I had admired the way his fingers tapped and rolled. When I was little, his hands had seemed so big, with long fingers, bulky knuckles, and round finger nails that caught tiny pieces of dirt beneath them if my father had been out digging in the garden. If he had been writing in his office all day, his fingers smelled of cigars.

As I watched my father drum on the grimy table of Phebe's, I did what I had always done with Daddy. I gave in. "Okay, Daddy. Okay," I said quietly. "I'll come Saturday night."

"Good, great. It's all set then. Great."

He reached over the table and took my hand in his. I held it weakly, uncertainly.

"Come sit over here, love. Come sit next to your old dad."

Slowly I moved around the table and sat down next to him.

"I have some coke," he told me. "Do you want some?" My father reached into his pocket and pulled out a tiny tinfoil square. "Go on. Go into the bathroom and have a little snort. It'll do you good."

"No thanks, Dad."

"Just a little snort won't do you any harm." He looked me in the eyes. "Just stay away from heroin. Don't *ever* do heroin. And listen, if you want drugs, get them from me. It's not the drugs that kill you; it's what they mix them with. I know where to get pure stuff. Keep this. You might want it some time." He put the coke in my hand. It was my father's version of Nancy Reagan's "Just Say No" speech.

"Okay, Dad." I stuffed the tinfoil in my pocket, and we sat there silently for a moment, me defeated and confused, him puffing his cigar, sipping his drink, and thinking no doubt of his new life ahead. Then he turned to me. "I love you, Jessie. Trust me. Things are going to work out just fine." I didn't answer, but I wondered: *For whom?*

When we got back to the loft, I said goodnight to my father and crept up to my bed. I sobbed into my pillow until I fell asleep. Women's faces filled my dreams. The next morning I avoided my mother and left to get on the subway to school before my father was awake. I never made it to school that day. In fact, I never left the subway until well past three. I rode it from Astor Place to the Bronx and back again, lurching and swaying as the subway hurled itself up and down Manhattan. When I finally got off the No. 6 train around 3:30 P.M., I left the untouched tinfoil packet of coke on a seat.

I still didn't want to go home. I couldn't face my mother, knowing what I knew. The thought made me want to scream. So I found a pay phone and tried calling Krisztina. No answer. Then Jessica. Her mother told me she was over at our friend Marla's house and gave me the number. I asked Marla if I could come over. I didn't need to say more than "I don't want to go home right now." All of us understood not wanting to see our parents.

Marla and her mother lived in the meat-packing district on Fourteenth Street and Ninth Avenue. In open doorways on the way there, I could see cow carcasses hanging on hooks. The entire neighborhood smelled of steer blood or at least it seemed that way, considering that pools of it rested in the gutters.

When I walked up to Marla's loft, her mom was out, and she and Jessica were rolling a long Jamaican-style hash spliff. It was a delicate process that I found therapeutic, the sort of distraction that seemed better than any high. Besides, I only pretended to smoke it. I didn't want to appear uncool in front of two girls who I admired so much. I had been at Marla's an hour or two, chatting, rolling spliffs, and listening to Prince Buster when the phone rang. It was my father. How he tracked me down I don't know, considering no one was ever able to find him.

"Why aren't you home, Jessie? I told you, you were *not* to go out tonight."

"I'm sorry. I forgot." I didn't feel like telling him the truth.

"You need to come home. This is unacceptable. You cannot abuse all of us like this. You are so incredibly self-involved that you never think about how you are abandoning our family!" This from the man who told me the night before he was leaving my mother for another woman?

For a moment I considered shouting that I would *not* be coming home, then or ever! That even if he stood outside Marla's door, I would tell my friends to bolt it. Or I'd hide in Marla's loft bed and stay there until I was ready to go, which would be never! He would have to tear me kicking and screaming from my safe haven of the blood-filled meat-packing district. But as usual, I said nothing of the sort.

"Okay, fine," I said coldly. "I'll be home in a minute."

I told my friends I had to go, and Jessica and Marla made sympathetic noises about how shitty parents could be. All the way home I wondered how I would face my mother. *Had he told her? And if he hadn't, what could I say to her?* I was angry that I had been summoned home, and as I walked back to the loft, I resolved that this time, I would have it out with him. This time, I would tell my hypocritical father just what I thought. I stormed up the stairs of Twenty-five East Fourth Street full of fire.

9.

MOM

WHEN I BOUNDED INTO THE LOFT, I LEARNED FROM my mother—whose eyes I could not meet—that Daddy had gone out. As always, he'd be "home soon." It shouldn't have surprised me. He'd often summoned me home, only to disappear himself. From what I could tell, he hadn't told her about the other woman. It would be another of our secrets.

By the next day, I had lost my nerve to confront him. Instead, I gave in to my dad's repeated requests that I come to the party for his latest newspaper parody, *Not the Wall Street Journal*. That's where I would meet his "friend." It was a typical literary event at someone's uptown home: a lot of wine, champagne, cheese, and probably coke if I had been looking for it. When I got there, my dad greeted me with a startled look, as if it were dawning on him that having his daughter and his girlfriend at the same place at the same time was not such a great idea. Left to himself, he never would have introduced us, and I would have gone home unsure which of the many women in the room she was. I must have been there for a half hour making small talk with some acquaintances when I noticed my dad in a corner with a pretty woman who looked about twenty-five. She was clearly bawling him out. Finally she turned around and walked toward me.

"I'm Carla," she said without a smile. "I was waiting for your dad to introduce us, but he's being an asshole, so I'm going to do it myself."

Her directness caught me by surprise. I didn't want to like this person whose very existence was going to inflict such damage on my mother. But I appreciated her "don't-fuck-with-me" attitude. Maybe this was the kind of woman my father needed, someone who wouldn't take the shit that had buried us long ago. I didn't know what to say. "Hi, I'm Jessie," was all I could manage. I left the party a few minutes later.

I spent the next few weeks avoiding everyone. Kathy was graduating high school and busy applying for student loans. She'd need them. She had gotten into Barnard College. Daddy was gone almost every night, so he was easy to dodge. With Ma, I just stayed silent. I even managed to graduate the eleventh grade. But of course, I couldn't stop thinking about Carla and the moment when my dad would finally come clean. *How could he have put me in this situation?* I must have asked myself that every morning I woke up, every time I walked past Mom. One night Carla even called the loft looking for him. I heard my mother talking to her as if she were just another acquaintance.

I suppose there is no good time or place to tell your wife of twenty years that you are leaving her for someone almost half her age. But of all the possible situations, my father chose a "family" weekend in the country, a choice that seemed to me to be particularly sadistic. It would have been easier on my mom to tell her in the city and then let her make a fast exit out of the loft. As it was, Dad made a big deal about us all going to New Jersey to "celebrate" the Fourth of July weekend, and he invited some friends too. I wonder what my mother would have cooked for lunch if she had known what all those friends already knew—that she was about to get dumped.

My dad told her after the baseball game on the lawn was over and the guests had started driving back to New York. Amid the empty wine bottles and French bread crusts that littered the lawn, he took my mom off for a "talk" down at the bottom of the garden. I went to hide in the barn and played with the woodchips from the winter logs that had been stored there, making them into piles and circles. I couldn't witness what was happening outside.

When I finally emerged, my mother was lying on the grass, sobbing and pulling huge clumps of weeds and earth from the ground. My father had begun packing up the house in preparation for the two-hour car ride back to the city. We would have to endure it together. What better way to make sure we were all involved in this mess than to pack us into a car. My mom sobbed in the front seat, and Kathy and I clutched each other's hands in the back. Dad drove, stoic, silent, but I imagined him whistling Mozart's "Jupiter Symphony," just as he had the night that he'd told me.

After the longest car ride of our lives, my father pulled up to the door of Twenty-five East Fourth Street. Kathy and I helped our mom out of the front seat. Dad sped away to return the rental car to Hertz, then presumably on to his new life on the Upper West Side with Carla.

I fell into bed that night knowing my mother was pacing. The next morning Kathy and I awoke to her tears. Being the kind of woman my mother was, she did not take to her bed in a dramatic collapse. As Churchill might've said, she just buggered on, got dressed, and cried into the coffee she let cool in her cup. Then she cried as she swept up the grounds that had fallen on the floor. Then she cried as she and I walked to the grocery store on Bleecker Street. Then she broke down in the yogurt section as she tried to decide between Dannon and Yoplait. I ushered her out of the store and onto the street. Her despair built a wall around us that even the panhandlers refused to scale. I worried about Ma standing too close to the windows in the loft. Would she jump when I turned away? I worried if she walked too close to the curb. Would she throw herself under a bus when I let her out of my sight? It seemed as if the tears she had repressed for twenty years were flowing freely, that the dam had finally ruptured and the torrent would not stop. I looked at her red nose, her swollen eyes, her gray skin and felt overwhelmed by my inability to help her—to say one word that would assuage her grief. More than that, I had become painfully aware that I did not know this woman. I had come from her body. I had called her Mom for seventeen years. But I did not know her at all. My father, even in his absences, had taken up all the space in the house, and there had been no room for us to get to know each other or even to talk. I went to work at the clothing store (where I had increased my hours for the summer), leaving Ma scrubbing the counters with more tears on her sponge than water.

Of course, I was in no shape to be of much help to her—neurotic as I was, anxious, bulimic, emotionally immature. I even had a dream that my mother and I were alone in an empty room. Before my eyes she got smaller and smaller until she was a tiny, crying baby. I picked her up and wrapped her in a blanket; she slid under the folds and shrunk so much that she disappeared entirely.

Adding to my worries, I felt guilty. Unlike Ma, I was relieved that Dad had finally left. When I saw or spoke with him in the weeks immediately after, I had little to say. Then, again one night, Carla called the loft looking for him. Luckily I picked up the phone. I wonder if Carla would have hung up had my mother answered. "Do you know where your dad is?" she asked. "No, sorry," I said cordially. My father's whereabouts were Carla's problem now.

I knew if Mom could just get through her mourning—if she could just set aside her pride—she would see how much better off she was without this man who had so dominated her life—*all* of our lives—day after day after day. By the end of summer, Kathy had fled for a new life at Barnard College. Left alone in the loft with my mother, I suggested we escape too.

"What would you say to getting out of the city this week?" I asked her.

She studied the Tetley tea bag she was dunking. "I am not going out to the country, not the way things are."

"No, not to New Jersey. I was thinking Cape Cod."

"Cape Cod?" She looked up as if I had suggested a trip to Pluto.

"Why not? I found out about the fares—it's cheap. We can fly to Boston."

"You're going to fly?" She knew I was terrified of flying.

"Yes," I said with certainty. "We're going to fly to Boston, take another plane to Provincetown, and stay there for a few days to get out of this crappy city."

My mother made the typical excuses. She didn't have enough time. She didn't have a bathing suit. We couldn't afford it. But I could see the idea appealed to her, and I think she understood how important it was to me. After all, I was offering to *fly* there, and she knew how much I hated flying. Besides, the whole jaunt had an air of bravado to it, as if it defied the fact that she had been abandoned. We began getting cautiously excited about going. I showed her the brochure that I had requested from the Cape Cod Chamber of Commerce, and we perused possible bed and breakfasts, pictures of the beach and shop signs spelled ye olde English way—with double p's and an e on the end.

We left on Labor Day morning, and I felt more lighthearted than I had in months. My mom looked young, almost vibrant again, and we headed to the gate at the airport hand in hand, as if we were two college students on an adventure. I fell apart on the plane to Boston, nearly taking my mother's arm off I was squeezing it so hard during takeoff. When the flight attendant asked me what I wanted to drink, I felt like screaming, "I am thousands of feet above the ground! What the fuck do I care if I have Coke or Sprite!" But I let my mom do the ordering and ended up with tea.

Our B and B was a weather-beaten New England house with a shingled roof. My mother and I were to share a room, and I think the desk clerk assumed we were a lesbian couple on holiday until I said "Mom." The assumption would follow us all over Provincetown and became a joke between us. How odd, I thought. When I went out with my father, he would joke that I was his date. And now, I was my mother's lover.

The first day, we walked into the early morning mist coming off the Atlantic and had breakfast at a local café. There, my mother asked the owner the best way to get around. "Well you can lease a car." We shook our heads. "There are buses," she told us, "but the best way to get around P-Town is by bicycle. They're easy to rent. Just walk up the street, and someone will fix you ladies up."

My mother looked a bit pale.

"C'mon, Ma, let's give it a try."

"Jessie, I haven't ridden a bike in years."

"Let's just give it a try."

We walked up to the bike rental place. I picked a red bike; my mother chose blue. She sat on the seat looking as if she might lose the Golden Sunrise Granola she'd had for breakfast.

"Don't worry, Ma, you never forget how to ride a bike."

She frowned.

"Just get going then you'll be fine."

She looked down Main Street toward the beach, determined, pushed off the sidewalk, and put her feet on the pedals. But she hadn't gathered speed, and she tottered and swayed so much that I was positive she would come crashing down and we'd be looking up bus routes around the Cape. Ma almost came to a complete stop before something miraculous happened. Okay, maybe it wasn't miraculous, but it seemed like it then. Something must've clicked, some body memory or something, and she straightened and picked up speed. The pedals turned swiftly and smoothly, their metal catching the sunlight as my mother zipped off toward the beach. When I finally caught up, her face was flushed "This is great!" she called.

"I know! I know!" I called back.

My mother and I rode our bikes all over Provincetown. We pedaled to the beach and braved the freezing water and to the dock to catch the whale-watching boat on which I got sick and my mother had the sea legs of a pirate. We pedaled to movie houses and watched *E.T.* and *The World According to Garp* while demolishing packets of red licorice. We sped by galleries showing far too many paintings of the surf. Then we threw our bikes in the dunes and collected only the best of the best shells.

I got to know my mother in those three days in Cape Cod better than I had in the entire seventeen years I had lived with her. We had, at least for this weekend, escaped from the loft, from my father, from a life that had always been his and never been ours. And away from all that, we had become friends.

I feared two things about going home: flying and the possibility that the second she hit New York, Mom might lose her new-found bloom. I refused to get on the Cessna to Boston and had a tantrum on the tarmac before giving in. And my mother's glow did fade a bit at the sight of the loft. But it didn't entirely disappear. In fact she began to talk about looking for new editing assignments and how she would make out all right on her own. Like riding a bike, she was remembering all the things she knew how to do. She even went on a date with an artist who had worked on the renovation of our loft. Dragen was Eastern European, with dark hair and eyes reminiscent of Vlad the Impaler. He had exhibited pieces constructed from ordinary lead pencils that had to be honed by hand, with a knife, never with a sharpener, and Krisztina and I made the odd dollar sharpening No. 2 pencils to Dragen's exact specifications.

Despite the stare, he was a nice man. I took the precaution of staying over at Krizstina's house that evening, as a discreet roommate might do, and I was too shy to ask my mother if she took advantage of my absence. But when I got home in the morning, her unmade bed looked as if it had slept two. And there were the remains of a cup of black coffee on the counter. My mother took milk. Dragen didn't become a fixture in the loft, but I knew the attention had been good for my mother

As for me, while sitting on a stoop on Saint Mark's Place, I had fallen in love for the first time.

He was a tall kid, English of course, wiry with spiky hair and a tattoo of a snake up his arm. The snake might have been an attempt to make him look tough; in truth, he was a sweet boy from a genteel part of North London whose parents were in the theater—she an actress and he a prominent director. Like English boys from good areas of London whose parents had worked hard on their BBC voices, he spoke with a slight cockney twang that was more affect than heritage.

And he was perfect for me. He loved the same music I did. He hung in the same scene but wasn't remotely self-destructive. In fact, he was kind. Absurdly enough, he was also named Jesse, just absent the "i." Jesse and I were known as Jess 1 and Jess 2 or "Jess(i)e squared" when we were together. After maybe two dates, Jesse and I became inseparable. It wasn't hard, either. Mom, unlike my dad, had no issues at all with a boy at our house day and night. Often we went to Jesse's brownstone in Park Slope. There, we were alone much of the time; his parents were commuting to London. Sometimes, we saw his older brother, Joe. But he was almost too cool for me. When I first met him, he was dating Madonna.

Now that my father had vacated the loft, Jesse became part of our household. As if to make a point of it, I locked the fire escape door once and for all. It wasn't much of a sacrifice. I never needed to sneak out anymore, anyway. I just told Mom where I was going and that was that. Still, things were hardly perfect. I kept secrets from Jesse, even though I loved him, and he never knew about my bulimia, which I took great pains to hide. It wasn't until a year or two into our relationship that I told him what my father had done. It was one thing to tell my girlfriends, but telling a guy . . . that was much more difficult. My on-again, off-again shame about sex and desire were incredibly confusing to Jesse. To him, sex was nothing less than everything. He wrote me X-rated love letters that I found thrilling—and unreadable. It amazed me that everyone felt so relaxed about the one thing that made my stomach tighten—sex. Even my father, after what he had done, seemed to carry no shame. It wasn't that I didn't enjoy sex in the moment. With Jesse, I did. But the enjoyment only intensified my guilt. If I enjoyed sex, did that mean that maybe I had wanted what had happened with my father? That maybe it *had* been my fault?

One night my dad and I arranged to meet at the loft (he still had the key). We could talk, and he could pick up some of his things. My mother purposefully went out for the evening. I stayed home and waited. And waited. And waited. Finally, Jesse called from a pay phone outside a bar. Would I come meet him? I had been waiting for my dad for more than two hours. Time meant nothing to him. His schedule, whatever it was, reigned supreme. So I walked down to the Holiday on St. Mark's Place and had a drink with Jesse and two other friends, a cockney kid named "Scrapper" and another guy named Mark.

When I got back to the loft a few hours later, I gasped. We'd been robbed. The potted plants had been thrown on the floor. Dirt was everywhere. Two standing lamps were in pieces, and shards of glass stood in the living room rug. Dishes had been torn from the cupboards and papers strewn around.

Then I found the note. The person who had ransacked the place was my father, and he had left his calling card on a piece of cardboard that he'd set in the middle of the rubble:

I CANNOT BELIEVE YOU DID THIS I CAME BECAUSE
YOU SAID YOU MISSED ME AND OF COURSE I MISSED
YOU. IF YOU DON'T THINK THIS IS IMPORTANT YOU
HAVE THE FEELING OF A CHECKER CAB. THIS SHIT WAS
ONE OF THE REASONS I COULDN'T STAY HERE. YOU
STINK!

10.

CELIA'S

I SPRINTED DOWN THE STEEP WOODEN ESCALATOR OF London's Kings Cross station, certain I was going to miss the train that would take me to the North of England—to a Christmas weekend at the home of my aunt Celia. My father was coming from New York and would be there with Carla and my baby half brother.

Eight years had passed since Daddy told me that I stunk, and I had no hard evidence that he felt much different today. I can't say that I disagreed with him, either. I considered myself a failure, consumed by my problems, and angry that I gave them so much control of my life. But I couldn't see a way out.

I was living in Jesse's parents' house in Hampstead. He and I had long broken up, but I remained quite close to his mother. Jesse was in New York, and I was poor, so I had taken up the offer of a room while I finished my second year at Central School of Speech and Drama. In fact, I had another love, a Spanish painter named Pablo, whom I had met in New York but who now was back in Spain.

We had been together for almost five years, often in different countries, but we were young and full of self-important enthusiasm for our "art." Pablo and I had frequent debates over which was more important: our romance or his painting and my acting. I might have chosen marriage, but long-term commitments made Pablo nervous. Soon after I reached England, he returned to Madrid. He said he was having a crisis in his work that could only be solved by going back to Spain. Then to Paris for a while. Then to Russia. Now, he was considering a trip to Chile. Even small commitments worried him. When we ate out together, he would agonize over what to order, turning pale and stammering at the waiter's unavoidably direct question: "And what would you like sir?" That was Pablo, a smart, talented guy who had a chronic inability to make up his mind. Of course, who was I to judge?

Here I was, running for a train I half-hoped I wouldn't catch. It had been awhile since I had seen my dad—about a year—and I had hoped the time away might heal all wounds. Instead, it had made them hurt even more. I not only couldn't forget what had happened with Daddy that night in New Jersey, but as I grew older, the memories had become overwhelming. I couldn't concentrate in some of my classes—particularly voice classes, when we were told to lie on the floor and breathe. Each time I closed my eyes, I saw my room in that majestic old house, my bunk bed, and my father's silhouette. But how could I bring it up with him after all these years? And why? I had lived with my memories since I was seven. Why bring them up now, just because they were haunting me?

I made the train and convinced myself that it would be better this way. *Enduring my father would be better than listening to him rant about my failure to show up for Christmas.*

I found a seat next to a British businessman. His blandness appealed to me. I wouldn't mind some blandness in my life. Whether it was a Spanish painter or a middle-aged man in a Marks & Spencer shirt, I was always looking for someone to save me. From what? Myself, I assumed. I pulled out my copy of *Look Back in Anger*, which I was supposed to be studying for a scene we'd do in class. But the play lay in my lap as I stared out the window, wondering as I did every day if I might ever feel in control of my life, of myself. When I might start keeping the daily resolutions I had made for the last ten years. When I would finally stop bingeing and purging. I had made and broken so many resolutions that, at twenty-four, I felt exhausted.

My turmoil seemed so out of place in the serene countryside outside, the villages and soft English hills. I remembered how George Orwell described the same terrain when he was coming home from the Spanish Civil War in *Homage to Catalonia*—"all sleeping the deep, deep, sleep of England, from which I sometimes fear we shall never wake till we are jerked out of it by the roar of bombs." Now I yearned for that sleep, or something like it, if only to escape the inescapable past.

The house where Celia lived with her husband and two young boys sat on the outskirts of the town of Newark. I couldn't get over the name and how little this northern English red brick town shared with its American namesake. Newark was full of Victorian buildings surrounded by flat, misty, deep green countryside. The house itself was ancient, long and vast with a curved, red shingle roof, with parts of it from the sixteenth century and "recent" additions from the eighteenth and nineteenth. I stood outside with my aunt and uncle, hesitant to enter. Already I could hear my father's voice from the sitting room. I couldn't make out exactly what he was saying, but by the tone of his voice and the rhythm of his words, I knew he was telling a story that no doubt had engaged the small audience of relatives. At just the right moment, he would pause to puff on the long cigar I was sure he was smoking. Then he'd slowly exhale, making his listeners wait for the punch line, just as he had done with us growing up, just as he had done that night he told me he was leaving my mother.

"Come in, Jessie. It's freezing out there." My aunt took my hand. Celia was an intelligent, understated woman with a quiet sense of humor. I liked her. Besides the faint aroma of cigars, the house smelled like tea and toast with a hint of pine, the scent of the season. I followed my aunt into the sitting room, where my father perched on the sofa. I hadn't seen him in months, but he looked the same. His hair was perhaps a bit shorter, his face a little puffier. But the big eyes were as prominent and intense as ever.

"Treasure, it's great to see you." He stood and gave me a kiss. Carla peeled the baby off the Christmas tree and brought him over.

"Hi, how are you, Jessie? This is Nick."

He was a strapping boy, and the chubby red cheeks and blond hair showed he hadn't inherited Carla's dark Italian looks. His blue eyes belonged to my father, just as mine did. And my dad gazed at him with paternal pride radiating from every pore.

"He looks a lot like you when you were a baby, Jessie."

I felt awkward. My cheeks grew hot, and I hid them by leaning down and giving the baby a kiss on the forehead. He smelled of baby powder and shampoo.

That night I lay awake for a long time listening to the voices from downstairs, my father's clearer and more distinct than the rest. It was cold in the room, and I pulled my nightshirt up over my chin, a habit that I had inherited from my mother. I remembered a photograph my dad took of her years ago, asleep with the sheet up to her mouth and clenched tightly between her teeth. I was her child too, and that gave me some solace.

The next day was one of preparation, of baking pies and Yorkshire puddings, of decorating. I tried to ignore how uncomfortable I felt there, chatting with Carla, my aunt, my uncle, and my grandmother. I played with Nick. Then I helped set the table for dinner. But when we sat down that night, something in me snapped. As Celia's husband began carving the roast, I looked across the table. There Daddy sat, hungry, eager. Suddenly, the strong, strange taste in my mouth, that taste that made me gag when I wasn't yet seven, came rising up fast, as if everything that had happened that night had happened just seconds ago. I tried to stop them, but tears filled my eyes and fell onto the red, holiday tablecloth. Everyone turned from the roast and toward me.

"I'm sorry. Excuse me. I'm sorry. . . ." I rushed from the dining room and up the stairs. Just in time I made it to one of the bathrooms, lifted the lid of an antique white porcelain toilet and vomited. The irony of what had just happened did not escape me. I was a bulimic who spent much of her time trying to make herself vomit. Now, my body—simply because I had been sitting across from him—had done it on its own. My tears surprised me because they wouldn't stop. The taste of bile stayed in my mouth, and I felt cold. I reached up from the floor and pulled down a towel, which I wrapped tightly around me. I had to go back downstairs. Everyone was worried. But I gave myself a few more seconds. Finally, I stood and rummaged in the drawers for some toothpaste. I squeezed a blob and ran it over my teeth, then splashed water on my face, took off the towel, and hung it back where it had been. I did everything as slowly and deliberately as possible. But it felt as though I were looking at myself from a great distance, as if I were watching myself in motion. When I went back into the hall, my father was climbing the stairs.

"What's wrong, Jessie? What is it?"

He seemed genuinely concerned, how he had sometimes looked when I was little and had fallen out of a tree or slid in the mud. Before I even realized the words were out of my mouth, I said, "How could you have done that, Daddy? That night in New Jersey. How could you have done that?"

He looked stricken, and his face flinched as if I had hit him. But he wasn't confounded. I knew he remembered. He remembered as well as I did.

"Jessie, I am sorry."

I felt a huge weight begin to lift. Maybe there was hope that this could be resolved in some way. Perhaps it would get better.

"Treasure, this is not the time to talk. We will talk about it; I *want* to talk about it, but not here, not with everyone waiting downstairs and worrying about you. We'll talk tomorrow. Come to Mass with me in the morning, and on the way home, we'll talk. I promise."

We'll talk! I felt more elated than relieved. Finally, he would own up to it. I needed more than an apology. He had told me that before. I needed to know that I had done nothing to deserve it. That I hadn't asked for it. That the guilt I felt should be his, not mine. But we were going to talk!

He took my hand and led me down the stairs. Everyone at the table asked if I was all right, but they were much too embarrassed by my outburst to want to do anything other than ignore it. I would guess most of them chalked up my behavior to being an overly emotional American. This time, I sat next to my father, and he put his arm around me. *We would talk,* I just kept reminding myself. I ate very little, for once not thinking about every bite. My dad ate a lot and drank even more, but that was nothing unusual. I went to bed anticipating the talk we were to have in the morning.

The next day dawned cold, with a gusty wind and a light rain. My dad barely said a word on the way to church, and I was too hesitant to bring up anything until he did. The brick church was rather ugly, and I could tell the service was not up to my father's standards. He hated any Catholic service that wasn't full of ritual and solemnity. I have always wondered if it was ritual that he craved from Catholicism more than a relationship with God.

He looked dark as we left Mass. Outside the wind was so fierce that we had to battle it. We trudged along the road that would take us back to my aunt's, and my father's continued silence troubled me. Finally, after a half a mile or so, he opened the subject.

"I know you want to talk about what you said last night."

"Yes, Daddy, I do. It's really bothering me."

"Well, first of all, my advice to you would be to stop picking at your wounds, Jessie. It's a bad habit to make other people responsible for your failures in life."

My wounds? My failures? Mine?

"What do you mean?"

"I mean that you are sitting around picking at old scars, bringing up history, so you can make excuses for yourself. If you have problems, they are yours, not mine. Stop being so self-involved. Much worse things have happened to children."

I stared at him, incredulous, as we walked on. *Where was he going with this? Where was the father who just yesterday said he was sorry?*

"Think about the Holocaust, for fuck's sake," he continued. "Babies being gassed to death. And in Cambodia, the Khmer Rouge bayoneting six-year-olds in the rice paddies."

The Holocaust? The Khmer Rouge? What did this have to do with what he had done?

"Stop being self-indulgent for a change. You're lucky to have the life you have. So think about that and stop blaming other people if you are a failure."

I felt ambushed, unsteady. He had framed his argument masterfully. As always, he had left me little ground.

"I don't think I had it worse than children in the Holocaust. That's not what I'm talking about! I just want to get over this, so I don't have to think about it anymore." My voice wavered.

"Well, if you *really* want to do that, stop opening up the same cut over and over again. Leave it alone and grow up. Life is not always what you want it to be. Think about that."

Life is not always what you want it to be . . . and that was true. It wasn't. *But I hadn't had a choice,* I thought. *Not when I was seven. Not when he crawled into bed with me. Not when he pushed my head down and told me what to do.*

I said nothing for the rest of that long walk. I just thought about what he said. I had never compared my pain to that of others. And he was right. Others *had* suffered worse. But he was simply trying to evade the most important issue—taking responsibility for what he had done. And until he did that, until he took responsibility, I could never feel that what happened wasn't my fault. Until I stopped blaming myself, I couldn't stop being ashamed. He had used the night to craft his response. I suspect he was proud of what he came up with.

I headed back to London feeling worse than when I arrived at

Celia's. I hated myself, not only for what had happened with my dad, but also because I couldn't get over it. I felt weak and stupid, just as Dad told me I would. Bulimia took over my life. I loved school and acting, but there were days when I gave up, "bad" days when I would walk up to Hampstead High Street and buy pastries and chocolates. I took them home to my small room in a new flat I shared with some girlfriends, locked the door, and sat in bed eating and eating and eating. Then I would cry over the empty wrappers and bags until my regret pushed me into the bathroom to throw it all up.

To make matters worse, I worked part-time at a tea house in Hampstead—a shop filled with creamy éclairs, croissants, homemade cakes, and other delights. Putting a bulimic behind the pastry counter was like leaving a Vicodin addict in charge of the pharmacy. Often, the temptations overwhelmed me. My finger might skim the icing off a cake I was wrapping for a customer. Or I might pilfer a cookie when the boss wasn't looking. I sometimes ate crumbs off the floor. And on quite a few occasions, I rummaged through the large garbage bins in the back of the shop, cramming the half-eaten scraps of a patron's chocolate gâteau into my mouth. I hated myself for doing it, but I was used to hating myself by then. Instead of using the employee bathroom for purging, I'd simply wait until I got home. That way, I could have all the time I needed with my head over the toilet and my finger down my throat.

I gave up on resolutions; I knew I would never live up to them anyway. Most days I thought I would rather be dead, but I didn't have the guts to follow through.

Now and then I had a "good" day when I managed to resist bingeing, but they were few. Pablo and I talked on the phone from wherever he was. I wondered if things would be better if we were together. But I knew he wouldn't be able to help me. I had already told him years ago about what my father had done. He seemed shocked and confused. He had always been enamored of Tony Hendra. "How am I supposed to treat your dad knowing this?" he asked me. I certainly had no answers. After all, I didn't even know how to treat my father. In the end, Pablo behaved as though no such thing had happened.

When Pablo and I were apart, he dated other women and I dated other guys—a Tango superstar visiting from Argentina who wore white linen suits and spoke no English; a nice Jewish premed from Yale who was working in London for a year, a cockney boxer, a musical prodigy three years younger who asked me to be his "first" (why not?) and, a motorcycle rider who turned out to be a coke head. By the summer, I was fooling around with an older married man. I met him in the North London wine bar where I waitressed. He wanted to set me up in my own "mistress flat" and would pay the rent and put me through school. In the diary I kept, I debated taking him up on his offer:

It's hard to be moral in the traditional sense when one of the greatest moral taboos, incest, has been part of your life. Maybe I am so immoral because I have to find a way to accept what happened to me, to normalize it. I can't normalize it if I make everything into "morals." Also, what's the big deal about marriage? Everything seems so secondary in the face of incest, a much more horrible and confusing sin than infidelity. Growing up in such a fucked up household has made me a complex person morally. In one sense I feel guilty about everything; in another I have no strict sense of morality as such. My father transgressed every boundary of morality; why shouldn't I do the same? Why shouldn't I get my own back on morality and treat people with the same lack of morals as I was treated? Why be the victim? Why not victimize other people? All these feelings though are ugly feelings because they come from anger. Anger that I was fooled, that I went along with it, that no one told me what it was about or what would happen to me.

I ended up sleeping with Steve. The next morning, after he had already left, his wife called. She was looking for her husband. She said she found my number on a matchbook and asked me to leave him alone. They had a little girl. She didn't sound angry, just desperate. I got the feeling it wasn't the first such call she had made, and I thought of my mother and my father's many mistresses. I promised Steve's wife that I wouldn't see her husband again. As it was, he never called me after I gave in to his requests to spend the night. Gone were the flat and the school tuition, even if I had decided to take them. He avoided the wine bar, and in a fit of anger, I tried to pawn the Rolex he had left by my bed. The tough-looking pawn-shop owner laughed when I asked him what it was worth. It turned out to be a fake.

I had to get out of London. The pattern of my life had become so self-destructive that I knew it was time to leave. I had made friends and contacts in the two years at Central, and, because I had British citizenship through my parents, I could work in London. But I began to feel as though I were on such a downhill slide that getting away was the only thing that might help. I was too poor to see a private shrink, but I did attempt to see someone through England's National Heath System. The receptionist told me politely that it could take up to three months for me to get an appointment. If I waited three months, I might be under a double-decker bus.

To save on rent, I had left my flat and squatted, with permission, in a house in Ladbroke Grove that an old family friend, the comedian

John Cleese, was renovating. My mattress lay on the floor of an up-stairs room, and the half-demolished kitchen had a working stove. In the dusty living room, surrounded by planks of wood and nails, sat a baby grand piano. It was the only piece in the room. Each morning, I would come down to find workmen tearing apart more and more of the house. I don't know what they thought of me in my white robe, making tea, surrounded by total destruction. At one point the house had no back walls and stood open to the London rainstorms. I didn't care. It had a roof (most of the time, anyway), and it was free.

Mine was not an unusual lifestyle for students at my school. In fact, I knew quite a few kids who "slept rough" as they called it, spend-ing nights on park benches or in squats. I thought one boy must be well off because he had a car. Then I realized he lived in it. But all of us took a certain pride in the poverty of student life. We were still young enough to think that being poor was glamorous. One roguishly handsome, gifted actor carried his toothbrush, not a silk handkerchief, in the top pocket of his jacket. "You never know where you might spend the night," he explained with a wink.

I was feeling poor but not glamorous. Disgusting, really. It wasn't so much my surroundings but the constant battles with myself. I made a desperate call to Pablo, who was in Madrid. "Please come get me," I begged. He said he still loved me, but our on-again, off-again relationship—and my emotional crises—were too much for him. I could come to Spain. He would be happy to see me, he said. But he wasn't coming to England.

A few days later, I packed and headed to Paris and then to Madrid. My mother was now living with a war photographer—a man who would become her second husband. Conveniently, he had a loft in the same building as ours. She planned to meet me in Spain, and we would go back to New York together. Pablo and I spent a few weeks traveling. We saw a Romanesque church in a small Andalusian village where we thought we might have our wedding. But I could tell we both had our doubts about whether that day would ever come. My mom joined us. Then, with the usual anxiety, I got on the plane to New York. It was good to be back, but I found that I hadn't left my problems in England.

I was once again in the same city as my father. I saw him and Carla, but I didn't dare raise what we had talked about at Celia's — and, of course, neither did he. I got a restaurant job, a few theater gigs, and made new resolutions about my bulimia. I started running every day and, though that didn't solve my eating problems, it seemed to help. Running became a way of escaping, of being in control if only for an hour or two. When I ran, I felt like a machine, freed of the guilt and self-loathing. I began to live for the early mornings.

I'd get up early, well before Mom, and head to the kitchen of the loft to make a cup of coffee that was strong enough to give me a mild heart attack. I'd down it fast, and tie my running shoes. Then I'd race down the familiar dusty stairwell of Twenty-five East Fourth Street, out the front door and into the usually freezing wind that came off Broadway and blew down the street. Rain might hit me in the face. The potholes might turn to miniature ice rinks. Snow, yellowed by dogs, might pile in heaps along on the curbs. But I would run. In me, my father's addictive personality came out not in a drug-and-drinking habit but in this solitary passion. One of my favorite routes was down Lafayette Street toward the Brooklyn Bridge. I ran through China-town, skirting delivery men as they unloaded heaps of bok choy and red cabbages from the trucks double parked in front of Chinese gro-cery stores. On to TriBeca, where hung-over kids emerged from the clubs I used to go to myself. Past the all-night diner on Canal Street, where Krisztina and I had often gone to smoke and drink coffee at four in the morning. I ran through the weekend emptiness of the streets around City Hall until I made it to the bridge and up the wooden steps to the walkway that led to Brooklyn. The planks clattered under my feet, and the wind off the river was often so strong that it would blow me back toward Manhattan. I loved looking up at the spider web of cables that supported the bridge. When I got to Brooklyn, I turned around and faced the Manhattan skyline.

Other days, I headed uptown for a different scene. Along Madison Avenue, I ran amazed by the fur coats and high-heeled boots the Upper East Side ladies wore just to get their morning coffee or walk their tiny, yapping dogs. I crossed Fifth Avenue and followed it past the Metropolitan Museum of Art and into Central Park, where I joined other puffing, sweating New Yorkers as we casually tried to outpace each other along the six-mile route.

No matter where I went, I ran for miles, and I loved my dirty, worn out shoes, loved the feeling of pounding the pavements. I wasn't fast or graceful, but I was dedicated and obsessive. And I didn't feel ashamed about this.

I began traveling for regional theater, to Philadelphia, New England, Florida, wherever I could make a few bucks acting and get a shitty place to stay free. I actually liked going to different places and meeting a new cast. I felt hopeful whenever I stepped off a train (I refused to fly) or a bus in some place I didn't know—and some place that didn't know me. But my habits traveled alongside.

I was thrilled to be cast in a play at The Williamstown Theatre Festival in the Berkshire Hills of western Massachusetts. A few years before, when I was about twenty-five, I did my first play there. Mel

Gussow from the *New York Times* came to review it, and I was delighted when he gave me a good mention. I met my dad in a bar in New York on my day off. He never came to see one of my shows at Williamstown, but then I'm sure he was busy. I showed him the review and pointed to my name and the positive line about my acting. He nodded and didn't seem at all surprised. "I know Mel very well," he said of the reviewer. "I'm sure he recognized your last name."

Williamstown was a summer stock for stars. The 1992 main stage production featured Linda Pearl and Michael York in Ibsen's *A Doll's House*. *The Waiting Room*, for which I was cast, was being done in Williamstown's more experimental second stage. The play took place in different time periods, and I played a Victorian woman who had nervous ticks and was subject to fits of hysteria. It wasn't a stretch. Another character was a Chinese woman whose feet had been bound so tightly they were mush. Actor Kurt Fuller played a big-time, modern-day businessman making dirty money in pharmaceuticals. The plot centered on a woman with breast cancer. It was a comedy.

I was nervous on the day of the first rehearsal. The rest of the cast had been flown in from L.A. and had already performed the play with great success. Only my part had been recast. The other actors had much longer résumés than mine. And almost everyone at the festival recognized Kurt from the movies he'd been in—*Wayne's World*, for one. When I walked into rehearsal, I had no idea who he was. I was from NoHo. I didn't go to see big Hollywood movies, though I had seen my father in *Spinal Tap*. I was used to the hole-in-the-wall theater spaces on Avenue A and sitting through intermission-less productions of *King Lear* in which the actors outnumbered the audience. I went to independent film festivals at the Angelika Film Center on Houston Street. I read a lot of subtitles.

But I was struck by Kurt nonetheless. He was so tall—all long legs and arms and huge green eyes. Twelve years older than me, he was balding but handsome. Charismatic. And funny, funny, funny. Self-deprecating and yet confident. Witty and sarcastic but still kind. That impressed me. Shocked me even. Funny people were not, in my experience, kind.

On that first day of rehearsal, Kurt was the only cast member who made a point of introducing himself. He seemed to understand how awkward I felt being the new girl. As he told me later, he also had fallen in love with me.

11.

SONG OF SOLOMON

AS REHEARSALS CONTINUED, WE SPENT MORE TIME together backstage. Kurt declined the festival's minimal housing (a bedroom and bathroom with a *very* shared kitchen) and rented a house on the town's golf course. He said he came to Williamstown more for the golf than for the theater. One day, he brought to rehearsal a Victoria's Secret catalog that had been sent to his rental house. During our off-stage time, he began reading it aloud to me in a sort of mocking announcer's voice.

"The bra top—our original sexy basic with very secret support. The genius is in what you *can't* see. Hidden bralette shaping for comfort. Our cleavage-enhancing padded push-up tops have removable pads and underwire cups. Be your best shape ever. . . ."

Given that I played a Victorian woman, I wore a corset, and I giggled so much that the laces started to pop. This only made us both laugh harder. I doubled up in hysterics and the whole corset ripped up the back. After that, the wardrobe woman forbade Kurt to bring in any more catalogs. Seriously.

Despite what I now see was heavy-duty flirting, it never occurred to me then that Kurt was attracted to me. It didn't seem odd that he would miraculously turn up at the gym when I was working out, happen to eat at the same restaurant, or even stroll into the post office when I was buying stamps. I rode a bike all over town (being a city kid, I had never learned to drive), and I had no idea that Kurt was scouting the town for my chained-up, bright blue ten-speed.

A few days before the play was to open, I arrived at the theater to find that a large, gold bike with a very high seat had been locked next to the spot where I parked mine.

I went into the theater and peeked into the men's dressing room.

"Hey, you got a bike," I said to Kurt.

"I got it yesterday. It seems like the best way to get around."

"It is," I said, as though I had converted him. "I'm thinking about going for a ride this afternoon. There's supposed to be a really nice lake about ten miles away. Do you want to come?"

"Sure," he said, "but are there any dogs?"

"Any dogs? I don't think so. I mean, I don't know. I don't think there are packs of wild dogs roaming around Williamstown, Massachusetts, if that's what you're asking." I chuckled. Kurt didn't.

"No. What I'm asking, smart ass, is if there are any dogs that are going to run out of their houses, come barking across their lawns, and bite me in the leg while I'm trying to ride away." He said it in a sardonic, self-deprecating way. "That's what I'm asking, because in case you haven't noticed, Jessica, I am a tall man. I have a long way down to the ground. I don't need some mutt chasing after me because it can't tell a bike from a live animal. So I'm asking, are there any dogs?"

"I don't know, Kurt." I smiled. "But I'll protect you."

He returned the smile. "Very good then. Perfect. You ride in front, and we'll do fine."

After rehearsal, Kurt and I climbed on our bikes and rode off down the tree-lined roads of western Massachusetts. We didn't see any dogs, but there were a lot of cows. And green fields full of hay. And tall maples and oaks. And sunshine, red barns, and chickens. We never found the lake, but it didn't matter.

After a few miles, we stopped at a general store to get drinks. I made Kurt stay outside while I went in. I told him he was so drenched in sweat that I was afraid the store-owner might get scared and call the paramedics. He laughed and sat down in the grass to battle the gnats.

While we drank Diet Cokes, I told Kurt about Pablo, how our long distance relationship had gone on for years, and also about John, whom I was seeing in New York but whom I knew was too young for me. Kurt asked if both of them had a lot of hair. Then Kurt told me about the woman he was living with in California. She had just broken off their engagement for the third time. Eventually the cool of the late afternoon got us back on our bikes, and at the corner of Main Street and some lane named for a tree, it was time for us to part.

"Thanks for coming," I said.

"Thanks for asking me," Kurt answered.

There was an awkward moment. *Should I give him a kiss on the cheek? A hug?* I considered more but assumed we were just friends and opted for the hug. "Bye," I waved, and rode off thinking what a nice afternoon we had had.

Kurt was thinking the same thing. But whereas I'm a waffler, he's a

man of action. He turned his bike around and took after me. As he began to catch up, he remembered later, he watched my legs (and my
ass) as I pedaled along. Lost in a fantasy of what might happen if he
ever caught me, he failed to notice a small tree branch that had fallen
on the road. He hit it and went flying. His bike flipped and all six-feet,
five-inches of his long body came smashing to the ground. He broke
his wrist and bruised both his ribs and his ego. Completely oblivious,
I rode farther and farther away. Kurt said later that he lay there in
blinding pain, waiting for help and wondering if this might be an
omen of our future.

The next day, he came to the theater with a cast on his wrist. His
dreams of playing golf all summer were over. A week later, another actor broke his arm, so the play opened with two of the male leads in
brilliant white plaster casts. It must have looked to the audience as if
we had had quite a rigorous rehearsal process.

Opening night meant a party, which also meant a few glasses of
wine. A few glasses of wine meant that when Kurt and I found ourselves
alone in someone's spacious garden on a perfect New England summer
night, we conceded we might be more than friends. And despite a cast
that almost whacked me in the face, Kurt managed to kiss me.

He walked me to the Williams College dorm room that the festival had assigned me for the summer. We decided it would be better to
wait before I visited his house or he spent the night on my single bed,
never mind that his feet would hang off by at least a couple of inches.
We both had concerns. He worried that, because I was younger, it
might appear he was taking advantage of me. I worried that I might
take it all too seriously and be really hurt when he flew back to L.A. —
and to a woman who was still, technically, his fiancée. But I was grateful there was no wife or child involved. Kurt was a rare man — almost

forty and never married but not committed to remaining a bachelor. His most recent relationship had almost resulted in marriage, but his girlfriend called off the wedding at the last minute, and Kurt said it was probably best for both of them. No matter what happened with us, he told me, he was going to end his relationship with her as soon as he got home. I believed him.

I wanted more than the lovers I was used to. For once, I wanted someone that was solid, not confusing and not long distance. I knew Pablo was seeing someone in Madrid, but we still had never completely severed our relationship. I felt I had used people—and had been used by others. It was a habit I hoped to break. "All the men in your life are interchangeable," one of my passing boyfriends once told me. "In the end, none of them means anything to you." In a way he was right. But when you're unhappy with yourself, it seems impossible to really love someone else. You're searching for someone to save you, and too often, you become an emotional opportunist.

I was beginning to see that about myself, and I didn't like it. I had an instinct that Kurt was someone whom I should take more seriously than anyone I had met before. Still, I had only known him a few weeks. We held out for almost the entire run of *The Waiting Room* and then "made out like teenagers," as Kurt now recounts it. The night before the play closed, I told him I wanted to go back to his house after the show. "Are you sure?" he asked. I nodded and smiled. By the end of the night, I wonder if he wished I had said no.

Our first time together became a scene of emotional high drama in the rented-out bedroom of a Williams College professor who had gone to Europe for the summer. After we had sex, made love, whatever you will, I fell apart. I was overwhelmed by shame. This was nothing new. But instead of hiding my emotions that night, I let them out. I buried my face deep into the professor's pillow until Kurt finally pulled me up by the shoulders and turned me around.

"Jessica, what's wrong?"

"I feel so ashamed!"

"Ashamed of what? Of being here with me?"

"No, it's not you. It's me. I feel so horrible, so bad, like I am a bad, bad horrible person."

"What are you talking about?"

"Things . . . things that happened, that I can't forget that make me feel dirty, stained, like I have a black thing on my soul that will never go away. Sometimes I just want to tear myself into little pieces."

"What do you mean?"

"Some things with my father, and when we were here, together, I saw it in my head. I saw his face; I saw everything. And I just feel like it will never, ever go away."

Kurt looked at me. There was no sarcasm, no effort to find a witty line. "Do you want to tell me about it?" he asked, gently.

"I can't."

Kurt paused for a moment. Then: "How old were you?"

"Around seven. The first time, around seven."

He sighed and moved toward the end of the bed with his hands over his face. "Oh God."

"I feel ashamed."

"Listen to me." His hands were back by his side and his voice seemed almost angry. "You have *nothing* to be ashamed of. You were a child. It was *not* your fault. It was your *father's* fault, completely and utterly. You have nothing to be ashamed of. Not. One. Thing."

There they were . . . the words my father would never say. That's all I had wanted him to tell me—that *he* was to blame, not me. And here they were, coming from this other man who barely knew me. A man who didn't know how badly I needed those words. A man to whom I explained so little but who knew so much. *Daddy, why couldn't you just say that? Why?*

"I wish I could believe that," I said through my tears.

"You can because it's true. Did you tell your mom?"

"No."

"I think you need to tell someone exactly what happened. It doesn't have to be me, but you need to tell someone. This isn't something you can get over by yourself, Jessica. You need help."

I knew he was right, and I wondered if maybe I should tell him about my bulimia too. It was a secret that I'd never told anyone. But I realized how much I was laying on Kurt. He seemed like someone who could handle anything, but even I could see that all these revelations might be a bit much for a man I still was getting to know. I didn't want to ruin my chances with him and send him off to L.A. thinking I was too messed up. *If I wanted to see him after the summer,* I thought, *I'd better keep to myself a bit more.*

In the morning, Kurt took me to breakfast, held my hand along the streets of Williamstown, and then sat backstage during intermission with his arm around me. I never felt for a moment that what I had told him changed his feelings toward me. I was grateful. We didn't really talk about it again, but we didn't need to. I suddenly felt very close to him.

The play ended. Kurt began packing to go back to California. And I started to doubt the wisdom of saying so much to a man whose life was all the way across the country. I took the taxi with him to the local airport, said good-bye, and tried to believe him when he said we would see each other soon. I felt small and lonely on the ride back and thought of him sitting in his cramped seat and wondering if he might be better off with a woman who had a less complicated life. I stayed to do the outdoor production of Shakespeare's *As You Like It*, but it wasn't the same without Kurt there. He called every day. He told me he'd left his fiancée. But still, he seemed far away.

I went back to New York and started looking for a job. Kurt and I made plans to meet in Washington, D.C., at the end of October. We had a wonderful weekend, and I met his close friend Rudy Maxa. But I went back to New York, and Kurt started work on a series in L.A. A few weeks later, I was letting myself into my studio apartment when the phone rang. It was Pablo.

I wasn't surprised that he was calling. I hadn't seen him in a year, but we still talked now and then. The last I had heard from him, he was involved with someone and was planning his life in Spain. But now . . . now, he was coming to New York—to see me. And he was wondering if we might be able to work things out. He even mentioned the subject he had always avoided—marriage.

I told Pablo that I had started seeing someone who lived in L.A. But he seemed as determined as I seemed confused. When he hung up, I decided that I needed to be honest with Kurt. I had no idea how I felt about Pablo's tentative proposal. I just knew I needed to tell Kurt. I called him on his car phone as he was driving to work on the freeway. I told him what Pablo had said.

"Listen, I have to pull over. Just wait. Do not put the phone down. Do not put the phone down!"

I heard the screech of brakes and "watch out, asshole!" Then sardonic Kurt was back on the line. "Okay, great. So this guy with all the hair is turning up in New York to get you to marry him, and I am not even there. He'll speak to you in that goddamn Spanish accent, and it will be good-bye to Kurtie." I could tell he felt hurt—and angry.

"Kurt, I've known Pablo for nine years. You're in L.A. I'm here. I don't know what to do."

"I'll tell you what to do. Do not make any decisions. Do not do anything until I get there. If he's coming, so am I. I am going to finish this job here and then get on a plane to New York. Don't say you will marry him until I get a chance to prove to you that you should marry me."

His decisiveness amazed me. Within a week, both Pablo and Kurt were in New York. Pablo stayed with a friend; Kurt took a hotel room. Pablo arrived first. He was happy to see me again, but as soon as the glow wore off, I could see his indecision creeping back. The image he had created of me during our time apart and the reality he now faced were very different, and he started hedging. He wasn't ready to leave Spain. I would have to live there if we were married. Maybe I should come to Madrid with him for a few months and we could see how things went?

But I felt it was too late for us, that as much as I had loved him once, I had never really been intimate with him, not the way I was with Kurt. And there was the issue of my father. Pablo seemed afraid of what had happened to me; Kurt faced it head on. If I married Pablo, it would be unmentionable, and I would bear it on my own. If I married Kurt, there would be no taboos, particularly this one. I had never lived with him, known his family, seen his house, or met most of his friends. But I knew I needed him.

Pablo went back to Spain alone—and relieved, I suspect. Kurt stayed and formally proposed one afternoon while we were running side by side on the hotel gym's treadmills. We decided to get married straight away and gave ourselves two weeks to plan the wedding. After that I would move to Los Angeles, since I had little to offer in New York besides a studio apartment.

My mother seemed happy to hear I was engaged. My father was not. He favored Pablo. He knew Pablo admired him, and he sensed Kurt never would. It wasn't as though Kurt were antagonistic toward my dad when they finally met, but he wasn't warm either. Before we went to have a drink with my father and Carla one evening, Kurt warned me what to expect. "Jessica, I will meet Tony if you want me to," he said. "I will even try to be nice. But there is only so much I can fake with a man who is capable of doing what he did to his own daughter. I don't like him, and I will never, never trust him."

Privately, Dad made some not-so-subtle attempts to dissuade me from marrying Kurt, telling me what a better match Pablo would be. I was under his influence enough to almost believe him. But a voice in my head, for once louder than my father's, told me I was making the right choice. Dad said he would only pay for the wedding if I got married in a Catholic church—a ridiculous demand given that my father was divorced and had married Carla in the garden in New Jersey. Besides, Kurt was Jewish. But it didn't matter. I didn't want him to pay for the wedding anyway. I wanted the day to be only about Kurt and me. My mom paid for part of it, and Rudy, with his connections, got us the second best suite at the Mark Hotel on Fifth Avenue for the price of a room at a Holiday Inn. It helped that it was Christmas Eve, not a big night for tourists or weddings.

The ceremony came five months after Kurt and I had met. My mother and father were there, keeping their distance. Carla was invited but said she couldn't leave her children at Christmas, perhaps an excuse to avoid being in the same room with my mom. Rudy was best man; my sister, Kathy, was my maid of honor, and Krisztina, Iana, and other old friends were there too. Kurt and I found the Universalist minister by calling an 800-number.

My father announced to the congregation that he had had Kurt "investigated" before allowing us to marry. I assumed he was joking. Then he began reading a Biblical passage of his choosing—one that he hadn't told me about.

As he read from the "Song of Solomon," my stomach turned. "Thy two breasts are like two young roses that are twins, which feed among the lilies," he announced. And then: "I sleep, but my heart waketh. It is the voice of my beloved that knocketh, saying, Open to me, my sister, my love, my dove, my undefiled, for my head is filled with dew, and my locks with the drops of the night."

He didn't stop. "My dove, my undefiled is but one; she is the only one of her mother, she is the choice one of her that bare her. The daughters saw her, and blessed her; yea, the queens."

And then: "How fair and how pleasant art thou, O love, for delights! This thy stature is like to a palm tree, and thy breasts to clusters of grapes. I said, I will go up to the palm tree, I will take hold of the boughs thereof: now also thy breasts shall be as clusters of the vine, and the smell of thy nose like apples; and the roof of thy mouth like the best wine for my beloved, that goeth down sweetly, causing the lips of those that are asleep to speak."

"I am my beloved's, and his desire is toward me . . ."

I tried my best to smile, but I couldn't believe my father failed to make the connection that was so obvious to me, to Kurt, and to my friends in the room that knew. I began to feel nauseated, as I usually did when those memories flooded back. I looked toward Kurt and felt better.

Anyone looking through the wedding album might think Kathy and I were two happy sisters with our happy parents. Sometimes, the thousand words a picture speaks are better if not truthful. Kurt and I stayed at the Mark that night. Early on a snowy Christmas Day, Kurt awoke to find his bride gone. I was up at 6:30 A.M., had procured a cup of coffee from the downstairs staff, and was tromping through a snowy Central Park in my running shoes. It was the first of almost 3,700 mornings since we got married that Kurt has woken up alone.

My new husband now faced his greatest challenge yet: getting me to L.A. We were set to leave on New Year's Day, but on New Year's Eve, I made the mistake of talking to a friend about the harrowing trip she had just taken from Florida. They had flown through a thunderstorm. "I was sure the plane was coming down," she told me. "The sky was blazing. I saw lightning strike the wings, and the whole plane bounced up and down. They even had us take our emergency positions!"

I looked mournfully at Kurt, as if to say, "How can you subject me to a plane trip, you heartless man!" But he was oblivious. The next morning, I started getting edgy. I looked pale and cringed at the mention of the trip. My mother recognized the signs and took me aside. "Jessica, you had better get on that plane, Kurt is not someone who will take a lot of nonsense."

She was right. A few hours before the flight, as we were getting ready to leave, I started weeping, saying that I was scared to get on the plane and wanted to take the train instead. Kurt looked at me as if I were crazy.

"I'm getting on that flight," he said, matter-of-factly. "But if you're nutty enough to spend three days in a train instead of five hours in a plane, fine."

He didn't seem angry at all. He simply kissed me on the cheek, went out the door to get a cab to the airport, and arrived promptly in Los Angeles five hours later. I spent seventy-two hours by myself on a scruffy leather seat looking out of an Amtrak window and feeling like the biggest idiot in the world. Kurt picked me up from Union Station. He looked rested and chipper. On the way to the car, he made cracks about how I was a mail-order bride and suggested that next time, I might want to travel by covered wagon.

Kurt took me back to my new home, a townhouse in Santa Monica, long enough for me to drop my bags. It had been more than twenty years since I had left L.A. behind, heading out of Laurel Canyon in the VW with my parents. Now, I found the city vast and hard to understand. Was it a city, a suburb, or a mass of strip malls with sun and palm trees? We drove north to Carmel for a honeymoon and came back to Santa Monica on the afternoon of January 16. That night I went to sleep in Los Angeles for the first time in twenty-two years. Early the next morning, at 4:30 A.M., I awoke to the sound of breaking glass. The bed tossed and bounced exactly as it had when I was five. This time I recognized straight away that Daddy wasn't playing a trick on me. The earthquake, we found out later, had registered 6.7 on the Richter scale. I had left L.A. after one major earthquake to return years later, just in time for another.

Being in L.A., being married, and having a person like Kurt in my life made me want to change, to make a real commitment this time. My bulimia was the most obvious place to start. Kurt still didn't know, and though I hadn't told him the truth, I rationalized that I hadn't really lied about it either. He just hadn't asked. I had been trying to control my eating for years. This time I was determined to get a handle on my problem. Eating disorders are tricky; you can't just cut food out of your life, as you might with drugs or alcohol. You have to find a way to manage what you eat.

I made a vow to change once and for all. For the first couple of months in L.A., I stuck to a diet and did not binge. I felt in control for the first time I could remember. But controlling what I ate—precisely and obsessively—became my new addiction. Starving myself made me feel "clean" and "good." I was proud of not being bulimic anymore, but after a few months in which I dropped twenty pounds off an already thin frame, my sense of being worthy and virtuous became hollow. I had traded bulimia for anorexia.

I'd had an illusion as a bulimic that if I could master my eating, I was of value to myself. What I came to realize after I became anorexic was that I didn't value myself any more than I had before. Food was not the issue. I knew that. It was my past, my self-loathing. In one sense, trading bulimia for anorexia seemed a positive step, if only because I realized my problems needed real attention this time. Anorexia was the end of the line. If I had stayed wrapped up in the cycle of bingeing and purging, I might never have hit that wall.

And thankfully, anorexia showed. I couldn't hide the weight loss as I could the vomiting. After a few months, I was down to about ninety pounds, gaunt and boney. But like all anorexics, I still thought I was chubby. When I looked in the mirror, I saw a woman who could easily lose a few more pounds. I was running six to eight miles a day, and most of the time, I was so exhausted and dizzy that I felt faint. It wasn't that I never ate. For months I ate exactly the same food at precisely the same time of the day, every day, seven days a week. I had an apple for breakfast, cut up into tiny pieces that I ate with a fork to make it last longer. I put a clock on the lunch table to make sure it took me at least forty-five minutes to an hour for me to finish a salad (without dressing, of course). Kurt got to the point where he couldn't bear to eat with me, the meals were so nerve-racking. I chewed every morsel of my salad fifty times, putting down my fork for exactly one minute between each bite. Kurt anxiously watched the woman he loved shrink away, but I thought I was doing fine. After being bulimic for fifteen years, anorexia seemed like an achievement. Everything about food was now strictly controlled, and as long as I stayed obsessively within the limits of what I could eat and when I could eat it, I would be able to ward off the danger of binges.

I lost an acting job because I was too thin. I looked so bad that the casting director asked my agent if I had a terminal illness. I had no energy for anything but my early morning run. Kurt tried everything. Compassion, jokes, begging, even tough love. Nothing worked. I was starving myself and felt panicked by the thought of breaking the "food rules" that I'd made. My priorities were a mess—it was more important for me to eat my salad in fifty-chew increments than to be able to function. Kurt must have wished that he had never set foot in Williamstown.

Then one day, I collapsed. I was leaving our condo building and fainted outside the garage door. No one was around. I must have come to pretty quickly, but I was still too dizzy to stand up. I crawled from the garage to our unit, stood and held on to the door jamb as I unlocked the door. I staggered inside and lay down on the sofa. I was scared.

Everything spun slightly, and I had a terrible headache. I found the phone and tried calling Kurt, but he was working on a set somewhere. Then I tried Laura, a New York friend who had migrated to L.A. and who also suffered from an eating disorder.

"Laura, I just fainted downstairs." I'm sure I sounded weak.

"Oh my God, Jessica, are you okay?"

"I am now," but I didn't sound like it.

Then she asked me the question all anorexics hate.

"Jessica, did you eat anything today?"

"I ate an apple this morning."

I said this as if the apple were a full stack of pancakes with a side of sausage. "Jessica, you have got to see someone about this. You are going to die if you don't."

Yes, yes, of course, I told her, though as soon as I put the phone down, I made no effort to follow through. But Laura did. That evening, she called Kurt and told him she had spoken to the head of the eating disorders unit at a Los Angeles hospital. His name was Dr. Jason Shaffer, and he was expecting me to call to make an appointment. I didn't want to, but I agreed to see him. I knew my marriage would be in serious danger if I didn't.

I arrived at the hospital the next day. The eating disorders unit was in the psychiatric wing of the hospital, which already freaked me out. Worse, Dr. Shaffer's office was adjacent to the in-patient unit for anorexia. As I got off the elevator, I saw a bunch of teenage girls talking in quiet, exhausted voices. All had rail-thin frames, sunken checks, and sagging clothes. Their hands had turned to claws, and their heads seemed disproportionate to the rest of their sunken, starved bodies. Kurt and I came to call them "the big headed girls," and "big headed" became our euphemism for anorexia.

I walked down the hall to Dr. Shaffer's office. The girls straggled back through the swinging doors and into the in-patient unit. *Well, at least I'm not one of them!* I thought defiantly. The office was locked, so I sat outside on a bench waiting for the doctor to arrive. I watched the swing doors of the unit to see if I could catch sight of any more anorexia patients. I was fascinated by these girls and their POW physiques. In some ludicrous way, I admired them. They were even better at anorexia than I was.

Then a small man with dark hair appeared and began opening the door. I got up and introduced myself. Dr. Shaffer and I shook hands and walked inside. The office had a dark brown sofa, matching brown chairs, and a desk. On a side table, tissues had been set out for patients. Around the room were photos of Dr. Shaffer's adolescent daughters who, in my expert opinion, did not look like they had eating disorders. Books on anorexia and bulimia filled the shelves.

Dr. Shaffer and I went through the preliminaries—age, medical history, and, of course, weight. I stood 5-foot-5 and weighed 90.4 pounds. I pretended I didn't know it; in fact, I knew to the ounce. It was 10:00 A.M., and I already had weighed myself three times that day. Dr. Shaffer took me into the unit, and my heart pounded as I stood on the scale, trying to see what it said. But Dr Shaffer knew better. He had me stand on the scale backwards.

The first two or three visits were spent getting to know each other. I told him some of my background, but not the most important things.

I told him how I thought about food all the time, wondered what other people were eating, counted every calorie, and couldn't stop weighing myself. Dr. Shaffer told me it was quite rare to have such a severe onset of anorexia at my age (I was then twenty-eight). And I explained that I had been bulimic for years and that I considered anorexia a step in the right direction. He looked unconvinced. Shaffer felt that I would do better out of the ward, but he warned that if my weight went down much more, he would admit me as a patient.

I liked Shaffer. He was easy to talk to without being patronizing, and he was understanding without being condescending. He also seemed completely unsentimental without being cold. He was reserved but had a sense of humor, and he knew or could anticipate every anorexic trick. He told me to add three Power Bars a day to my diet, knowing that I might add a half of one. He said I must get rid of the scale in our house and got me in touch with a nutritionist whom I was to see twice a week. And I thought often about what Kurt had said that night in Williamstown—that I needed to tell someone what had happened with my father.

Finally, I decided to do it—to tell him the whole story. All the details. Everything I had left out before. I was terrified that Dr. Shaffer, this objective psychiatrist, would blame me for what had happened. So I turned around on the couch, faced the wall and began to gather my story.

I remembered my life backward, from the last time I had confronted my father at Aunt Celia's, back to my teenage years, when he slipped me some coke the night he told me he was leaving my mother. Back to the days when I first started bingeing and purging. Back to the night just before I turned seven. Back to the piece he had written for the *Lampoon* just a few months before. He had called it "How to Cook

Your Daughter," and it started this way: *A recurrent problem facing the gourmet who wishes to prepare this excellent dish is the difficulty he experiences in obtaining a daughter.*

"When I was really little, I remember one night in the country, in New Jersey, when I was sleeping in my bunk bed." I paused for a moment to see what Dr. Shaffer might say. He said nothing, and I closed my eyes and saw it all again.

. . . People so often ask, "How do I tell when my daughter is ready for the table?" Well, there's always some little variation, but generally the exact age falls somewhere between the fifth and sixth birthdays. . . .

"It was just before my seventh birthday," I continued, "and it was dark, except for some moonlight that was coming through the window." I opened my eyes. I was still on the brown, cloth couch in his office. I closed them again and was back in the bunk.

"I thought I heard voices from my parents' room." I spoke to the wall in Dr. Shaffer's office, my eyes still closed. "It was right next door to ours. There was just a door between our rooms, no hallway or anything. Then I saw my dad open the bedroom door and close it behind him. I remember his silhouette, but I could tell he was dressed even though it was late. I knew he was going out, maybe even all the way into the city, and that I'd spend the whole night worrying about him and wondering if he was okay, and that in the morning . . . in the morning I would ask my mom when he would be home. And she'd say she didn't know."

. . . During this period the daughter acquires a smooth firmness totally free of flab or muscle, especially in the shoulders, buttocks, and thighs, areas which are the gourmet's delight . . .

"So I sat up in my bed and called out to him quietly." I could see him stop and look toward my bed, then walk toward me. "He came and stood by the side of the bunk bed, and I said, 'Where are you going, Daddy?'" I could hear myself say it in that little-girl's voice. "And he said, 'I'm just going out for a minute love.' I told him I didn't want him to go, and he said he would come lie down with me." I stopped for a moment and took a deep breath.

"I snuggled into his arms, and he asked for a kiss," I told Dr. Shaffer. "But then he kissed me again in a way that was . . . really hard." My voice shook. "On my lips."

I paused and breathed deeply again. "He undid his pants and pulled out his penis." I began to cry as I sat on my therapist's couch, and I closed my eyes so tightly I was scrunching them shut.

. . . *Signs that the daughter has reached the ideal point are: The flesh will be soft but resist a pinch somewhat, returning to its full shape immediately upon release* . . .

"He put his hand under my nightie, and I asked him not to because it made me feel so cold, his hand was so cold." I paused again. The next part seemed the hardest, and I could feel my father next to me, even here on the couch. "Then he whispered into my ear, 'Take off your nightie, Jessie.' But I wouldn't. I didn't want to. So he said it again. 'Take off your nightie, Jessie. Take it off or I won't stay here. I'll go out.'"

I remembered how confused I had felt, as though I knew he was doing something wrong. But it was Daddy. And if he told me things were okay, I believed him. I'd do almost anything to keep him from going out. I think he was counting on that.

. . . . *An ancient and surprisingly accurate test of readiness is to hold the buttocks one in each hand and squeeze gently. If the daughter says "Grrrugchllllchlll," she is not yet quite ready. If she slaps your face, you have missed your opportunity . . .*

"I started whimpering, but I sat up and pulled off my nightie." I was talking so low now that I wasn't even sure Dr. Shaffer could hear me. "Then my dad told me to take off my underwear. I didn't want to. I told him that. But he said he'd leave if I didn't. So I pulled off my panties."

. . . . Now turn your daughter on her tummy in a kneeling position so that her head rests on her hands. . . . If she giggles at this point, reprimand her. Then scatter the sliced papaya all over her and rub the liqueur wherever you like . . .

I took another breath, this time deeper than all the others, and went on. "My dad started . . . feeling around my body and then, then he put his finger in my vagina and pushed it up a little bit. And I remember he whispered, 'You're too small.' So he took my hand and put it on his penis."

. . . . Unless you're really abnormal, you will find that during this preparation the daughter becomes increasingly appetizing . . .

As I told the story, I started to feel sick, like I was going to vomit. My body shook. "It was all hard and kind of sticky, and I was terrified. He moved my hand up and down it a bit. Then he took my head in his hands and pushed it toward his penis and whispered for me to put my mouth on it." This time I sighed—a huge, painful sigh, as if I were breathing my last breath. "I said I didn't want to, but he said it was okay because that's what people do if they love each other. So I did what he said, I put it in my mouth. It tasted . . . strong, and I was so scared."

The tears streamed down my cheeks.

"Then I tasted this sticky stuff, and it oozed out of my mouth and down my chin. I swallowed some of it and felt myself gag. And then I remember wiping my chin on my patchwork quilt." I pulled a tissue from the box of Kleenex and wiped my eyes.

"My father pulled me back to him and held me. He hugged me and stroked my hair. I was crying, and he said it again; he said 'It's okay, love. That's what people do when they love each other.'" As I spoke, I held my head in my hands and tried to wipe away tears that wouldn't stop. "He kept telling me everything was okay, but even then, I knew that it wasn't."

. . . . *At this point, the daughter will probably want to get up and go to the bathroom or play something else like prince and princess. If so, let her get up off the platter and give her some chocolate. If not, eat her.*

"After awhile, we went downstairs to the kitchen together, and he got me some water. The kitchen was cold and dark, and I remember thinking that it must've been very late by then." I sat up a little straighter on the couch, feeling as though the worst was over. "I remember my dad was just wearing a towel, and he made himself a drink, and I think I felt a little better. I wanted so much to believe him when he said it was what people did when they loved each other."

I needed Dr. Shaffer to understand. "I loved him so much. Then I got tired and told him I wanted to go to bed. So he came and tucked me in."

There. It was over. But my tears wouldn't stop. I sat with my back to Dr. Shaffer, still facing the wall, crying and crying and crying. It had been so shocking for me to hear the story out loud, to hear myself telling it, to see it all again in my mind's eye. And now, Dr. Shaffer would tell me what I always knew: that it *had* been my fault, that I *had* asked for it. I remember thinking, or maybe I said it aloud, *Kathy never would have taken off her underwear. She would have just let him go out. She was always stronger than me.* But I couldn't stop sobbing, and Dr. Shaffer said nothing.

He just let me cry.

PART IV

JUNE 2004

THE DAY AFTER HE SENT MY PIECE TO THE *NEW YORK Times*, I heard back from Rudy. The opinion's page editor said he was "absolutely shocked," Rudy told me. And the editor, David Shipley, thought my letter merited a full-blown story. I knew what I had written could not have been published as an Op-Ed piece. It was just too incriminating (not to mention too long). Rudy had sent it to Shipley more as a place to start than because we thought he would consider publishing it as it was. I knew that claims such as mine would and should be investigated. I was scared about what might happen next. But I also was grateful. The *New York Times* was treating what happened to me more seriously than my father ever had.

It had been eleven years since I had recounted for Dr. Shaffer the details of what happened. Like Kurt, he had told me in the days and weeks after that it hadn't been my fault. But much as I wished for one,

I hadn't had a miraculous recovery. In fact, I lost even more weight, and Dr. Shaffer threatened to hospitalize me. I called my mother and asked her to come to Los Angeles. She knew how sick I was. On the first of our joint visits to Dr. Shaffer, I told her that Daddy had molested me, but I didn't offer any details. She took it in as she always had—quietly, soberly. Kurt also came with me to see Dr. Shaffer a few times. But the person who should have been there was not.

Dr. Shaffer thought it might be helpful to confront my father again. I had told him of my father's Jekyll-and-Hyde reaction in England during the trip to Celia's, but we decided I should write Dad a letter, if only to see how he responded. I did, and the reply was blistering. Just like the e-mails we exchanged after *Father Joe* was published, he didn't deny what he had done. But in the letter, he launched into a tirade about how I wanted to see myself as a victim, how I longed to be part of the "Sally-Jessy-Raphael culture," how my problems were not his fault, how I needed to conquer my disorders by myself. Dr. Shaffer and I read the letter together. After a moment, he looked at me. "I don't think you will ever get the response you want from this man, Jessica," Dr. Shaffer said. "He is a true, textbook narcissist, not able to empathize with you or really take responsibility for anything. He is not capable of it."

I knew Dr. Shaffer was right, but I refused to give up. I wrote back and so did Dad—this time with a response that essentially said I was making a big deal over nothing. Then he admonished me to never, ever say a word about it to his wife, Carla.

Finally, one last letter came. Kurt and I were set to travel to New York for my sister's, Kathy, wedding. Dad would be there, as would Carla. The afternoon before we were to leave, FedEx delivered his latest missive, this one telling me once and for all that I was a failure, a pathetic whiner, and that he was blameless. I couldn't stand to be there with everyone, so I cancelled our tickets and called Kathy to tell her I wasn't able to come. I told her why, what had happened with Daddy, but again not in detail. Kathy tried to be sympathetic, but I could tell she was angry. As she reminded me, she had made a lot of effort to come to my wedding.

I realized that unless I relented, unless I simply did as my father suggested, I would always be the family spoiler. And so I tried to move on with my life, just as Daddy wanted, just as he had told me in England after Mass, in letters back and forth, in the tone that he took, in the words that he used.

With Dr. Shaffer's reluctant permission, I took a part in a play in a regional theater in Sonora, a city five hours north of Dr. Shaffer, my husband, and L.A. I would be on my own, and unable to make our counseling sessions. But Dr. Shaffer acquiesced, as long as I agreed to drive back to Los Angeles now and then and to check in on the phone once a week. Kurt also would be coming to visit, and Dr. Shaffer trusted him to assess my situation.

I brought my habits with me to Sonora. I'd been given housing by a supporter of the theater, a seventy-something widower who settled me comfortably in his guest room before heading east to visit his grandchildren. Before he set out, he told me to help myself to anything in his house. I investigated the "bad" foods in Bob's kitchen and swore not to touch the cookie dough ice cream or Twinkies. Instead, I continued to slice my breakfast apple into tiny pieces, each to be eaten with a fork. For lunch it was salad. For dinner, a plain bagel that I cut it into four equal parts—one section to be eaten before the show, one to be nibbled during intermission, and the remaining two for after the curtain fell. The cast must have noticed the way I parceled out my lone bagel, but, of course, I found my behavior unremarkable. I continued to run six miles a day, and came home exhausted, my head spinning from lack of fuel.

I called Dr. Shaffer each week, telling him the same things I had told him in his office: how scared I was to gain weight, to break all the food rules I had set for myself. I told him how I wanted to be someone with no needs at all—for food, for love, for anyone or anything. I told him how I thought my need for my father's love had made me complicit in his molestation of me, that if I had been a "stronger person" it never would have happened. I told him I still felt weak, that, even at age twenty-nine, I hated myself for my neediness. And I told him how I simply wanted to be invisible, to take up no space in the world, to become a tiny, emotionless thing. During the calls, I worried out loud that if I began to eat more, I would simply binge and become bulimic again. Dr. Shaffer suggested I try Prozac, but it only made me feel nervous and even more anxious than usual. I had two car accidents in a week. And when Kurt told him that I hadn't gained a pound, Dr. Shaffer decided to make a "house call" to northern California.

We sat in a small cafe in town, and Dr. Shaffer told me that I had come to the proverbial fork in the road. The path I chose was up to me. I couldn't get better for him or for Kurt, for my mom, or my friends. I had to do it for myself. I had to take a chance on breaking my life-threatening food rules, to be brave enough to believe in myself. And if I couldn't . . . there wasn't much that he or anyone else could do for me. I knew he was right. I had to stop punishing myself for what had happened with my father.

That night I returned to the house and lay on the floral bedspread in the guest room, thinking about what Dr. Shaffer had said. In Kurt, I had been given a huge gift: someone who loved me despite the dirty secrets of my past. Now, here I was, squandering that gift, taking Kurt's love for granted. I thought about how I had told my secrets, and how both Kurt and Dr. Shaffer had supported me. Then I began to wonder: *What would it feel like not to be dizzy all the time? Or sick? It has to be better than this!* I got up from the bed and headed to the kitchen. I felt as though I were moving in slow motion, watching myself, just as I had that evening at Celia's, when I threw up in her bathroom. When I finally got there, I reached into the cupboard and pulled out a bowl. Then I opened the freezer door and took out the cookie dough ice cream. I put two scoops in the bowl, and sat down at the kitchen table. But I was too nervous to eat. I knew I needed to talk to the one person in my life who would understand what it meant for me to eat a bowl of ice cream. I called Kurt.

I told him what Dr. Shaffer had said, how I felt it was time to break my rules, and that I needed him to talk to me while I ate.

"What do you want me to talk about, Jess?"

"Anything . . . what you did today, how work was, anything to take my mind off what I'm about to do."

"There's nothing wrong with eating some ice cream," he reassured me. "Nothing is going to happen to you if you do. It's just a first little step, a little step that might be the beginning of you getting better."

"I know, but I'm scared."

"Just eat," he said, "and let me talk."

And so Kurt chatted on about this and that, told me a funny story, then an ironic anecdote. I laughed a little, ate deliberately, and felt that each spoonful that went into my mouth was part of a long journey toward the bottom of the bowl. I wished I could just be a normal woman and enjoy my dessert.

Finally, I finished.

"How do you feel?" Kurt asked.

I thought for a moment. "Okay," I told him. "I actually feel okay."

"I'm very proud of you, Jessica. I know how hard that was."

Kurt said good night, and he told me that he loved me. And I went to bed feeling hopeful. I vowed that in the morning, I would not skip breakfast to make up for being "bad." That I would finally add the PowerBar Dr. Shaffer had been urging me to eat. That I would take baby step after baby step. That I would recover. In the morning, I kept my promise, and in the weeks that followed, I started to gain weight.

The bulimia hadn't returned, and I began to see my body differently. Now, I *wanted* some flesh. I *wanted* to take up space. The scale still scared me, but I felt as though I had turned a critical corner—that, maybe, I had begun to free myself.

My neuroses resurfaced whenever I'd hear Dad's voice or see his face, but I tried my best to set them aside. We even traveled to France to visit his new family. Kurt lurked in the bushes whenever Dad took our girls out to play. I hated myself for seeing him, for pretending to be okay when I wasn't. But what choice did I have?

Then, *Father Joe*, a book that I couldn't help but see as an attempt to bury our secret once and for all. If I didn't speak now, if I didn't correct my father's "record" of our family history, then I would never be able to live with myself. He had chosen to let the world believe he had bared his soul to save it. He even had the gall to dedicate the book to his first family. I simply couldn't let it stand. Here I was, telling the *New York Times* details of something I never wanted to make public. But Daddy only had himself to blame—for what he had done and for what he had written.

It was the end of the week, and Rudy told Shipley that I was coming to New York on Monday. Shipley would call me Tuesday, he told Rudy, after he met with the other editors and figured out the best person to cover the story. That Sunday, a girlfriend in New York called asking me if I had seen the *Times*.

"I live in Los Angeles, now, remember!" I told her. I was a little tense. So she e-mailed me the letter. It was written by Michael McKean, perhaps best known for cowriting the movie *This Is Spinal Tap*.

> To the Editor,
>
> In his review of Tony Hendra's *Father Joe* (May 30), Andrew Sullivan refers to the author as "an architect of the peerless parody rock documentary *This Is Spinal Tap*. I wonder where Sullivan picked up that phrase.

McKean wrote that my father "stands apart" as the only actor to have tried to claim credit for the movie, even though he had neither written it nor conceived of it. McKean ended his letter this way: "I think Tony Hendra is at least one confession away from salvation."

I could feel the frustration and anger in each word that McKean had written. Even today, having authored "one of the best spiritual memoirs ever," my father was still trying to pull a fast one. And one that Michael, Chris, and the other writers of *This Is Spinal Tap* had called him out on before. They must have been shaking their heads, just as I was, thinking *Tony hasn't changed. He might have* said *on the cover of his book that his soul is saved, but the guy hasn't changed one bit.*

I think Tony Hendra is at least one confession away from salvation. Yes, I thought. *At least one.*

My mom, the girls, and I flew to New York on Monday. Kurt stayed behind to work. Mom had sold the loft and moved to California shortly before my youngest daughter had been born. She wanted to be close to her grandchildren. Her new husband, my stepfather, watched their house in Topanga—and their gigantic dog-child, Dave.

I went through my usual anxiety about getting on the plane. But I had important reasons to get to New York. First, to take Julia and Charlotte to the American Girl Store on Fifth Avenue, and second, to tell my story to the *New York Times*.

My mother kept a studio apartment on East Thirty-fifth Street, and we arrived there late. The girls were thrilled to be back in the city. All of us crowded into the studio, Charlotte and I sleeping on an air mattress on the floor, my mom and Julia in the bed.

I didn't hear from David Shipley on Tuesday, and I began to wonder if perhaps they had second thoughts about pursuing the story. The notion left me disappointed—and relieved. When I checked my voicemail on Wednesday, I had three messages. Two were from my father, asking me again if we could meet privately and talk. The third was from Shipley. He wanted me to call.

When Shipley and I finally connected, I was on my way up Thirty-fourth Street with my mom and the girls, looking for a bagel place. I stopped on a "quiet" corner and, pressing my cell phone to my ear, strained to hear him. He told me how much my piece had affected him and how he thought it was important to handle it correctly. He wanted my permission to pass it on to the Metro editor, and if I agreed, they would assign someone to the story the next day. I didn't think twice and gave my permission. Shipley said someone would be in touch with me soon. I told my mother the gist of the conversation. She felt as I did—gratified and scared shitless.

On Thursday morning, I heard from John Kifner, the reporter who had been assigned the story. My mother remembered him as an old friend of my stepfather's (my stepfather had been a well-respected photographer and had worked with a lot of reporters). She wondered if we should remind Kifner of this or whether he might remember himself. I suspect he remembered because, a few hours later, he called me again and cited "a family emergency" that would prevent him from being able to follow the story. He said someone else would be calling me within a few hours.

We had planned to take the girls to the Metropolitan Museum of Art that afternoon. I thought it was unfair for them to sit at home waiting for a phone call. So we made our way to the number 6 train and headed to Eighty-sixth Street. Just as we crossed Fifth Avenue and walked toward the main entrance of the museum, my cell phone rang. The number came up as 1111111111. Could it be my father?

"Hello?" I answered reluctantly. The voice on the other end said his name was Sonny Kleinfield and that he was from the *Times*. He sounded so unassuming that I feared I'd been passed on to someone junior. I had no idea that he was one of the *Times'* best, most experienced investigative reporters, and that he would turn out to be, as one of his colleagues later noted, "the instrument of providence."

"When could we talk, Jessica? I can meet you somewhere, or you can come here. Whatever you prefer."

"What about tomorrow morning? That would be the best time for me."

"I was hoping we could meet today."

"It's just that I am on my way to the museum with my daughters. . . ."

I saw my mother making gestures at me.

"I'm sorry. Can you hold on one second?"

"Sure," Sonny said.

I put my hand over the phone and turned toward my mother. "What?"

"Jessica, I'll take the girls to the Met. Go and meet this guy if he wants to meet now. You need to get this over with."

"But look what I'm wearing!" I had on shorts and a tank top.

"Just say you will meet him. No one in New York dresses in the summer."

"But I don't have my notes or anything." I had been trying to anticipate the interview by writing down some thoughts.

"You don't need notes."

"But I'm not prepared!"

"Jessica. . . ." My mother looked straight into my eyes. "You have been preparing for this your whole life. Just tell the guy the truth."

I took my hand off the phone.

"I'm so sorry to have kept you waiting. I can come now. My mother is going to take my girls."

"Okay. Where would you like to meet?"

For a second I had an image from some 1940s movie. "Thank you for meeting me, Mr. Kleinfield," I would say in a deep, raspy voice. The reality was I had no idea where to meet. At that moment I felt incapable of remembering a single diner or coffee shop in the entire city.

"I'll come to the *Times* building. It's easier."

"Great. Call from downstairs when you get here. I'll come and get you."

We hung up, and I turned to my mom. "I'm going to meet him at his office."

"Good," she said.

"I just worry that I look like a complete flake coming to the *New York Times* building in shorts!" I looked myself over. "And a tank top! Mom, what if he thinks I'm not credible?"

My mother took off the Ann Taylor cardigan she had slung over her shoulder, drew my arms into it, and buttoned the sweater over my tank top. It was like she was dressing me for the first day of school.

"Here. Now go."

I was nervous as I kissed her and the girls good-bye and took the steps into the subway.

As I emerged twenty minutes later on Forty-second Street, I imagined meeting my father coming out of the news buildings around Times Square, having just given an interview about *Father Joe*. Or perhaps he would be coming from a leisurely lunch with his agent during which they discussed the size of the checks they would both be receiving if *Father Joe* stayed on the bestseller lists. I felt like a traitor to him.

I walked in the lobby of the *Times* building, and the security guard, large and gruff with a big mustache, greeted me. I called up to Sonny in the newsroom. He said he'd be right down to get me.

I paced in the lobby and tugged at the legs of my shorts, trying to make them seem longer. I wished I was wearing a nice pants suit (I didn't even *own* one, but never mind). Finally, a fair, slight man came out of the elevator wearing jeans and discreetly holding a notepad and pen.

"I'm Sonny Kleinfield," he said, extending his hand.

"I'm Jessica Hendra," I said, shaking it.

"Do you want to go and talk in the cafeteria here or out somewhere?"

"I don't know," I said somewhat sheepishly. I mean, what was the best spot for denouncing your father?

"Let's just go to the cafeteria."

"Fine."

Sonny signed me in, and I followed him to the elevators.

"I'm sorry I'm so casually dressed. I was expecting to be taking two small children around the hot city today." I sounded a bit shaky.

"Don't worry about that," he said. "No one in New York dresses in the summer." Mom was right.

Sonny and I took the elevator to the cafeteria and chitchatted about the security in the building since September 11. When we got there, I excused myself and went into the ladies room to splash some cold water on my face and pull myself together. Sonny waited patiently, and when we walked into the cafeteria together, we stopped for coffee.

Do I pay or does he pay? I felt I should offer, but strangely, I didn't want him to think I was buying him off. Sonny paid. Then he asked me where I wanted to sit. I chose a table at the very back of the cafeteria. Even though I was about to tell more than a million readers of the *New York Times* what my father had done, on that day I didn't want anyone but Sonny to hear my story. It was as though I had blocked out the reality of what I was doing and still treasured the illusion of privacy. I took one sip of the coffee, gagged slightly, and left the rest to get cold on the table.

I wish I could remember all the questions Sonny asked me or even how he began his interview. I only recall how nervous I felt and how skillfully Sonny drew the story out of me. He didn't push me into saying anything, and he was considerate of the difficult details of my past. I don't even remember when I realized he was taking furious notes. I just remember telling him my story, as clearly as I could. And objectively, even. Despite all that had happened, I felt I needed to be fair-minded. The truth, after all, was on my side.

"I have the piece you sent to the Op-Ed page," he told me. "You talk about what happened with your dad in great detail in it. I'm not going to ask you to recount all that again right now. But is it okay for me to just quote from what you have already written?"

"Yes. That would be much easier for me." I felt relieved. "Thank you."

We talked for more than three hours, and Sonny sympathetically scrutinized everything I said. It seemed as though he believed me but needed to be sure. And who could blame him for being skeptical? I had come to the paper on my own volition. I had initiated this. And I was increasingly aware that I was taking a huge risk. Sonny might believe me. Or he might not.

He asked if he could talk to Kurt, my friends, and two therapists— Dr. Shaffer and the woman I was currently seeing in Los Angeles, Dr. Tracy Studdard. And also to my mother. I promised to call him with a list of numbers from my phone book after I got back to Mom's apartment. I also said I'd ask my mother if she would consent to an interview. But I cautioned him that Kathy "wasn't going to want to get involved."

Sonny also wanted to see the e-mails my father and I had exchanged after *Father Joe* came out. And as I had over and over again since that day, he bemoaned the fact that I had destroyed the letters my father had sent me ten years ago, when I was in therapy for my anorexia.

"Does your dad know you're talking to me?" I knew Sonny would ask. I felt awkward about my dad not knowing and answered, simply, "No."

"You know that I will have to contact your father later in the process." Sonny seemed so matter-of-fact about it, so clinical.

"Of course you will," I said. "You should. You have to." I'm sure he didn't need to be reminded. "I understand that."

"What do you think he will say?"

I had asked myself that very question since I thought about doing this. "I don't know," and I didn't. "I can't imagine he could deny it. . . ." Not exactly true; I could *imagine* it. Vividly. "But I guess he will."

"Yes," Sonny answered, "I guess he will."

We exchanged e-mails and phone numbers and agreed to talk soon.

I walked from the *Times* building and onto Forty-third Street. The late afternoon sun still blazed but with a tad less intensity. I even felt a very slight breeze. I called my mother on my cell phone. She had arranged for us to have dinner at a friend's apartment that evening. I didn't ask what excuse she had given our hostess for me being so late.

"How was it?" she asked quietly.

"It was fine. Hard. Very hard. But fine."

I told her I'd make my way to the Upper East Side to meet her. "It may take me awhile. I really need a walk."

I ducked into a Starbucks for a decent cup of coffee and spotted a stack of the *New York Times* at the counter. *In a few days, my story might be sitting there, for sale in this very Starbucks.* I wasn't sure what to think about that. It just felt . . . strange.

I walked to East Eighty-second Street—wandered, really, past buildings and stores that seemed familiar. *I guess this made sense,* I thought. *To come back to New York to tell my story.*

My mother buzzed me into her friend's apartment building, and when I came out of the elevator, we had a muffled conference about how we "would talk about it later." I stepped into the living room where the girls were playing Sorry! with the daughter of our hostess, and I worked hard to set aside the day's events, even for a while.

That night, I told Mom about my talk with Sonny. She seemed proud of what I'd done, and she said she would be willing to go to the *Times* the next day. I checked my messages. My father had called twice. I spent the night tossing on the air mattress.

Sonny and I talked in the morning, and I asked him if I could call my friends and doctors before I gave him their numbers. I wanted to let them know why they might be receiving phone calls from the *Times*. That's fine, he said, but he wanted the go-ahead to start calling people as soon as possible.

That afternoon, my mom went to Forty-third Street while I roamed around Manhattan with Julia and Charlotte. She returned late in the afternoon, after she and Sonny had spent almost two hours discussing what I had told him. My mom corroborated dates and places. She gave details about her life with my father and what my childhood had been like. And she said she made at least one thing very clear to Sonny: She believed me.

I left messages for everyone on my list, none of whom I managed to reach on the first try. The day was as sweltering as the day before, so I took Julia and Charlotte to the park on East Thirty-fourth and Second Avenue to cool off. I knew there were sprinklers there, and the girls loved to run through them. My phone rang just as I was trying to find Charlotte's sandals to walk back to the apartment. Before answering, I made sure it wasn't my father.

Dr. Shaffer was returning my call. In a muddled narrative, hindered by the fact that I had to crawl under a bench to retrieve the lost sandals, I explained what was going on. I was in New York, I told him. I had gone to the press. And the *Times* was working on the story. "I was wondering," I asked. . . . "Could I give the reporter your number? I know it's a lot to ask, but it would be so helpful if you could talk to him."

"Jessica, the hospital has very strict rules about this sort of thing," he told me. "There is a whole public relations process that has to be gone through for me to allow them to publish my name and the name of the hospital."

Dammit! Now Sonny will never believe me. I would have to call him and tell him that my psychiatrist couldn't talk to him. My voice was full of disappointment.

"I understand," I said, and part of me did. "But if you don't talk to him it makes me seem . . . not credible." I must've sounded pathetic. I was pleading. I knew that. "That's the thing. I want him to know that I'm not making this up."

Shaffer paused. "Jessica, listen. I know you are credible. But I can only talk to this reporter anonymously. I cannot give permission for him to publish my name or use the hospital's name in the story. But if it helps you, I will talk to him."

Then: "You can give him my number."

I thanked him profusely, and about ten minutes later, repeated the conversation with my other therapist, Dr. Studdard. Like Dr. Shaffer, she would agree to talk to Sonny, but only if her name wasn't published.

That night, I reached two very old friends. The first was Gage, who was at home in Philadelphia. Gage once had a theater company in Philadelphia and had directed me in at least six or seven shows. We hadn't worked together since we started having babies. But we were still close, and I had told her years ago something about what had happened with my dad.

"Jessica, I have been thinking about you!" she said the moment she heard my voice. "The other day I was listening to *Fresh Air* on NPR, and I heard the most nauseating interview with your father."

"Yeah, I heard about that," I groaned, remembering that day at Charlotte's preschool.

"I was storming around the house at every word out of that man's mouth. And Terri Gross was practically crawling into his lap. 'Oh Tony,' she kept saying." Gage spoke in falsetto, and I couldn't help but laugh. "It was revolting. How could he dare to write a book like that! You must be going insane."

And then I grew serious. "Actually, Gage, that's why I'm calling. . . ."

"Of course you can give him my number," she told me after hearing what I had done. "Your dad should not be able to get away with this."

Then I called Alison, my closest friend in Los Angeles. She and I had known each other in New York long before we both ended up moving to L.A. I had told her about my father when we were in our twenties.

She and I had been talking almost daily since the book came out. She knew I had contacted the *Times*. Now I asked if they could call her. Like Gage, she was supportive. "Absolutely, Jess. Absolutely he can call me."

The only friend left to call was my soul mate, the girl who had been with me during some of the worst of times: Krisztina. But it was four in the morning in the French village where she lived with her husband and children. That call was going to have to wait until the next day. I got up early to catch her at home. She was just sitting down to lunch.

"Krisztina, I need to talk to you about something serious. I want you of all people to understand what's going on here and how I feel." I explained about *Father Joe*, which had yet made its way to rural France. Her reaction told me so much about how nothing between us had changed.

"How did your dad have the guts to write a book like that?" she asked incredulously. "Doesn't he have any conscience?"

"I guess not," I answered. *A part of me still wants to defend him!* I thought.

I told her about the *New York Times*.

"I'll talk to whoever you want me to," she said. As always, she had come through for me.

Later that morning, I called Sonny to give him the go-ahead to call whomever he wanted. Then I took the girls to Chinatown. Again, my father called. Again, I did not answer.

The weekend proved quiet—no calls from my father or from Sonny. Then on Monday, Sonny and I must have been on the phone at least four or five times.

I knew he was hoping to get the story out by the middle of that week. And my father's messages were piling up in my voicemail. It was time. I had to return his call. He would have one last chance—one final opportunity to come clean himself before I went any further with the *Times*.

I called him at home, but he wasn't able to talk. So we arranged that I would call him that night, on his cell, at 10:00 P.M. sharp.

A few minutes early, I headed into the tiny bathroom of my mother's studio apartment, locked the door, and crouched on the floor. *I'm thirty-nine and still scared of him*, I thought. I felt as if I might vomit.

But this . . . this would be his chance—his *last* chance, I promised myself—to do what he hadn't done for thirty-two years, to finally take responsibility for what he'd done to me. I would call him and tell him that I had gone to the press, that a reporter was working on a story. I would tell him that I couldn't keep the secret any longer. And he would say, "Jessie, treasure, I'm so sorry." He'd tell me that it wasn't my fault. He would promise he'd get help. He'd tell me to do whatever I needed to do, that he understood.

And I felt sick because I knew it would never happen that way.

Outside the bathroom door, my mother played Go Fish with Charlotte and Julia. She knew what I was about to do, and I could tell she was concerned; her face said so.

I punched in the number he had given me, written down on an old grocery receipt. "Dad cell," it said. The phone rang twice. Then, my father: "Hello."

"It's me, Dad." Three words and I felt exhausted.

"Hi Jessie." I could see his face—those huge blue eyes, the puffy cheeks, the thin blond hair combed back behind his ears. He might have been sixty-two, but the features never aged. I could see his hands, those sinewy hands, and smell the thin cigars he smoked since before I was born. I stood for a moment with the phone to my ear and looked in the mirror over the sink. They were *his* eyes that stared back at me, *his* hair that fell on my shoulders.

I can't do it, I thought. I sat quickly on the floor, pulled the phone from my ear and put my hand over the mouthpiece. I closed my eyes and took a deep breath.

He had wanted to see me, but I needed the distance, the insulation. I heard him tell someone that he had to "take this call in private." Then the background sounds faded, and my father said my name again. Not the name I had now. Not my grown-up name. Not Jessica, but Jessie.

"Hi Dad," I said flatly.

He thanked me for calling and told me he was devastated that I was upset by *Father Joe*. "I wrote it to make amends, Jessie."

"Dad, how can covering up what you did to me make amends?"

"Jessie, it's not a *comprehensive* confessional." Not a "comprehensive confessional" was *such* a Tony Hendra-ism.

He asked me what I wanted him to do.

"I want you to go to all the people who have bought, read, and believed in your book and tell them what you left out, Dad. That's what I want." My heart banged on my chest. *I was telling him. I was saying what I needed to say.*

"That's impossible, Jessie," he said. But what about this? he wondered. Perhaps the two of us could write a book together?

"I don't want to write a book with you, Dad. I want you to tell the truth, *now!* And if you don't, Daddy . . ." My heart banged harder. "If you don't, then I will."

"Is that a threat, Jessie?"

"No, Dad, it's not a threat." I felt so tired, so worn down. "It's just how I feel. It's just . . . how I feel."

"But this is something between *us*," he said forcefully. "I am *not* going to tell the media about this."

I paused a moment, closed my eyes and realized that once I told him, my relationship with my father—the one that I had struggled with and agonized over for the last thirty-two years—likely would end. It came out almost casually. "Well, Dad, I went to the *New York Times* and told them everything."

Silence. And then, in the highest register of his usually mellow voice: "Jesus Christ, Jessie! Oh Jessie, what did you go and do that for!" It was the first and last time I have felt sorry for my father since the day when I first read the *Times* review of *Father Joe*. But I couldn't let my guard down. Not this time. I knew what was coming, and I was right: the counterattack.

"You've ruined Carla's career, Jessie. You've brought nothing but pain, misery, and suffering on to the lives of countless people by doing this, Jessie."

Neither statement made any sense to me. *Carla? Why should what my father did long before he met his new wife reflect at all on her? And how could something that he always told me was not that big a deal suddenly, because other people knew about it, become so devastating? Why was it never devastating when it was just* me *who had to suffer it?* But I said nothing and just sat in that small bathroom with my heart drumming against my chest, my head leaning on the sink, my eyes closed.

"The media is not objective," he said, which made about as much sense to me as the comment about ruining his wife's career. And then his voice softened. "Did someone put you up to this, Jess?" A *way out!* I thought. *He's giving me a way out!*

I had tried his ways before. They left me hating myself, bulimic, anorexic, and wishing I were dead. It took me three decades to learn there was only one way out: to simply tell the truth. To tell everything. To make the secret go away. *How could he not know that? Wasn't that the point of his bestselling book? Confess and forgiveness and salvation can be yours?* "No, Dad," I said. "I did this by myself."

Another pause.

"We will never speak to each other again on this earth," he said, and with that, he hung up on me for the last time.

Into the line that seemed as dead as my relationship with my father, I said only one word, softly: "Okay." And I was sure, perhaps for the first time since I was seven, that it would be.

I listened to the silence on the other end for a second. Then I opened my eyes, looked at my cell phone and saw the word "END." I pressed the button, turned off the phone, and hid it beneath a towel on the floor. Then I lay down as well as I could in the tiny space and waited to cry.

Suddenly, I felt the hardness of the floor, my body lying there, hands cushioning my head. I remembered the worst stage of my anorexia, how I wanted to be so small that no one would even realize I was there. How I wanted to vanish. How I hated myself.

The tears never came, but I guess I wasn't surprised. What had just happened was inevitable. For thirty-two years, I had tried to have a relationship with my father, and pretending I could almost killed me.

There would be no more lies. No more secrets. I owed my father nothing.

I knew too much—I'd gone through too much—to be a little girl anymore, silent, timid, and afraid of Daddy. Now, at thirty-nine, it was time to grow up.

The next morning I told my mom that I didn't think Dad was going to take responsibility for what he had done, that I was sure that when he got the call from Sonny, he'd find a way to creatively—and convincingly—deny everything. Mom said nothing at first. Then she stood and walked over to where I sat. Her face looked tight.

"Jessica, I should have told you this years ago, and I am *deeply* ashamed that I didn't." I looked up at her. "Tony confessed to me. Not about when you were seven but about the time when you were older. When he touched you in the bathroom."

I stared at her, stunned. She came closer and whispered so that the girls wouldn't hear.

"He told me he was in the bathroom with you and that he made you masturbate him. He said he was 'a monster.' And then he cried. I didn't know what to do. I thought maybe he was making it up, or that he was drunk or stoned, and that he was being dramatic. I'm so sorry."

She sounded almost desperate, as though she had also been keeping a secret for him for decades. I couldn't believe what she was saying.

"This has been on my conscience for years," she said a bit louder now. "I should have told you when I came with you to talk to Dr. Shaffer ten years ago. But I was ashamed. I was just too ashamed to tell him that I knew and didn't do anything. And I lied to Sonny too. He asked me if I knew, and I didn't tell him the truth."

I put my hands over my face and closed my eyes. *Dad confessed to her? Not all of it, no. But some of it anyway. He confessed it.* I was too shocked by my mother's revelation to be angry at her for never having told me. And I understood why she hadn't. I knew about keeping secrets, about being afraid to tell. I imagined the night he told her, that he almost certainly was drunk or high. I imagined him collapsing on their bed in the front room, crying, beating his breast. She must have been terrified. Maybe she considered going to the police that night, but I doubt it. And when he woke up the next morning, hung over and silent, she reasoned that if she said anything he would only deny it. And so, as I had tried to do for so many years, she simply let it go. I knew that she had tried to make it up to me, that she was trying to make amends now by finally telling the truth. Perhaps that meant more to me than it should have. It was something my father never had done.

"Ma, you have to tell Sonny," I implored. "I'm not angry. But you have to tell Sonny."

"I know."

She picked up the phone, and I recited the number as she dialed. I heard her tell Sonny that she needed to talk to him about "something very important." Then she tried to hide from her granddaughters—not in the bathroom, as I had done the night before, but near the front door of the apartment. I distracted Julia and Charlotte as best I could while she talked. All I heard were her opening words—the same ones she had just said to me: "I am desperately ashamed of this."

When she finished, I asked her about Sonny's reaction.

"He asked me why I hadn't said something before now." She looked relieved, almost freed. "I felt as if he were the voice of God."

I kissed her. "Thank you, Ma." And I wondered what Sonny was thinking at his desk in the *Times* building. Did he feel as though he had unwittingly become a member of the chorus in a Greek tragedy? I could see him watching all the Hendra secrets come to light in front of him, shaking his head, and saying "What a family. What a family."

EPILOGUE

IT WILL BE YEARS BEFORE I TELL MY DAUGHTERS what happened to me as a little girl, years before they know the real reason we don't see their "Grandpa Tony" anymore.

Today, it seems they never will be old enough to hear about incest and what happened to their mother. And until I can tell them, I will have to make up reasons why we no longer visit my father's apartment on trips to New York, why we never returned to his home in France, why the elaborate gifts that my stepmother used to send on Christmas stopped coming. There will be lots of questions from both my girls about why I don't talk to my daddy, and for now, I will just have to give them that irritating answer: "I'll tell you when you're older."

But there will come a time when I can finally pull out the article from the *New York Times* and hand it to them to read. They'll see that their grandpa denied molesting me. They'll see that he called me unstable and pathological. And of course, they'll know the truth. And after they take turns reading it, they'll look at me, and it will be my turn to explain.

I'll tell them that I did what I did not only for myself but for them. And without trying to make myself into some sort of martyr, that I came forward for anyone who was sexually molested. Because, as I'll tell them, I believe that the only way to stop such abuse is to tell. Since I went public with my story, I've heard from others who suffered as I did. As one of the incest survivors wrote, "Never again. No more silence." Perhaps I'll show my daughters those letters.

I'll tell them how I thought a lot about what kind of mother I wanted to be as I considered whether to challenge my father's book— that I wanted them to see me as a woman they could emulate, someone who would stand up for herself despite her fears. And then I will tell them that watching them as little girls with their daddy taught me to forgive myself for what had happened with mine. I see how they sit on their daddy's lap, just as I had with mine. I see the easy way they snuggle with him, the instinctive way they hold out their hands for him when they're about to cross the street, the way they reach out when they're tired or scared. How I hear them call out for him when they wake up after a nightmare. How I see their wonderful innocence and how I know that it is our job as parents to protect it.

In a decade or so, I will tell my daughters that the love they have for their father shows me the truth in what my therapists and close friends insisted: When a little girl who's not yet seven loves her father, believing what he tells her is natural. And I will tell them that there was a reason I had girls who looked like me. I will tell them that they were my second chance and that I tried to do for them what I only now have been able to do for myself: make a place that was safe.

When I began writing this book, I came to understand so much about my father. I received e-mails from old family friends— colleagues of my dad's at the *Lampoon* who had listened to his banter in the 1970s and now realize they should have taken his words more seriously.

One of them, Ted Mann, recounted a stroll with my father. He wrote to me: "As we walked down Madison Avenue, Tony remarked, 'I have fucked three women today.' I asked, 'Was any of these your wife?' Your father responded, 'No, but one of them was my daughter.' I assure you," he told me in an e-mail, "I gave the remark no credence at the time."

Another former friend of my father's, Valerie Marchant, e-mailed me a letter that she was sending to a New York newspaper after she read the *New York Times* story. Valerie, who remains close to my mother and me—and who had, those many years ago in our yard in New Jersey, pounded on our barn with a croquet mallet—wrote that "everyone who knew the family had witnessed Tony treating Jessie in social situations in a way that was very disturbing. She was his girl. Nothing you could report to a police officer, but something that made you very uneasy and would be identified in later years as emotional incest."

Valerie's boyfriend at the time, long-time *Lampoon* editor Sean Kelly, also wrote me. He recalled my dad coming into a *Lampoon* staff meeting after it had started. "Sorry I'm late, lads. I was home playing hide the bologna with the daughters." Sean wrote that he had "developed something of a theory" about my father, whom he refers to as T. H. "It's why I absolutely believe you," he wrote, "and how I can't feel anything but painful hate for him.

> I think that when he was an adolescent, those Catholic monks
> really did get to him—that is, they exposed him to a marvelous (if
> imaginary) universe—something like Middle Earth or Dungeons

and Dragons, or the Great Game of Kipling's Kim. A Universe with a fantastic, intricate (and feudal) back story, a Universe you can only access by learning a secret code language (Latin), a Universe in which Ultimate Evil is the opponent, and only a few vulnerable, misunderstood heroes are fighting against it: the Catholics, including you. The problem with all of that is that as you begin to grow up, it gradually—or in a flash—occurs to you that the whole business in utterly preposterous. And still you long for it—the certainty about what's Good and Evil, an understanding of "what it all means." The Big Picture.

I think (from any number of things T. H. said and did in my presence) that he wanted to prove the existence of Good by establishing the existence of Evil. If he deliberately and gratuitously lied—and he did, all the time—it implies the possibility of Truth. If he repeatedly cheated and stole (and he did) it was to suggest that there is, out there somewhere, Honesty.

If he betrayed everyone close to him—wife, friends, collaborators—it establishes the possibility of Loyalty. Overindulge in every substance—food, drink, dope—and your gluttony suggests that there must be such a virtue as Temperance. If you know there's a Hell—because you live there—it at least proves that there must be a Heaven. In my experience, T. H. would size up any situation, and invariably proceed to do the WORST POSSIBLE THING under the circumstances—and all to prove the Existence of Good Old God.

I have never blamed the church for my father's behavior, not after coming to know Father Joe and the boundless love he offered Dad and me. Still, Sean made me see how my father might be intent on *using* his religion, as though he wished to do harm—to himself and to others—if only so that he could repent.

I also learned a great lesson from my father's failures—a lesson that has helped me find the morality that was once so absent in my life. Now, I have an overwhelming desire to call people I haven't spoken to in years and—just like a member of Alcoholics Anonymous might—make the sort of amends that my father never considered. And for the first time, I started seeing incest as something that happened to more people than just me. I found the statistics on the Internet and read the newsletters of survivors. The numbers horrified me.

Late this summer, my mother came over to my house with two grocery bags. Inside were pictures from my childhood, some letters, and some old diaries. Two were mine; one was my father's. My mom put them down and said, "I thought you might like to go through this stuff, Jessica," but instead we both simply stood there, looking down at a past we still couldn't understand.

I thought of my mother packing all these remnants of her twenty-year marriage when she moved from the loft in New York to her new house in California. I imagined her sitting on the floor, picking up each picture of my father, and wondering whether to toss it or keep it. I thought about how she called me after the *New York Times* piece came out, and I remembered the catch in her voice. "I'm scared, Jessica," she had said. "I thought Tony was out of my life and now he's back because of all this. I feel like I'm back in the whole nightmare." I knew that I would have to be the one to go through the bags. Later that night, when everyone was asleep, I did.

The pictures of my sister and me as children made my heart hurt. We both looked so vulnerable, so young. I looked at my school picture from when I was six or seven, and it made me want to cry. There I was with my crossed eye, my crooked smile, and my wispy white-blond hair. I wanted to crawl into the picture and hold the hand of that little girl, take her on my lap, and tell her that she'd done nothing wrong. In her school picture, my sister, Kathy, looked awkward and chubby, with thick glasses and stringy hair. I don't believe my father ever sexually molested Kathy, but his words had beaten her down, year after year. I wanted to crawl into her picture too and tell her the things that my father never said: that she was beautiful and smart. That she was loved. I put the pictures back in the box and walked through the house and into my daughters' room. There they lay, sleeping, with hot faces and wrinkled nighties. I kissed them both. Then I went back into the office and picked up my father's diary.

Masking tape secured the book's broken binding. Its cover was light purple with block letters that read Schooltime Compositions. Beneath it, next to NAME, SCHOOL, and CLASS, my father had written TONY HENDRA, LIFE, and UPPER MIDDLE. I opened it slowly and saw the first entry, dated June 1981. I recognized my father's elegant but almost illegible handwriting in various colors of ink. I closed the diary and put it on the floor. *Should I read it?*

I felt overwhelmed by the predicament. It was his *diary*, for God's sake—his private thoughts and feelings not meant for others to read or to judge. *But what if it contained a confession?* Even though it was from 1981, about ten years after he first molested me, perhaps he might refer to what he had done. It would prove he was lying when he denied it to the *New York Times*. It would prove that I was telling the truth. And maybe, just maybe, even if there were no confession, it might finally help me understand my father.

I picked it up again, but this time, I didn't open it. It didn't seem right, but it also didn't matter. I put it in a brown envelope and wrote my father's address on it. I'd had enough of my father's words to last me a lifetime. I had given him so many chances to speak to me honestly. His final words to me, that we'd never speak again on this earth, told me precisely where he stood. On this day and every day after, his words would no longer matter.

Instead, I decided to write him a letter that I suspect I'll never send.

Dear Dad:

I'm not sure how to start a letter that I know you'll never read. Maybe the best way is to just ask you all the questions you haven't been willing to answer.

Why did you molest me, Daddy? Why did you take me, your little girl who loved you so much, and hurt me so terribly? What were you thinking when you slipped beside me in my little bed and touched me like that? Did you hate me? Did you think I could erase from my memory the way it felt to be touched like that by my daddy? Did you ever really think it didn't matter?

I have asked myself these questions for thirty-two years, Dad. I have spent so much of my adult life trying to figure out who you are and how and why you did what you did. I still have no answers. Only you can answer those questions, Dad, and I know you never will. You are not brave enough to tell the truth. You will continue to hide behind the lie that you are not a man who is or ever was capable of doing such a thing. Instead, you will continue to call me crazy and unstable—pathological even. You will do what you have always done: make your sexual abuse of me my problem, not yours.

But now it *is* your problem, Dad. I hand it over to you. I have lived with it, thought about it, and relived it in my head. I have made myself vomit because of it, starved myself, and hated myself so much that I wanted to die. I give you back the shame, Dad. It always belonged to you. I know that now, and I am free.

I have spoken out and told my story, and I pity what you're now going through. I regret that people have to know this about you, but I could not keep your secret any more. Your secret almost killed me, and I'm sorry it had to come to this, Dad. But I gave you so many chances to accept responsibility, to even in some small way make things better, to help me when I came to you. Instead, you chose to discount what you did, to minimize it, to make me feel inadequate because I couldn't get over it. To my face, you never denied it, and I was grateful for that at least. But of course, by writing *Father Joe*, you took back whatever small solace that offered, and today you are denying it to the world.

I don't know whether there's anything you could have done to make up for what you did. Maybe the moment you touched me like that the damage was irreversible. But I am, despite it all, an idealist. I believe in what Father Warrilow, the man we both knew, preached: that everything can be forgiven. But first, there has to be acknowledgment, *real* acknowledgment, of the transgression. Only then can forgiveness be possible.

I don't hate you, Dad. I'm just sad. I wish I could look back at my childhood, at my life with you, and take the good things and leave the rest. I try embracing the interesting aspects of my *Lampoon* childhood, what it was like being the daughter of a brilliant and funny man, an educated and, in some ways, sensitive man. But in the end, I only feel confused. How do I reconcile the witty historian, the magnificent conversationalist, the wonderful storyteller with the reckless alcoholic, the drug abuser, the man who sexually abused his daughter? Did I ever really know you?

Your power over me is finally at an end, Daddy. I don't believe the things you told me anymore, that I just wanted to see myself "as a victim" or that I should be ashamed of myself for "continually picking at the same old wound." I believed what you said for years and years. But your voice is gone from my head, and I found my own voice now, Dad. It tells me that I'm not a failure or a loser or a victim and that I'm done suffering from my memories.

During that call in New York, you said we will never speak again on this earth. I accept that. I know now that the only way for me to ever see you again, to ever even try to have a relationship with you, would be for you to finally tell the truth. And I feel certain that won't happen.

So I say good-bye, Daddy, not in anger but with resignation.

I knew since I was seven that you'd be mad if I told.

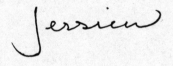

AFTERWORD

AFTER THIS BOOK WAS PUBLISHED I WAS OFTEN ASKED, with incredulity, if the sexual abuse really happened, why did I continue to have a relationship with my father for so many years? But that question misunderstands the nature of the shame victims of sexual abuse carry and how much we need and want for our abusers to take the burden of that shame. We keep going back because the abuser is the only person who can really, in some twisted way, relieve us of it. When a friend said, "If your father were to read your book it would change him," I wanted that to be true. However, I soon learned how stupid I was to think it could ever be.

Kristina, my childhood soulmate, called from France, frantic. She received a letter from my father's British lawyers. Unless she retracted the statement she made to Sonny Kleinfeld in the *New York Times*, that I told her about the abuse when I was twelve years old, my father would sue her in a British court for defamation. She was scared, and I felt a punch to the gut. I should have known better. I had taken my father's year of silence as a kind of truce, but in fact he had been planning, plotting. He was Hydra, one head cut off but growing another, breathing fire and spitting bile more viciously than before. Utterly deflated I asked Kristina, "Do you want to retract what you said? I will understand if you do." Kristina said, "No. I don't want to do that, Jess, because what I said is true." "Okay," I said, "in that case I will contact a lawyer and find out what our options are."

The next day, I was up at one in the morning Los Angeles time on the phone to London with a solicitor. He explained that my father was engaging in "libel tourism" by bringing his suit in Britain where the libel laws are more in favor of the claimant. Rather than sue me, or the *New York Times*, my father was suing Kristina because he knew she had no money. His strategy was to get a retraction from Kristina, and then use that to undermine the account in the *New York Times* and, ultimately, my book. In order to bring a defamation suit in the United States my father would have to prove not only that Kristina was lying, but also that she had intentionally sought to do him harm. In Britain, Kristina would have to prove she was telling the truth that my father molested me. The solicitor's next words literally brought me to my knees. "The cost of a defense in this kind of a case could be enormous." "How enormous?" I asked. "Upwards of five-hundred-thousand pounds—about one million dollars." I was speechless. The solicitor continued, "Of course if Mr. Hendra lost his case he would have to pay for any fees amassed on behalf of your friend. But for you to win a litigation like this would be very difficult." He had done it again, my father had beaten me again. I went back to bed and tossed and turned until the sun came up bringing with it another call, this time from my mother. She, too, had received a missive from London, she was being sued for defamation.

That night, my husband, Kurt, and I talked it over. We did not have a million dollars for a lawsuit. We are not reckless types who rush into what we can not afford, we consider for months if we really need a new washing machine before we finally cave in and buy one. But Kristina had spoken up for me, she could not be left to the mercy of Tony Hendra. Kurt and I made a crazy decision, the only thing we could do, we would hire a solicitor, take out a line of credit against our house, and fund a defense in the hope that we would win and the fees would be paid by the other side. It was insane, absurd—we did not have that kind of money, we had children, college tuitions in the future, a household to keep together, bills to be paid. Yet conviction pushed us to jump hand-in-hand into the void. My mother felt the same, staring at ruin, she and her husband, Bill, also took out a line of credit.

My father and I began the most protracted act of our shared tragedy. Instead of giving in to his bullying, I fought back. The lawsuit was a chess game, our moves against each other made by proxy. Technically, I was not being sued but I knew, and he knew, that I would have to be the one to make decisions. For months witness statements flew back and forth over the Atlantic, I was on the phone daily, addressing each of my father's claims, defending my sanity, my account of my life, my truth. I submitted letters, emails, any trace of my past. I handed over journals from my teenage and young adult years in which I wrote about the sexual abuse and its impact on me. My father's legal team suggested the three-hundred-and-something misspelled and blotted entries were forgeries. They demanded the diaries be ink-dated and the paper be chemically analyzed. I jokingly told our solicitor that if I was that good at forgery I might actually have the hundreds of thousands of dollars we already owed him. I said if my father wanted to pay for the diaries to be examined by an expert then by all means. The expert was never called in.

At the pretrial hearing the entire text of my father's *National Lampoon* piece "How to Cook Your Daughter" was read aloud in the High Court of Justice Queen's Bench Division. The black-robed, white-wigged judge shook his head in disgust as my father's solicitors tried to pass the piece off as "innocent fun." Old friends came to my aid and gave statements supporting my story; all my psychiatric records were divulged to disprove my father's claim that I had been hypnotized by my therapist and a false memory implanted in my brain.

Only weeks before my father and I were to face each other in the High Court of Justice Queen's Bench Division, the demands for retractions were abruptly dropped and the legal fees we had amassed—a stunning amount of money that my mother, Kurt, and I did not have—were quickly paid off. My father had gotten cold, icy-cold feet about going to trial. Despite relief that our stupendous legal debt was erased, part of me was disappointed. I wanted my day in court. The statute of limitations had long passed for me to be able to bring charges against my father in the United States. This British proceeding would have been my opportunity to take my place in the witness box, my only chance to publicly address, in a court of law, all the falsehoods my father would tell. But there were other people involved—Kristina, my mother, and Kurt: it would be selfish to insist on going to court. I took solace in that my father's most grandiose attempt to ruin me had failed. He was out a million dollars with nothing to show for it, and the whole ill-gotten enterprise had only made me stronger. If I had any hope of a reconciliation with my father I lost it in the months I countered the lies he told about me and anyone who defended me.

* * *

Victims stay silent because of shame, shame that belongs solely to their abusers. Yet that shame is almost always heaped on the victim. In the press, my story was called "stomach turning," "icky," "scurrilous," I was accused of "airing my dirty linen in public," and "engaging in repugnant he said, she said." During the lawsuit every aspect of my life was scrutinized by my father's legal team through the warped premise that only a psychotic liar would make a sexual abuse claim against her father.

The experience of sexual abuse isolated me for decades and bound me to my father with the most terrible kind of exclusivity. Keeping his secret burdened me, kept me small and quiet under the enormous weight of silence. Only when I spoke out did it begin to fall away. Because of the #MeToo movement society is finally beginning to understand that sexual abuse victims do not speak out for attention or because they are vindictive, but because they can not bear their burdens any longer.

The number of women and men coming forward may shock those who greet accusations with an instant "It could never happen." Those of us who have been victims of sexual abuse are not surprised by the explosion of stories—we know sexual abuse happens, and with horrible frequency. It is the rest of the world that must now accept the truth.

In this new moment where victims are finally being believed, I hope that the past routine of degrading and vilifying the abused is over. I hope women and men will never again keep their abusers' secrets because they fear embarrassment, legal retaliation, stigmatization, being beaten into silence by lawsuits and harassment; that no one has to face the humiliation of their truths being summarily condemned as fake, icky, disgusting, and stomach turning.

Traveling around the country talking about my book and interacting with survivors, I constantly encounter those desperate to heal. At the end of a reading in a small-town library an eighty-year-old women pulled me aside; when she was a girl her uncle took her to the basement, put her up against the washing machine and raped her. She asked me if I thought it was too late for her to get help. I said no.

After everything that has happened with my father—the accusations, the reprisals, and the lawsuit—I am still convinced it is never too late to speak out, to share your truths. My experience, though harrowing, has shown me that there are numerous forms of redemption and justice, and, despite everything, your story deserves to be heard.

ACKNOWLEDGMENTS

FIRST, MY DEEPEST GRATITUDE TO MY HUSBAND, KURT, for his boundless love and support. My warmest thanks to Blake Morrison, without whose guidance, encouragement, and dedication this book would not have come to fruition. Also to my agent, Sterling Lord, for his belief in this project; to my editor, Cassie Jones, for her meticulous eye and hard work; and to Judith Regan, for giving me the opportunity to tell my story. I salute my oldest and dearest friends, Krisztina, Iana, Alison, and Gage, for their loyalty. To Rudy Maxa, Jonathan W., Bob Faggen, Jim Gaynor, Valerie Marchant, Ted Mann, Sean Kelly, Michael Strober, Angela Bonavoglia, and Amy Solomon. To my stepfather, Bill Pierce; to my sister, Katherine, and her husband, Peter; to Al, Enid, and all the Fuller family—in appreciation for your compassion. Thanks to Rachelle Benveniste for inspiring me. Lastly, I wish to acknowledge my mother, Judith, for her courage.

–JESSICA HENDRA

Thanks to my wonderful wife, Bernadette, whose love, patience, support, and kindness make every day special. Thanks to my father and mother, Jim and Arline Morrison, for fostering in me a love of the language. Thanks to my agent, Sterling Lord, whose wisdom, encouragement, and belief in me proved priceless. Thanks to Cassie Jones, the sort of editor who elevates the work and the spirit, and to Vivian Gomez for the care she gave to every page. And thanks most of all to Jessica Hendra for allowing me to help her tell her story. As we worked together, Jessica, my respect and admiration for you only grew. I hope this book allows others to see the woman I have come to know: a fantastic mother, a loving wife, a trusted friend, and a forgiving daughter who values the truth above everything else.

–BLAKE MORRISON